Psychology and Learning

MASTER LECTURE SERIES

Psychology and Learning
Self-Study Instrument

NOW AVAILABLE

If you were unable to attend and receive credit for the 1984 Master Lecture Series on Psychology and Learning, you may obtain 10 hours of Continuing Education Credit through a self-study instrument developed to accompany this volume. For further information, please write or phone:

Psychology-Learning SSI
CE Program Office
American Psychological Association
1200 Seventeenth St., N.W.
Washington, D.C. 20036
(202) 955-7719

Psychology and Learning

Master Lecturers

John Garcia
Gregory A. Kimble
Leonard Krasner
Jack L. Michael
Lauren B. Resnick

Edited by
Barbara L. Hammonds

AMERICAN PSYCHOLOGICAL ASSOCIATION
WASHINGTON, DC 20036

Library of Congress Cataloging in Publication Data
Main entry under title:

Psychology and learning.

   (Master lecture series; v. 4)
   Bibliography: p.
   1. Learning, Psychology of—Addresses, essays, lectures.
I. Kimble, Gregory A.   II. Hammonds, Barbara L., 1943–
III. Series.
BF318.P77   1985   153.1'5   84-73343
ISBN 0-912704-93-4

Copies may be ordered from:
Order Department
American Psychological Association
P.O. Box 2710
Hyattsville, MD 20784

Published by the American Psychological Association, Inc.,
1200 Seventeenth Street, N.W., Washington, D.C. 20036
Copyright © 1985 by the American Psychological Association.

Printed in the United States of America.

CONTENTS

PREFACE
Barbara L. Hammonds
1

THE PSYCHOLOGY OF LEARNING ENTERS ITS SECOND CENTURY
Gregory A. Kimble
5

APPLICATIONS OF LEARNING THEORY IN THE ENVIRONMENT
Leonard Krasner
49

BEHAVIORAL ANALYSIS: A RADICAL PERSPECTIVE
Jack L. Michael
95

COGNITION AND INSTRUCTION: RECENT THEORIES OF HUMAN COMPETENCE
Lauren B. Resnick
123

EVOLUTION OF LEARNING MECHANISMS
John Garcia and Rodrigo Garcia y Robertson
187

PREFACE

At its annual convention in 1974, the American Psychological Association introduced the Master Lecture Series, a series of lectures presented by leading scholars and designed to provide a forum for the presentation of theory and research in selected areas of psychology. Each year five lectures focus on topics of social and ethical importance and of broad interest to the profession. At the presentation the audience is invited to participate in a discussion of these issues.

As one of the Association's most prestigious and significant activities, the series attracts large audiences at the APA Convention. It also reaches a broad audience through the distribution of tapes of the lectures and, more recently, through the production of an edited volume of Master Lecture papers. This volume, *Psychology and Learning,* is the fourth in the series of bound volumes derived from the Master Lecture presentations.

The Master Lecture Series was initiated and organized by the Committee on Program Innovations of the Board of Convention Affairs. This committee sponsored the series from 1974 through 1976. When the Continuing Education Committee of the Education and Training Board was established in 1976, it was given responsibility for administering the Master Lecture Series. That stewardship began with the 1977 series.

Titles for the Master Lecture Series have included the following:
Physiological Psychology (1974)
Developmental Psychology (1975)

Behavioral Control (1976)
Brain-Behavior Relationships (1977)
Psychology of Aging (1978)
Sex and Gender in Psychology (1979)
Cognitive Psychology (1980)
Psychotherapy Research and Behavior Change (1981)
Psychology and the Law (1982)
Psychology and Health (1983)
Psychology and Learning (1984)

In 1985 the title for the Master Lecture Series will be *Psychology and Work,* and in 1986 it will be *Cataclysms, Catastrophies, and Crises: Psychological Knowledge in Action.*

Psychology and Learning

Five lectures on the theme of psychology and learning were presented at the 1984 APA Convention by leading scholars in the study of animal and human learning. The lectures in this volume are by Gregory A. Kimble, Leonard Krasner, Jack L. Michael, Lauren B. Resnick, and John Garcia.

In the first chapter, Kimble compares the early scientific studies of learning done by Ebbinghaus, Pavlov, Thorndike, and Locke with the contemporary psychology of learning. The psychology of learning in its early stages was dominated by a view of behavior in which the organism was a passive tool of the environment, a helpless product shaped by the accidents of experience. Investigation by psychologists, however, has led to a new psychology of learning that differs from the earlier one in that the organism is now recognized as an active agent in the learning process. It is now recognized that heredity and prior experience affect basic processes such as acquisition, extinction, generalization, and discrimination, as well as modifying the influence of such variables as number and magnitude of reinforcements and stimulus intensity.

Krasner discusses the derivation of learning theory applications in the environment—what he calls "LTE"—focusing on concepts and issues with environmental impact, such as instrumental or operant conditioning, reinforcement, shaping, situational influences, consequences of behavior, social learning, contextual components, and research design. The broad framework of this chapter is the psychology of behavior influence, which focuses on the process of change (via learning).

Michael considers the origin and current characteristics of the behavioral approach that is most closely related to the work of B. F. Skinner, and he includes a discussion of theoretical and philosophical issues, basic behavioral concepts, and the field known as applied behavior analysis. In addition to describing the current and potential contributions of this approach, Michael clarifies some common misconceptions and discusses frequently raised objections to Skinner's "radical" behavior analysis theories.

Recent research in cognitive science is shaping new conceptions of human mental functioning and suggesting new ways of thinking about the processes of learning and instruction. Resnick outlines some of the most important current theories of how people acquire and use complex cognitive capabilities and considers their implications for the theory and practice of instruction. In fundamental domains of instruction, such as reading, writing, mathematics, and science, research has shown that learning is dependent on a complex mix of already established knowledge and general processes of thinking. Special attention is given to the questions of whether general learning abilities and higher order skills can be taught and what the most effective ways of teaching them might be.

In the final chapter, Garcia reviews the evolution of learning mechanisms based on biological adaptation. It is now recognized that organisms are subjected to selective pressures that apparently have led to at least two types of specialized defense mechanisms. These mechanisms operate under different learning principles that cannot be explained by traditional learning theories. Garcia maintains that learning must be characterized as a series of adaptive subsystems, each characterized by particular input, output, and parameters of association, and each designed to carry out specific strategies in the face of ecological challenges.

The thrust of these lectures, taken as a whole, is that the psychology of learning is changing through research and new applications in ways that were not foreseen by the pioneers who first studied learning in a scientific manner. These changes have broad implications for the fields of instruction, behavior change, social psychology, and further study of human learning.

I am indebted to the Continuing Education Committee including Clyde Crego, Deanna Chitayat, Lucia Gilbert, Thomas Boll, and Kurt Salzinger for the selection of timely topics and preeminent lecturers for this series. I also thank our lecturers whose cooperation in submitting excellent first drafts made our job less formidable than it might have been. Their diligence and thoughtfulness are much appreciated.

Finally, special thanks are due Amado Padilla, Kurt Salzinger, and Deanna Chitayat for their assistance in contacting the lecturers; Rosemary Beiermann of the Continuing Education Program Office for assistance in preparing materials for the Master Lecture Series in this volume; and Brenda Bryant, APA's Manager of Special Publications, for technical assistance.

Barbara L. Hammonds

THE PSYCHOLOGY OF LEARNING ENTERS ITS SECOND CENTURY

G regory A. Kimble, Professor Emeritus of psychology at Duke University, has been a member of the American Psychological Association for nearly 40 years and a fellow since 1951. He is a member of Divisions 2 (Teaching of Psychology) and 25 (Experimental Analysis of Behavior) and a fellow of the Divisions of General Psychology, Experimental Psychology, Evaluation and Measurement, Physiological Psychology, and History of Psychology. He has served on numerous governance units of APA, including the Council of Representatives, the Policy and Planning Board, the Publications and Communications Board, and the Board of Directors. He is currently chairperson of the *Psychology Today* Committee.

Kimble is also a member of several regional psychological associations, as well as the Society of Experimental Psychologists, the Psychonomic Society, and the American Association for the Advancement of Science. He has authored 13 books, nearly two dozen chapters, and more than 50 articles on topics ranging from general psychology to learning and conditioning.

After receiving his PhD from the State University of Iowa, Kimble began his teaching career at Brown University, moving from there to Yale University, Duke University, University of Colorado, and back to Duke University as Chair of the Department of Psychology. In 1973 he was a NATO Fellow at Cambridge University. He is a member of Phi Beta Kappa and Sigma Xi and is listed in *Who's Who in America.*

GREGORY A. KIMBLE

THE PSYCHOLOGY OF LEARNING ENTERS ITS SECOND CENTURY

A hundred years ago in 1884, Herman Ebbinghaus, in Germany, must have been nearly finished with the research that appeared in *Über das Gedachtnis,* or, translated roughly, *On Memory* (1885/1913). This research consisted of a series of studies of the rote memorization of nonsense syllables, in which Ebbinghaus inflicted upon himself the role of sole subject. In his report Ebbinghaus introduced psychology to the use of statistical thinking; he demonstrated the existence of remote associations; he dealt with the length–difficulty relations in rote learning; and he pointed to the importance of meaningfulness in verbal learning, which for him was a problem, one that he solved by reducing, as much as it is possible, the meaningfulness of the materials to be learned.

Less than a decade later in Russia, Pavlov began his studies of digestion that led to the discovery of the classically conditioned reflex. Begun in the early 1890s—well before the appearance of Twitmeyer's dissertation in 1902 (see Twitmeyer, 1974), which some chauvinists have cited to establish American priority in the study of conditioning— Pavlov's research was reported in *Lectures on the Work of the Principal Digestive Glands* in 1897. An English translation of the book appeared in 1902 (Pavlov, 1897/1902). In this book Pavlov reported observations that would later be called the acquisition and extinction of conditioned reflexes and interpreted in terms of "temporary connection," "internal inhibition," and "external inhibition."

In 1897, the year in which the first Russian edition of Pavlov's book on digestion was published, Edward Lee Thorndike at Columbia had already completed the pioneer experiments, which were reported in 1898 in an article entitled "Animal Intelligence: An Experimental Study of the Associative Processes in Animals." In this article Thorndike described his studies of cats escaping from a puzzle box to obtain a bit of food outside. These were early experiments on what was later called operant conditioning or instrumental learning. In the interpretation of his findings, Thorndike put forth a stimulus–response interpretation of learning (learning by doing) along with early versions of continuity theory (gradual learning) and what, unfortunately, came to be called reinforcement theory (the law of effect).

Methodological Climate

The foregoing capsule history shows that by the turn of the century, substantial progress had been made in the study of human rote learning, classical conditioning, and operant conditioning. A scientific psychology of learning appeared to be in the making. The earliest treatments suggested that the science of learning would be a very general science. Almost nobody was concerned with a question that today seems both obvious and important: Can there be a completely general psychology of learning? Given that the studies of Ebbinghaus, Pavlov, and Thorndike used very different methods, different materials to be learned, different species of subjects, and different forms of interpretation, what, if anything, do these studies have in common? Are they really just different versions of the same process? Is it proper to call them all by the same name?

The reason that these questions were not asked suggests the probable answer. In the early 1900s the great schools of psychology, structuralism, functionalism, behaviorism, and Gestalt psychology, were beginning to take form. In spite of their basic disagreements, these schools shared a common outlook. They all attempted to develop very general explanations of behavior. Although it is important to understand that the functionalists and behaviorists were much more interested in the early studies of learning than the structuralists and Gestalt psychologists were, none of them had much difficulty in making the facts of learning fit their interpretations: association of ideas for the structuralists, reacting to total situations for the Gestaltists, adapting to environmental requirements for the functionalists, and forming neural connections for the behaviorists.

It has often been argued (Kimble, 1973) that this new science captured and was captured by the themes that had come to dominate all psychology in those days: empiricism, elementism, associationism, and mechanism.

Empiricism refers to the idea that all knowledge comes from experience. For psychology this idea had two important consequences. One is that it gave the learning process a special significance for the field, for if all knowledge comes from experience, everything that people know and do, even what they are, must be the result of learning. The other consequence was a directive on the nature of scientific procedures: They must be objective and based on observation rather than on authority and intuition.

Elementism maintains that the proper scientific method is analysis. The elementist breaks a phenomenon down into elementary units and then attempts to discover the rules of synthesis by which these elements combine to create the observed phenomenon. In the early psychology of learning, stimuli and responses were the elements. Even Ebbinghaus's nonsense syllables were conceived in these terms.

From the time of Aristotle, *associationism* has referred to the process that hypothetically joins psychic elements together. This process was referred to as stimulus–response connections by Thorndike, as temporary stimulus–stimulus connections by Pavlov, and as verbal associations by Ebbinghaus.

Mechanism endows an organism with machinelike properties. In the mechanistic viewpoint behavior is seen as the inexorable consequence of influences over which an individual has little or no control.

This list of impersonal characteristics makes me wonder why a psychology defined by such terms was accepted. Such a psychology robs behavior of its wholeness; it destroys the concept of personal control; it takes away all possibility of people's being constructive and creative; and it leaves them submissively obedient to the laws of association. Lately I have come to suspect that this cold-blooded psychology never did catch on and that the methodological "isms" I have summarized are the lowest common denominators of the psychology of the 1900s. They are like the fundamental tones that make up the pitches of a melody. Analysis reveals that the tones are there and that they are indeed fundamental, but what makes the melody worth listening to is the richness provided by a pattern of overtones. Thus in this chapter, I concentrate on what was more clearly unique to the psychologies that grew out of the work of Pavlov, Thorndike, and Ebbinghaus.

This chapter is intended to be a review of the field of learning. My discussion of classical conditioning and operant conditioning provides brief histories of the research and theories in each subfield. I then progress to a discussion of human information processing. I have also tried to limit my discussion to generally accepted facts and interpretations. There is little in this chapter that is faddish or controversial. I have tried to be comprehensive; I deal with 80 or 90 basic concepts and ideas, and my coverage of most topics is consequently sketchy. I have provided references to other sources that contain more complete discussions. Key terms are introduced in italics in order to aid the reader.

Classical Conditioning

Pavlov's demonstration of *classical conditioning* is so well-known that my description of the method can be very brief. A neutral *conditioned stimulus* (CS) such as the ringing of a bell was presented a few seconds before the delivery of some non-neutral *unconditioned stimulus* (US) such as food. The food produced an *unconditioned response* (UR). After several pairings of CS and US, the CS would dependably begin to evoke a *conditioned response* (CR) that resembled the unconditioned response. In the 40 years following his first demonstrations of conditioning, Pavlov discovered most of the major phenomena of conditioning: acquisition of the CR, extinction, spontaneous recovery, generalization, discrimination, inhibition of delay, conditioned inhibition, and higher-order conditioning.

Pavlov (1927) interpreted these phenomena in terms of a quasi-neurological theory. Considering only the most basic phenomena, he took the *acquisition* of the CR to mean that a *temporary connection* had been formed between a cortical center activated by the US and another center activated by the CS, so that the CS came to function in the same way as the US did. Later writers would call this a *stimulus-substitution theory*. He explained *extinction* as the breaking of this temporary connection as a result of the accumulation of *internal inhibition,* which was produced whenever a temporary connection was not *reinforced* by the delivery of the US. *Spontaneous recovery* resulted from the disappearance of internal inhibition. *Generalization* occurred because of the process of *irradiation.* That is, the cortical activity produced by the CS spread outward from the focal center of cortical excitation, allowing stimuli that resemble the CS to elicit the CR. Because the level of excitation decreased with greater distance from the focus of excitation, however, the CR elicited by stimuli other than the CS would be weaker. This accounted for the existence of the *generalization gradient. Discrimination* occurred because irradiation to neighboring cortical areas was prevented by internal inhibition which also irradiated from the cortical locus of activity representing the nonreinforced negative stimulus.

Pavlov was a physiologist, and he was very critical of psychology because of that field's preoccupation with what he saw as fictitious entities like superego and attitude. The Russians take a materialistic view of behavior, and Pavlov objected to the immaterial nature of psychological explanations. It is at least amusing to note that none of Pavlov's concepts were any more materialistic than those he criticized, for he had never made direct observations of the hypothetical cortical events that were alleged to underlie conditioning phenomena. They, like the concepts he rejected, were inferences from observations of animal behavior and nothing more than that, except for the surplus meaning carried by the Pavlovian concepts. It was easy for psychologists to make this criticism, however, only after they had been exposed to the writings of the logical positivists and had recognized the importance of operational definitions. Pavlovian theory had other problems, many of which remain today.

What is Learned?

Pavlov's stimulus-substitution theory ran into trouble almost immediately, for rarely if ever was the CR identical to the UR. In most cases the CR was smaller and slower. Actually this was not a serious problem for Pavlov, because he took a very dynamic view of the conditioning process, and he maintained that the CS initiated excitatory and inhibitory processes simultaneously. Thus the more sluggish CR could have been accounted for on the ground that it was elicited against a background of inhibition that attenuated the reaction.

Paradoxical conditioned responses. A more difficult problem for stimulus-substitution theory grew out of the phenomenon of *paradoxical conditioning,* which sometimes occurred with the conditioning of drug-induced physiological responses. (See Eikelboom & Stewart, 1982, for a recent review and for a more detailed presentation of the argument that I am about to make.) In the experiments that demonstrated this phenomenon, the CR is the opposite of the UR. For example, in rats, an injection of alcohol results in a decrease in body temperature, but if the injection occurs as the US in a conditioning situation, the CR is an increase in temperature. What accounts for these paradoxical CRs, and can stimulus-substitution theory be salvaged from the threat that such observations seem to pose?

The answer to these questions was almost available in one of Pavlov's most essential notions, the idea that conditioning is a function of the central nervous system (CNS). Quite recently Eikelboom and Stewart (1982) suggested such an explanation. They proposed that paradoxical CRs develop when the UR is elicited by influences operating directly on the responding organ, or through efferent neural processes that do not involve the CNS. Under such conditions feedback mechanisms that do involve the CNS go to work to restore the body's function to its predisturbed state. These corrective processes that oppose the effect produced by the US are what gets conditioned in these cases. Thus if the response mediated by the CNS is taken as the true UR, there is nothing paradoxical at all about these conditioned responses.

A personal example that may be familiar to others who grew up in a cold climate will show how this conditioning process works. I remember that as a child, when my mother bundled me up before I went out into the subzero Minnesota winters, I often felt a sudden glow of warmth, and I worried about it because I thought that the outside cold would just seem that much colder by contrast. Much later on, somewhere in the literature, I discovered that this "flushing reaction" is a well-known physiological phenomenon. What apparently happens is that low temperatures acting directly on the body surfaces elicit the shivering and shuddering that are common responses to cold. These reactions lead the body to take corrective measures that counteract the threat of the loss of body heat. It is these responses that become conditioned and appear in response to the stimuli associated with going out into the cold.

Contiguity versus contingency. According to Pavlov's interpretation, conditioning consists of an association between the cortical events evoked by two stimuli, CS and US. More recent thinking assumes that the critical events are indeed the occurrences of stimuli, but that something additional is involved. It is not just the *contiguity* of the two stimuli, the fact that they occur together in time, that is important. Rather, it is when the learner perceives a *contingency* between them that the CS serves to predict the occurrence of the US. As with other developments in learning, which I will mention in this chapter, this theory makes the learner more of an active participant in the process than previous treatments had.

The definition of a contingency involves two probabilities, the probability of the occurrence of event B, given the occurrence of event A and the probability of the occurrence of event B, given the nonoccurrence of event A. In classical conditioning, events A and B are the CS and US, respectively. Plotted against each other, these two probabilities define the *Pavlovian contingency space* shown in Figure 1, in which p(US/CS) is to be read "the probability of occurrence of the US, given that the CS has occurred," and p(US/$\overline{\text{CS}}$) is to be read "the probability of occurrence of the US, given that the CS has not occurred."

The concept that CS–US contingency rather than CS–US contiguity is required for conditioning to occur can be made explicit with the aid of Figure 1. The diagonal line labeled "unpredictability" in Figure 1 represents the absence of a contingency. The probability of occurrence of the US is the same whether or not the CS has been presented. Everywhere else in the contingency space, some form of CS–US contingency exists. In the upper left-hand region of this space the contingency

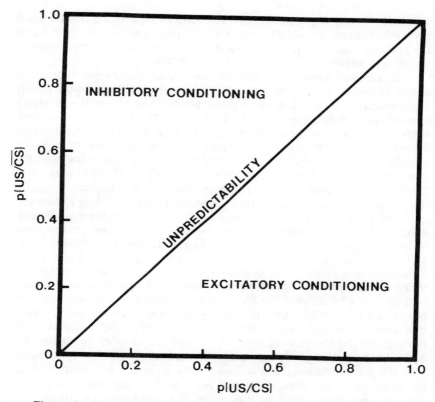

Figure 1. Pavlovian contingency space. A contingency is defined in terms of two probabilities, the probability (p) of the occurrence of event B (US) given the occurrence of event A (CS), or given the nonoccurrence of event A ($\overline{CS}$).

is a *negative contingency*. The occurrence of the US is more probable if the CS has not been presented than if CS has been presented.

This last point has a particular significance for choosing the appropriate controls to be used in performing a conditioning experiment. If the essential circumstance for the acquisition of conditioning is a contingency, then the appropriate control to use in an experiment designed to determine whether a particular CS–US combination leads to conditioning is one of zero contingency. The random presentation of explicitly unpaired deliveries of CS and US (formerly the standard control procedure) would not be appropriate because this procedure entails a negative contingency, and *inhibitory conditioning* would be expected to occur. A landmark experiment by Rescorla (1967) showed that this actually happens and that *excitatory conditioning* occurs when probabilities are arranged to provide a *positive contingency,* the CS and US probabilities shown in the lower right-hand portion of the contingency space.

An additional point of particular importance that needs to be made about Figure 1 is that the probabilities represented there are purely mathematical. Figure 1 says nothing whatsoever about the learner's appreciation of contingencies. To be specific, the fact that a zero contingency means mathematical unpredictability does not guarantee that a person will react that way. There is reason to conclude, in fact, that people tend to perceive predictability where none exists and that the strength of this tendency is one where great individual differences exist. Once more the contribution of the learner is more important than a purely mechanistic treatment of the learning process is likely to suggest.

Effects of cognition. Sometimes subjects in a conditioning experiment fail to get conditioned. If the subjects are human one can ask them about their understanding of the procedures. These unconditioned subjects may know a great deal about the experiment—that there was a little light that came on now and then; that it wasn't very bright; that there was a puff of air that hit the corner of the eye from time to time and caused a blink; that the little light and the air puff came together, but not on every trial; that trials were separated by about half a minute; that late in the experiment the air puff ceased to be delivered; that never once did the subject blink at the light before the air hit the eye; and that the whole procedure was a colossal bore. Obviously, subjects who do get conditioned know these same things, a fact that leads to the question of why these cognitive aspects of conditioning could have been ignored for as long as they were. Perhaps they were thought to be unimportant. If so that notion was eventually proved to be wrong.

There were demonstrations that both conditioning and extinction could occur in curarized animals, which suggests that cognition can mediate these processes. As early as 1949, Razran proposed that stimulus generalization entailed the categorization of stimuli by subjects. Razran argued that the smooth generalization gradients that had been reported by Hovland (1937) and others were *averaging artifacts,* and that, within categories, *generalization decrement* did not occur. Finally Spence (1956) and others employed cognitive interpretations when they proposed a generalization decrement hypothesis to account for the *partial reinforcement extinction effect,* where extinction following intermittent reinforcement is slower than extinction following continuous reinforcement. The specific hypothesis was that the switch to extinction is easier to perceive after continuous reinforcement than during partial reinforcement, hence the more rapid extinction in the first of these conditions.

Another suggestion of the importance of cognitive processes came from studies of the effects of varying *conditioned stimulus intensity.* To

Pavlov, CS intensity had been one of the most important variables that determined the effectiveness of a conditioning procedure. He had found that increasing CS intensity, at least up to some fairly high level, increased the speed of conditioning. American experiments on the same topic yielded little or no difference in the levels of conditioning obtained with differentially strong CSs. These different outcomes were eventually traced to the fact that Pavlov's experiments were usually carried out *within subjects*. The different CS intensities were used with the same dog, and this procedure gave the animal the chance to compare the various stimuli. American attention to unconfounded experimental design led to experiments that employed a *between-subjects* design in which each subject was conditioned with a single CS intensity, making comparisons impossible. Grice and Hunter (1964) performed the critical experiment in which they compared the between- and within-subjects procedures. Their results showed a strong difference in effect of conditioned stimulus intensity within subjects and no difference between subjects.

After attention was focused on CS effectiveness, two other phenomena that could be interpreted in cognitive terms, overshadowing and blocking, soon became matters of great theoretical interest. *Overshadowing* occurs when *compound conditioned stimuli* are used in an experiment where the CS consists of two or more stimuli, say a noise and a light, and one member of the compound may be completely dominant. Tested separately, only one of the stimuli turns out to be effective. One stimulus has overshadowed the effect of the other.

Blocking refers to overshadowing that is produced by past experience. In the classic experiment on blocking (Kamin, 1969), rats were first conditioned using one stimulus (e.g., noise) as a CS. In the next stage of the experiment, the original CS was paired with a second CS (e.g., a light) to form a compound, and conditioning continued. Appropriate tests showed that, although the second stimulus was potentially an effective CS, it did not elicit the CR in these experiments. The cognitive interpretation of blocking is that the second CS in the compound was ineffective because it carried no information; the original CS predicted the US as well as the two together. Such experimental results led to the appearance of powerful new theories of conditioning (e.g., Rescorla & Wagner, 1972) that easily incorporated such cognitive concepts as information processing, expectancy, surprise, and rehearsal.

Universality of the Process

Pavlov believed that classical conditioning was a very general process, possibly so general that any response an organism could make could be conditioned to any stimulus it could detect. This opinion was not without foundation. Pavlov and his associates had investigated the conditionability of a considerable array of responses to an equally wide assortment of stimuli and obtained only positive results (Bykov, 1957). Gradually, however, the assumption of grand generality began to be questioned.

The first of these questions arose with the recognition of the operational distinction between classical and operant conditioning and with the suggestion by some authors that classical conditioning might occur only with responses of the autonomic nervous system and that operant conditioning might occur only with responses of the skeletal nervous system. This hypothesis is now commonly regarded as wrong, partly because of the existence of the phenomenon of *autoshaping.* If a key in an operant chamber for pigeons is illuminated briefly and grain is made available soon afterward, the pecking that was originally elicited by the food is directed at the illuminated key. No special training is required. Operationally the autoshaping procedure is a classical conditioning procedure. The CS is the key light; the US is food; the UR and CR are both pecking, which is not an autonomic response. Hence, there is the current suspicion that skeletal responses are subject to classical conditioning.

Another type of threat to the complete ubiquity of the classical conditioning process came from studies of *taste aversions* (see chapter by Garcia in this volume). These experiments show that it is much easier to condition these aversive reactions to tastes than it is to condition them to other types of stimulation. One of the earliest demonstrations (Garcia & Koelling, 1966) showed that rats easily develop associations between tastes and sickness and between exteroceptive stimuli and electric shock, but they do not make the opposite associations: tastes with shock and exteroceptive stimulation with sickness. In these experiments, rats were first allowed to sample a substance with a novel taste—saccharin water, for example. Later on some rats were made sick with X-irradiation; others received electric shock. Tests conducted still later showed that those that had been made sick avoided the saccharin solution; those that had received electric shock did not. The reverse results were obtained with pairings of exteroceptive stimuli and sickness or shock. To repeat, it appears that certain stimulus–stimulus sympathies play a part in classical conditioning: tastes and sickness go together as do exteroceptive stimulation and pain.

At the same time that these studies called the complete generality of the classical conditioning process into question, they had the incidental effect of destroying certain faiths many psychologists acquired as undergraduates. One of these faiths was a faith in the classical *interstimulus interval function,* with its optimum at about half a second. In the taste aversion experiments, the CS (distinctive taste) and US (sickness) could be separated by hours, and still the conditioned aversive reaction was established. And as if that were not enough, the taste aversion conditioning studies provided examples of single-trial learning. It was obvious that Thorndike's *continuity theory* that learning is a gradual process does not apply universally.

Applications of Classical Conditioning

At the same time that some lines of research were producing a new understanding of classical conditioning, it was becoming increasingly clear that such learning had important everyday applications. The most famous study of conditioning after the original Pavlovian demonstrations helped to make this point. In this study Watson and Rayner (1920) conditioned the orphan boy "Little Albert" to fear a white rat by pairing the presentation of the rat with the production of an ear-splitting noise made by striking an iron bar hanging just behind the child's head with a hammer.

The announcement of this successful demonstration led many psychological theorists to conclude that all phobias were acquired through such conditioning. Fear of flying in some people could sometimes be explained as a result of their painful wartime experiences involving planes. Claustrophobia was explained in one case (White, 1956) as the result of the person's having suffered through pneumonia in an oxygen tent while an infant. And sexual anxiety was held to be the unhappy result of cruel, but not unusual, handling of childhood sexual interest and experimentation.

One form of support for the theory that phobias must be conditioned responses came from the evidence that they could be extinguished by *systematic desensitization.* An interesting point that is probably not well known about systematic desensitization involves its history, going back to the University of Iowa in the late 1940s with Kenneth Spence. Leo J. Reyna came to Iowa the same year that I did. We were office mates for a time and suffered together the drudgery of doing the statistical analyses demanded by one of Spence's wartime projects. Having come to Iowa with a master's degree in hand, I finished in 1945 and went on to a job at Brown. Reyna finished two or three years later when jobs in experimental psychology were even scarcer than they are now. He ended up in South Africa at Witwatersrand University. There he met a young physician whom he encouraged to practice Hullianism in psychotherapy, thus making him one of Spence's intellectual progeny. The name of Spence's improbable grandson, as the reader may have guessed, was Joseph Wolpe. Wolpe's method is so well-known that I shall not describe it. It demands notice in passing, however, because it was a landmark contribution in our field. It was soon to have the company of a number of other operant methods of behavior therapy to be mentioned after a more general discussion of operant conditioning.

Little Albert acquired his fear of white rats in a situation where pain and punishment were the predictable sequels to the presentation of the rat. The introduction of the newer, contingency view of the conditioning arrangement led psychologists to question the consequences of unpredictability, that is, where the contingency falls on the diagonal line in the contingency space in Figure 1. Answers to this question came from studies that used what is sometimes called a *triadic design.* There are three groups of subjects in these experiments. For those in the first group, the occurrence of punishment (usually electric shock) follows the presentation of a conditioned stimulus. For the second *yoked control* group, the shock is delivered without warning on the same schedule as for the first group and there is no CS to predict it. The third group receives no shock. The critical comparison in these experiments is between the subjects in the first two groups, for whom the only difference is the predictability of shock; everything else is the same. In one particularly important series of studies, Weiss (1968) demonstrated a much greater frequency of stomach ulcers in rats in the yoked control group than in the group receiving signaled shock.

The phenomena of conditioned taste aversions are common in human experience. In the introduction to *Biological Boundaries of Learning* (Seligman & Hager, 1972), Seligman tells this personal story.

> Sauce Béarnaise is an egg-thickened, tarragon-flavored concoction, and it used to be my favorite sauce. It now tastes awful to me. This happened several years ago, when I felt the effects of the stomach flu ... after eating filet mignon with Sauce Béarnaise. I became violently ill and spent most of the night vomiting. The next time I had Sauce Béarnaise, I couldn't bear the taste of it. [The acquisition of this powerful averson seems] to fit a classical conditioning paradigm: CS (sauce) paired with US (illness) and UR (vomiting) yields CR (nauseating taste). (p. 8)

There is now reason to suppose that taste aversions can accompany vitamin deficiencies (Rozin, 1968) and diseases such as cancer, in which nausea is a common symptom. Berstein and Sigmundi (1980), for example, found that rats implanted with a lethal tumor ate much less food than control animals and that they did so because they developed aversions to the tastes of the foods eaten while the tumor was developing. These authors point out that people also develop aversions to the foods that they consume while they are undergoing the chemotherapy and radiation therapy, which have well-known nauseating side effects.

As I have stated, Pavlov thought of classical conditioning as a totally general form of learning. He accepted a *premise of equipotentiality,* according to which any response can be conditioned to any stimulus and with equal ease. The taste aversion experiments challenged this interpretation and suggested that a *principle of preparedness* applies to the establishment of conditioned responses. Some responses are easier to condition to certain stimuli than to others. Evidence that this principle might also apply to human fear conditioning became available shortly after Watson and Rayner (1920) reported the results of their experiment with Little Albert. Attempts to repeat the experiment with other CSs were sometimes unsuccessful. For example, Valentine (1930) failed to obtain fear conditioning in a child when he used objects such as a pair of opera glasses for the CS. He suggested that fears might be more easily conditioned to furry animals than to other objects.

Öhman and his colleagues (Öhman, Fredrikson, Hygdahl, & Rimmö, 1976) have now provided more formal evidence of the correctness of this point of view in an experiment on the *galvanic skin response* (GSR), which is commonly used for the experimental study of conditioning with human beings. If an electric current too weak to feel is passed between electrodes placed on two points on the body, there is a measurable resistance to the passage of this current. The level of this resistance depends on several factors, the most important one for psychological purposes being emotional arousal. When the individual is emotionally excited, resistance decreases. This change can be measured with sensitive electronic equipment and recorded in ink on graph paper. This change in resistance is the GSR. When the GSR is used in the conditioning laboratory, the procedure usually consists of pairing a neutral CS with electric shock, the US. After very few such pairings, the CS usually comes to elicit the GSR.

The investigators conditioned the GSR to three different classes of stimuli—pictures of snakes and spiders, circles and triangles, and flowers and mushrooms—and they used electric shock as the US. The strengths of conditioning to these classes of stimuli were the greatest to snakes and spiders, the next greatest to circles and triangles, and the least to flowers and mushrooms. This suggests that the circles and triangles were truly neutral stimuli for the participants in this experiment, that human subjects are prepared to acquire a fearful response to snakes and spiders, and they are prepared not to acquire such a response to flowers and mushrooms.

Operant Conditioning

Until the mid-1930s psychologists made no sharp distinction between classical conditioning and operant or instrumental conditioning. Although Miller and Konorsky had argued as early as 1928 (see Kimble, 1967, p. 261) that the two forms of learning are different, Pavlov totally rejected this idea. Thorndike suspected that "associative shifting," as he called it, might be different from trial-and-error learning, but he seemed inclined to dismiss the former process as a mysterious and probably insignificant nuisance. Then in 1935 and 1937, respectively, Skinner and Schlosberg published important articles that brought the critical distinction to everyone's attention.

To use modern terminology, classical and operant conditioning differ operationally in terms of the procedures that define them. In operant conditioning, there is a contingency between the learner's response and reinforcement (reward or punishment). In classical conditioning, the contingency is between the experimenter's presentation of the CS and reinforcement. Figure 2 presents the *operant contingency space,* which is like the Pavlovian contingency space presented earlier as Figure 1. In this case p(RF/R) is to be read "the probability of reinforcement, given the occurrence of a response" and p(RF/$\overline{\text{R}}$) is to be read "the probability of reinforcement, given the nonoccurrence of a response."

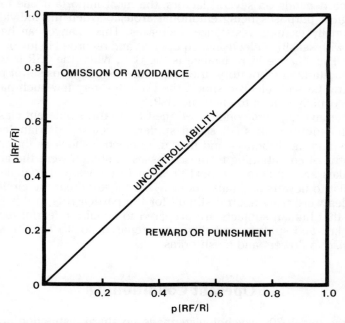

Figure 2. Operant contingency space. This space is defined in terms of the probability (p) of reinforcement (RF), given that some specified response has (R) or has not occurred ($\overline{\text{R}}$).

Types of Operant Conditioning

With the operational difference between classical and instrumental or operant conditioning established, finer distinctions among types of operant conditioning were soon proposed. Four of them appear in Figure 3: reward learning, punishment learning, omission learning, and avoidance learning. These distinctions derive from the possible combinations of positive and negative contingencies (which I have already discussed) and positive and negative reinforcers, which I discuss now.

Positive and negative reinforcers and reinforcement. Paraphrasing Thorndike, I define a *positive reinforcer* as something that an animal does nothing to avoid, often doing such things as attaining and preserving it. A *negative reinforcer* is something that an animal commonly avoids or abandons. With these definitions, I can now explain what is involved in the four types of operant conditioning that are shown in Figure 3. *Reward learning* occurs when there is a positive contingency between a response and a positive reinforcer (the response is rewarded). In *punishment learning* there is a positive contingency between a response and a negative reinforcer (the response is punished).

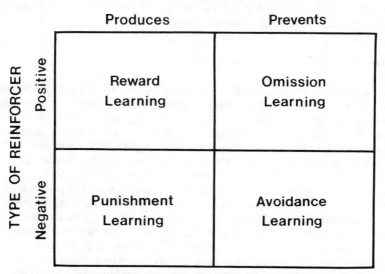

Figure 3. Response–reinforcer contingencies for four basic forms of operant conditioning.

Omission learning is occurring when there is a negative contingency between a response and a positive reinforcer (not making the response is rewarded). In *avoidance learning,* there is a negative contingency between a response and a negative reinforcer (not making the response is punished).

Data from a host of experiments show that subjects learn the response involved in reward learning and in avoidance learning; they fail to learn the same response (or they learn an opposing response) in the omission and punishment situations. If one takes note of the algebraic signs of the contingencies and reinforcers involved, the rules of multiplication provide sensible definitions of positive and negative reinforcement that are not the same as positive and negative reinforcers.

Positive reinforcement occurs when there is a positive contingency between a response and a positive reinforcer (plus times plus) or a negative contingency between a response and a negative reinforcer (minus times minus). Like signs multiplied yield a positive product in both cases. In negative reinforcement, there is a positive contingency between a response and a negative reinforcer (plus times minus) or a negative contingency between a response and a positive reinforcer (minus times plus). Unlike signs multiplied yield a negative product in both cases. A response that enters into a contingency will be learned only under conditions of positive reinforcement, that is, in the reward learning and the avoidance learning paradigms. Please note that this statement is merely a factual statement; it makes no commitment to any particular theory of reinforcement.

Basic Phenomena of Conditioning

These modern definitions of the four fundamental operant conditioning paradigms are couched in terms of probabilities rather than inevitabilities. An earlier definition of *reward learning,* in contrast, would have been the form of learning that occurs when a response produces a reinforcer. A definition of *avoidance learning* would have been the form of learning that occurs when a response prevents the occurrence of a negative reinforcer. The newer definitions are more comprehensive because they include an infinite number of combinations of possible probabilities of the occurrence of a reinforcer. These definitions also put more of a burden on the learner, who is expected to assess these probabilities in order to deal with them. There is substantial literature on the so-called *matching law,* according to which animals distribute responses among alternatives in proportion to the probability of obtaining reinforcement for each alternate response (see Schwartz, 1984, pp. 301–326 for a discussion). Such behavior suggests that animals are responding in terms of what they know about these probabilities. Research on the basic learning processes has revealed a number of other ways in which cognition influences are important.

Acquisition. At the halfway point between the time of the pioneering work of Ebbinghaus and now, C. L. Hull (e.g., 1943) was the dominant figure in the psychology of learning. Hull and his colleagues, John Dollard and Neal Miller (1950), who may have been most specific on this point, thought of the actions of reinforcers as being highly automatic and as being able to strengthen stimulus–response connections that could even be out of the learner's awareness and beyond control. Early demonstrations that supported this idea appeared in studies of verbal conditioning and the operant conditioning of visceral responses.

In the *verbal conditioning* experiments, subjects were rewarded for making some verbal response, which they were never told produced the reinforcer. In the most studied procedure, the experimenter said "good" whenever the subjects used the pronouns "I" or "we" in sentences that they created from words presented on flashcards. In these experiments, the percentage of "I" and "we" responses increased, although the subjects reported that they had not noticed the connection between making these responses and hearing the reassuring "good" voiced by the experimenter. At first these data seemed to provide strong evidence for learning without awareness.

Follow-up experiments soon challenged the without-awareness interpretation, however (see Erikson, 1962, for a discussion of the issue after this line of research had become controversial). It turned out that more careful questioning of the subjects revealed that they were usually aware of some response–reinforcement contingency, although they sometimes misperceived the connection and developed a *correlated hypothesis*—"he's saying 'good' whenever I make up a crazy sentence"—that increased the probability of using "I" or "we" in the sentence. After the subjects arrived at such an awareness, their motives became important; they increased the frequency of saying "I" and "we" only if they enjoyed the experiment's little game; otherwise, they did not. Obviously, the operation of the reinforcer was far from automatic in these experiments.

The study of *visceral conditioning* began as a test of a difference between classical and operant conditioning that had been suggested by a number of authors. The immediate provocation appears to have been some of my statements in *Hilgard and Marquis' Conditioning and Learning* (Kimble, 1961), in which I held that classical and operant conditioning procedures are effective with different classes of responses. I said that

classically conditionable responses are "involuntary" responses of the autonomic nervous system and that instrumentally conditionable responses are "voluntary" responses of the central nervous system. . . .

It appears that there is no evidence which clearly violates the rule that the organism is capable of two forms of learning and that they are differentiated in terms of the responses to which they apply. (pp. 100, 102)

Soon after those blunt statements were published—whenever it was that the annual meeting of the Psychonomic Society was in Niagara Falls—Neal Miller told me that he was pretty sure that I was wrong on this point. He said, in fact, that a student of his had evidence that at least the salivary response could be conditioned by instrumental methods. Other demonstrations were soon to follow (see Miller, 1969). In these experiments curarized rats, without control of possibly mediating muscular reactions, received reward in the form of brain stimulation for the production of some involuntary responses such as bowel distinction, salivation, increased or decreased heart rate, or an altered pattern of blood flow. The animals learned to control these responses that are normally both beyond control and out of awareness. These results provided strong evidence for the conclusion that it is possible to obtain direct, unmediated control over normally involuntary responses with the aid of operant conditioning procedures.

More recent clinical studies (Miller & Brucker, 1979) support the same conclusion. In these experiments, paraplegic patients who have lost control over the muscles of the lower limbs, thus excluding the mediating responses available to other people, have learned to manage the pattern of blood flow in these limbs through operant conditioning procedures. Again the evidence suggests that normally involuntary responses can be brought under direct voluntary control.

My own current opinion is that, although such learning may be possible, its occurrence is a rarity. For one thing the outcomes of these important experiments were not totally dependable. Soon after the successful demonstrations of visceral operant conditioning in curarized rats, there was a period of disheartening disillusionment. For reasons that are still not understood, the original investigators could not replicate the original results. Following a series of unsuccessful experiments designed to uncover the reason for these failures, Miller (Miller & Dworkin, 1974) finally advised against accepting the results at face value. Moreover, when such learning does take place, it is difficult and time consuming, much in contrast to the ease with which the same learning occurs with *biofeedback* methods that allow the use of mediating responses. Once more the active participation of the learner appears to be making important contributions.

Stimulus–response reinforcement theory. In the development of his influential theory of habit acquisition, Hull (1943) accepted all of Thorndike's major theoretical ideas: that learning consists of the development of stimulus–response (S-R) connections; that learning is gradual; and that the responses that an organism learns are those that are rewarded, punishment, according to later Thorndike, being relatively ineffective in weakening habits. All of these ideas came in for criticism. I have already mentioned one line of the research that led to a questioning of *continuity theory* (gradual learning) in my discussion of conditioned taste aversions. Criticisms of the other two hypotheses were often linked because evidence for learning without responding usually means learning without reinforcement as well.

One example of this linkage occurred in the famous *latent learning* experiment in which rats were permitted to explore a maze before the introduction of reward. Later on a reward was made available, and these animals often performed better than animals without the previous unrewarded experience. When such learning occurred, the importance of reinforcement and of responding was questioned. Reward had been eliminated—although there were always those who would argue that sources of reward remained—and the responses made in the original exploration of the maze would more often be responses that were not needed to run the maze efficiently than they were responses that were needed. These early demonstrations (e.g., Tolman & Honzik, 1930) gave rise to controversy and to a great deal of research that failed to put the controversy to rest. Latent learning frequently failed to occur, and when it did, creative theorists found ways to explain the phenomenon away if they needed to (Kimble, 1961, pp. 226–234).

More dependable support for learning without responding and without direct reward or punishment soon came from experiments on *observational learning;* the studies of *modeling* are one example. For example, Menzel (1973) allowed some chimpanzees to watch an experimenter hide 18 pieces of food in a large field, and then Menzel counted the number of pieces that the animals could find. The chimpanzees that saw the food being hidden found an average of 12.5 pieces; other chimpanzees without this experience found none.

Research on modeling showed that observational learning can affect socially important behavior like aggression and helping. In the best known studies, Bandura and his co-workers (Bandura, Grusek, & Menlove, 1966) let some children watch while an adult person kicked, punched, and verbally abused a "Bobo" doll. Other children did not have this experience. Later on, mild frustration was induced in both groups of children by taking toys away from them. Those who had witnessed the model's aggression were themselves more aggressive than were the other children. Such results show the importance of cognitive-perceptual processes in learning.

Extinction. Related changes of interpretation were taking place with respect to extinction. In 1939, Humphreys reported that an eyelid response conditioned with a schedule of randomly alternated reinforcement was more resistant to extinction than the same response when it was conditioned with continuous reinforcement. This partial reinforcement extinction effect (or just partial reinforcement effect) caused problems, for most theories accepted resistance to extinction as a measure of the strength of a habit and usually made habit strength a function of the number of reinforcements, ignoring pattern of reinforcement.

It now appears that several factors may contribute to the production of the partial reinforcement effect. First, a schedule of intermittent reinforcement during acquisition seems likely to produce frustration and to heighten the learner's motivation (Amsel & Roussel, 1952). Second, during acquisition on a partial reinforcement schedule, the individual learns to continue responding on trials without reinforcement. This learned persistence continues when there is no reinforcement at all. Third, the shift from partial reinforcement to no reinforcement is less noticeable than the shift from a continuous schedule to no reinforcement. Fourth, when individuals learn on a partial reinforcement schedule, memory traces of nonreinforcement become cues for responding. According to this more cognitive interpretation, the total absence of reinforcement provides cues to responding and resistance to extinction increases as a result.

Stimulus generalization and discrimination. When Hovland (1937) reported his classical studies of *stimulus generalization,* it was already recognized that the discriminability of stimuli might be the basis for this phenomenon. As a result, in his study on generalization along a pitch dimension, Hovland plotted his gradients as a function of *just noticeable differences* rather than sound frequency. The argument by implication was that stimulus generalization occurred to the extent that subjects failed to discriminate between training stimuli and those used to test for generalization. Blackwell and Schlosberg (1943) demonstrated *octave generalization* and provided an interesting bit of unusual evidence for such an interpretation. Although they differ markedly in physical terms, tones an octave apart are occasionally confused, even by people with perfect pitch. The phenomenon of octave generalization makes this same point for the laboratory rat.

The theory that stimulus generalization means a failure to discriminate was soon to come under attack, however. The strongest attack came from the important study by Guttman and Kalish (1956), who trained different pigeons to peck at a key that was illuminated by light of different colors and then measured the rate of key pecking at neighboring wavelengths. Guttman and Kalish found very little relationship beween the discriminability of training and test stimuli and the form of the generalization gradient.

In response to such criticism, one might say that the failure to obtain correspondence between generalization and discrimination is not surprising because Guttman and Kalish never told their subjects that they were supposed to discriminate. Perhaps if the pigeons had been clear on this point the expected relationship would have materialized. The way to communicate this idea to a pigeon, of course, is to carry out a discrimination experiment prior to testing for generalization. If one does such an experiment, the results show that discrimination training does make a difference in performance on tests for generalization. The gradient becomes steeper and two other new phenomena, a version of behavioral contrast and peak shift, occur (Figure 4).

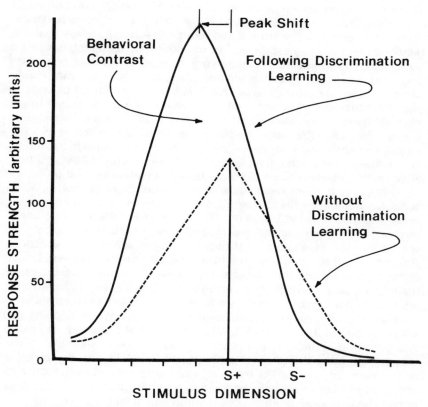

Figure 4. Effects of discrimination learning on generalization gradients. Note the increased amount of responding (behavioral contrast) and displacement of the gradient (peak shift) after discrimination learning.

Behavioral contrast refers generally to the fact that, in a discrimination situation, responding is more vigorous to the reinforced stimulus than it is to the same stimulus used alone as a discriminative stimulus. In Figure 4, the greater responding to S+ than to the same situation in the control condition makes this demonstration. *Peak shift* refers to the displacement of responding that occurs following discrimination training so that the strongest responding occurs to a stimulus that differs from the nonreinforced stimulus in the same way as the reinforced stimulus did, but by a greater amount.

Biological Constraints on Operant Conditioning

In my earlier discussion of the universality of classical conditioning, I described studies that demonstrated the existence of certain sympathies between predictive stimuli and reinforcers that make associations between them easy to establish. Let me now shift the emphasis just a bit to make the point that similar sympathies exist between responses and reinforcers. For example, anyone who has studied operant conditioning in the laboratory knows that it is very easy to train pigeons to peck illuminated keys to get food or to train rats to press levers to get food. Although it is possible, it is very difficult to train these same animals to make the same responses to avoid receiving an electric shock. The unfolding story has added a great deal to our understanding of constraints on learning, and separate chapters on positive and negative reinforcers describe somewhat different features of the plot.

I begin with a famous example in the first of these categories. Many years ago, Skinner (1948) described an important experiment on *superstitious behavior* in the pigeon. The pigeons were placed in a Skinner box, and the hopper was opened at fixed intervals, allowing the pigeons access to grain no matter what they did. There was no actual contingency between any response the birds made and reinforcement. Under these circumstances the pigeons developed individual patterns of ritualistic behavior, which they performed as though they believed that food was contingent on these particular responses. These responses consisted of things such as circling the chamber, bowing, flapping the wings, and stretching the neck, all in ceremonial sequence. Skinner's interpretation of these actions was that each pigeon repeated whatever it happened to be doing when the hopper opened. Its chance activities of the moment, reinforced by food, were automatically strengthened and organized into a chain of actions that the pigeon performed to bridge the temporal gap from one reinforcement to the next.

At first blush these data seemed to suggest that reinforcement dictated the selection of whatever movement the pigeon was making as food was offered. Later work was to show that important qualifications were still needed. Staddon and Simmelhag (1971) repeated Skinner's experiment on superstition, but they made much more detailed observations of the pigeons' responses. They obtained the same results as Skinner had, but with one important addition: The ritualistic sequences of behavior always ended with a feeding response. This response was pecking in every pigeon except one, whose reaction was to move its head toward the food hopper. Such behavior seemed to occur more and more dependably as training progressed.

A second example has an even longer history. In 1946, Guthrie and Horton published their report on a study of cats escaping from a puzzle box. In their report they emphasized the fact that the cats tended to use identical movements when they tilted the pole in the box that achieved release. They interpreted this result to support Guthrie's hypothesis that what an organism learns when it learns anything is a detailed set of movements followed by a dramatic change in the situation.

In 1979, Moore and Stuttard published a note in *Science* that puts quite another light on the matter. In brief, Moore and Stuttard showed that the movements produced by the cat, although stereotyped as Guthrie and Horton had found, were actually species-typical greeting responses probably directed at the experimenters, who were present in the room. In fact, Moore and Stuttard showed that they could turn these responses on and off simply by having an audience either present in the room or absent.

Species-specific defense reactions. The very last experiment I ever did on avoidance conditioning never got beyond the pilot stage. It was an attempt to train rats to press a lever and then release it after the presentation of a light stimulus to avoid electric shock. The press–release contingency was introduced to preclude the possibility of the animals' learning to lean on the bar, keeping it permanently depressed, and thus making it impossible to administer another trial. After 15 to 20 unsuccessful attempts with as many subjects, I gave up. Not a single animal learned the bar-pressing response. Early in the experiment most of them produced that reaction, but they soon gave it up. Eventually all of the rats reacted to the light by crouching and cowering immobile in a corner of the conditioning apparatus.

That was sometime in the early 1950s. Guided by then-current Hullian learning theory, I concluded that the time it took for the lever to return to the released position after it had been pressed (1/20 of a second or so) must have been enough for some response other than lever pressing to occur and to be reinforced by shock reduction. In 1984, these disappointing results are understood in different terms. The fact that the rats learned to crouch and cower instead of to press the lever in my aborted experiment shows, as Bolles (1970) has stressed, that animals find it very easy to acquire *species-specific defense reactions* in avoidance learning. Crouching, cowering, and freezing are very characteristic fear reactions in the rat, and the fact that the rats in my preliminary experiments produced these reactions instead of lever pressing would not be a surprise these days.

There are even fragments of evidence for such influences in human fear conditioning. Samelson (1980), for example, picked up the point, missed by all of us for years, that Little Albert in the Watson and Rayner experiment typically responded by plunging his thumb into his mouth and sucking it. Thumb sucking, of course, is a high-probability reaction to fear in many children. Also, the idea that reinforcers are effective over time spans during which responses can be protected from interferences has been proposed by several authors. For an excellent review of research on biological constraints on classical and operant conditioning, see Domjan (1983).

Applications of Operant Conditioning

Ties between the psychology of learning and the field of psychopathology have always been close. Until recently, it was the fashion to view mental disorder as being determined primarily by environmental factors—as disorders of learning. With this assumption, it was natural to think of psychotherapy either as a set of procedures that were direct applications of the methods used to promote learning or as procedures that could be understood in those terms. More recently biological interpretations and therapies have come to dominate work with what were called the psychoses prior to DSM-III. Learning-based behavioral methods remain the treatment of choice for other mental disorders.

Behavior therapy. Programs of behavior therapy that correspond to each of the operant conditioning paradigms already presented have been developed. Reward training has proved to be particularly effective with children. Even severely withdrawn autistic children have been trained to follow simple commands and to attain an improved adjustment. The most telling demonstrations of the power of reward training are found in *token economies.* A token economy is a broadly based institutionalized program of behavior modification in which the client receives some sort of token for desired behavior. These tokens are then exchangeable for specific gifts, commodities, services, or activities. Token economies have been successfully established in schools, mental hospitals, reformatories, and homes for the mentally retarded.

The parallel to omission training is usually designed to extinguish an undesirable response by withholding reinforcement whenever the response occurs and rewarding a specific desirable behavior, not just any other response, as in the laboratory version of omission training. For example, a child might be ignored after a display of undesirable whiny behavior and praised after a display of more mature interactions with adults. Avoidance training and punishment training have both been used as therapy for sexual deviations with some success. Because success means the extinction of some behavior, one could question the alleged ineffectiveness of punishment, which is the reinforcer employed in both procedures.

The myth that punishment is not effective seems to have originated in Skinner's (1938) study of the extinction of the bar-pressing habit in laboratory rats. Skinner's results suggested that punishment merely slowed up the process of extinction and did nothing that nonreinforcement alone could not accomplish. More recent work beginning with Solomon and Wynne's (1954) studies of traumatic avoidance learning in dogs showed that strong punishment is actually very effective (see Solomon, 1964, for a review). Only mild punishments have the effect described by Skinner.

Learned helplessness. When a strong punishment is uncontrollable, the consequences for the organism can verge on the disastrous. Support for this strong statement comes from a series of studies involving a triadic design resembling that which was used in the classical conditioning experiments that produced ulcers in rats. The most impressive data have been provided by studies where the subjects were dogs. The animals in one group received strong electric shocks that the dogs could turn off by turning their heads and operating a lever. The dogs in a second group were a yoked control group that received uncontrollable shocks on the same schedule as the first group. A third group, the naive control group, received no shock. Twenty-four hours later, all of the animals received avoidance training in a shuttle box. The group previously trained with a shock that could be escaped and the naive control group learned the avoidance response quite readily. Six of eight animals in the yoked control group failed to learn at all. Because they had received the same shock as the group to which they were yoked, it was not punishment itself that was responsible for this failure to respond. Rather it was the inability to control the shock. In a summary article, Maier and Seligmen (1976) cite a considerable amount of research with dogs, cats, fish, and rats to show that this phenomenon of *learned helplessness* occurs very generally.

Maier and Seligman proposed originally that three psychological processes contribute to the production of learned helplessness. The subject loses the motivation to respond in the aversive situation, develops a cognitive inability to see that control is possible, and becomes anxious and depressed and develops other emotional disturbances. These ideas have been extended by others to interpretations of important human reactions, including depression (Seligman, 1975), the effects of classroom failure (Dweck, 1975), and analgesia (Sherman & Liebeskind, 1980).

Human Information Processing

The tradition of research on human verbal learning that began with Ebbinghaus dominated the field for about 80 years and made many important contributions. These contributions included (a) the assessment of the meaningfulness of the materials to be learned in terms of

the likelihood of their eliciting associations; (b) the invention of mechanical devices like the memory drum to control the learner's method
of practice; (c) the discovery of such phenomena as the serial position
function, retroactive and proactive inhibition, reminiscence, and
learning to learn; and finally (d) the creation of interference theory, one
of the most elegant theories in the history of the psychology of learning.
In my opinion, this research tradition reached its highest point of development with the publication in 1964 of Jean Barnes McGovern's dissertation "Extinction of Associations in Four Transfer Paradigms,"
which had been carried out under Benton J. Underwood's direction.

But there was a fatal flaw in the approach that began with Ebbinghaus: Its scope was limited to the passive rote learning of materials
presented in discrete units. In particular, interference theory broke
down in its attempts to deal with memory for organized lists and prose.
In the volume of *Psychological Monographs* that carried the McGovern
dissertation, there were two other monographs with the phrase "information processing" in their titles. Information processing had already
become the preferred approach to the study of human learning and
memory.

The Structure of Memory

As happened in the fields of classical and operant conditioning, the new
approach to human learning and memory was one in which the learner
made more of a contribution—as a processor and storer of information.
The three-stage model of information processing that came gradually
to be accepted appears in Figure 5. Tracing the progress of information
through the three stages in this model presents its main features. In
order to keep this presentation manageable, I shall limit my example
to the processing of verbal materials presented to an individual in
written or printed form. The most important questions that need to be
addressed in order to describe this information processing model are
these four:

1. How long do materials remain in each stage of memory?
2. How are they represented there?
3. How much information can be stored in that stage of memory?
4. What determines the fate of the information at each stage; that
is, is it lost or retained for further processing?

The answers to these questions are presented in Figure 5.

Sensory memory. Information remains in sensory memory for a
brief time that probably depends upon the sensory modality involved.
This period is only a second or two in the case of visual information.
During that brief time, huge amounts of material are registered as a
sort of sensory image, and the individual has some choice of what to
pay attention to. What the individual does attend to survives for further
processing in short-term memory (STM).

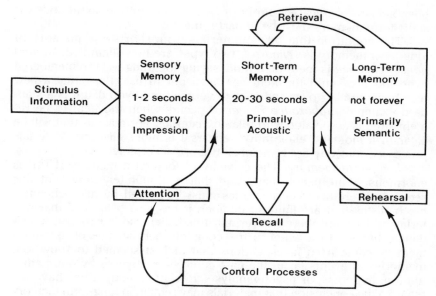

Figure 5. The information processing model of memory.

Short-term memory. In contrast to sensory memory, the capacity of short-term memory is small (seven items, plus or minus two), but the duration of this memory is something like 20 to 30 seconds. During this time, some materials in STM are lost as a result of interference. Materials in short-term memory exist in a form that is primarily acoustic.

At one time, it was believed that the representation of materials in STM is entirely acoustic, but experiments by Wickens (1972) on release from proactive inhibition (PI) have demonstrated that the representation is partly semantic.

In these experiments, subjects were presented with three related items (words, for example) to remember. On the first three trials, the words all belonged to one category, such as vegetables: *corn, pea, onion/bean, lettuce, radish/squash, potato, carrot.* On the fourth trial for a control group, the words were vegetables again: *pumpkin, spinach, turnip.* For an experimental group, the words were from another category, such as parts of speech: *noun, verb, adjective.* Over the first three trials, the amount recalled after about 20 seconds declined as proactive inhibition accumulated. Using the words on any trial after the first that belonged to the same category as those on previous trials created interference. The switch to a new category freed the subject from this interference and performance improved. Most importantly, what this phenomenon of release from PI proved is that the memorial code for short-term memory must be in part semantic.

The condition that takes materials from short-term memory to long-term memory is *rehearsal;* two types are now identified. *Maintenance rehearsal* is mere repetition, saying the thing to be remembered over and over until the item has been put to use. Repeating a new telephone number over and over to yourself until you dial it is a standard example. *Elaborative rehearsal* occurs when the item to be remembered is associated with related materials. For reasons that will be clear in a moment, elaborative rehearsal is more effective. Materials processed that way are remembered more accurately.

Long-term memory. The capacity of long-term memory (LTM) is enormous. Some people have said that it is infinitely large, but this seems unlikely because memories must be served by neurochemical mechanisms that are finite in number. It has also been said that materials in LTM are there forever, but this belief also is wrong. The evidence that led to a belief in the complete permanence of long-term memory came from investigations that at first seemed to show that memories of events far in the past could be recovered by brain stimulation, hypnosis, or psychoanalysis. Recent investigations have led many to the conclusion that materials may remain in long-term memory for years, but that they do disappear. For a very brief summary of current thinking, see Kimble, Garmezy, and Zigler (1984, pp. 194–195). The most important process that drives materials out of LTM is probably proactive inhibition.

The representation of materials in long-term memory is primarily semantic, but a part of the representation must be in terms of physical features. The latter features appear to provide the routes that are used to retrieve materials from LTM. The distinction between physical and semantic representation comes up frequently in discussions of information processing.

Research on *depth of processing* provides one important context for the application of these ideas. When one attempts to commit materials to memory, it is possible to study them in different ways, by attending to individual attributes of the materials to be learned. One can either process them superficially by attending to the physical characteristics of the materials or process them deeply by attending to meanings. Many experiments have demonstrated the superiority of deeper processing. As folklore understands, learning is far better when one studies materials for their meanings rather than their physical features. Because most verbal materials have meaning almost by definition, it is hard to imagine how they could be studied any other way or how they could be processed otherwise than deeply. In recognition of this general point, research since the earliest studies on depth of processing has suggested that a better expression than deeper processing may be more *elaborate processing.* Processing that adds meaning, makes connections to related ideas, and calls upon supporting information aids learning and subsequent recall (Stein & Bransford, 1979), presumably because such processing puts information into the type of code that is useful for storage.

Retrieval

Important leads to an understanding of how physical and semantic features function in the representation of materials in memory have come from studies of the *tip-of-the-tongue phenomenon*—those cases when we try to recall a piece of information that we know we know, but it refuses to be remembered. In technical terms, the desired information is available in memory but not accessible. Studies of the psychological states of people experiencing the tip-of-the-tongue phenomenon (Brown & McNeill, 1966) have produced very useful information about the process of retrieval.

As you know, one problem that one encounters in the tip-of-the-tongue state is that wrong answers come to mind, and they seem to prevent the occurrence of the right answer. An analysis of these wrong answers is revealing. Sometimes they are associated with the right answer in terms of meaning. More often, however, they merely sound like the sought-for term. Such data have led to a *generation–recognition theory* of retrieval. According to this theory, retrieval consists of a search through a region of memory where materials with a certain range of meanings are stored for an item with particular physical features. It is these physical features that permit the recognition of the correct answer when we find it and the rejection of all other items in memory.

The representational fate of physical and semantic features. Of necessity, information that finds its way eventually to long-term memory arrives at this information-processing doorway in physical form. Almost immediately this input acquires meaning. An important question is what the roles of physical and semantic forms of representation are from then on. Only the outline of an answer to this question is available presently.

Psychologists do know from work on the tip-of-the-tongue phenomenon that both physical and semantic information are stored in long-term memory and that physical features are important in retrieval. This is why Figure 5 shows information returning to STM—where representation is predominantly acoustic—in the process of retrieval. There is also reason to suspect that the form of representation in memory depends upon the type of processing that was used to store it. Most often people process materials for meaning. They store it as semantic information, and most of the superficial details disappear. Sometimes, however, people learn things under conditions that emphasize exact sounds and phraseology, that is, physical attributes. Learning "The Star-Spangled Banner" and Lincoln's Gettysburg Address for school-room presentation are examples. These memories tend to be stored in terms of exact phraseology (Rubin, 1977).

Episodic and semantic memory. Materials that are represented semantically in memory are at least close to what is commonly called "knowledge." Tulving (1972) has contrasted such semantic memory with *episodic memory,* which is memory for temporally dated autobiographic events. Semantic memory consists of facts, principles, relations, and strategies. The information in semantic memory has been coded in ways that allow it to be retrieved in a form that is different from the one in which it was stored originally. Episodic memory, by contrast, is tied to time and place.

The semantic–episodic distinction has existed for over a decade, and predictably, there are those who have turned against it. It is easy to show that the distinction is fuzzy. Most memories have both episodic and semantic components. In my opinion, however, this point should be taken as an observation on the nature of memory rather than as a criticism. The distinction sets the stage for asking questions about the acquisition of these two types of memory and about their interactions.

Acquired automaticity. One distinguishing feature of episodic memory is that some of its features, like the time and place where something happened, often register automatically, without attention or effort. Meanings, by contrast, are usually established by deliberate study. This distinction between automatic and nonautomatic processing identifies what I regard as the most important current issue in the study of human performance. The issue is important because automatic processing contributes in such a significant way to human adjustment. Activities that can be carried out automatically, without attention, take care of themselves and free the mind to deal with more important problems.

There are times of course when such automatic processing is a handicap. Consider this hypothetical example. While driving your automobile to work, you put yourself on "automatic pilot" and think ahead to how you will deal with a dishonest employee whom you will have to confront that day. Caught up in the details of a possible scenario, you run a stop light and cause an accident. Such breakdowns of a generally adaptive mechanism simply point up the importance of understanding more about the origins and operation of the automaticity of some behavior.

In recent years, there have been many publications (e.g., Hasher & Zacks, 1979) in which attempts have been made to list the distinguishing features of automatic and nonautomatic processing (Table 1), and there have been experiments that can be interpreted as illustrations of the way in which behavior that was originally nonautomatic can be automatized (Hirst, Spelke, Reaves, Caharick, & Neisser, 1980). In this connection, it may be important to mention two points. First, the distinguishing features of these two forms of processing remain a matter of disagreement. The list in Table 1 is only suggestive. Second, automatic and nonautomatic behavior are probably ends of a continuum rather than categories. There are degrees of automaticity.

Context Effects

It has been suspected for a long time that the situation in which learning occurs has some control over what is learned. Recent research has revealed some characteristics of such control. I begin by describing a study that will give the reader the big picture, and then I turn to some of the more detailed questions the study raises. Anderson and Pichert (1978) had subjects read stories from different points of view and then attempt to recall the story, sometimes from the viewpoint in which they originally read the story, sometimes from a different viewpoint in which they originally read the story, sometimes from a different viewpoint. One of the stories is as follows.

> One passage was about two boys playing hooky from school. They go to one of the boys' homes because his mother is never there on Thursdays. The family is well-to-do. They have a fine old home, set back from the road, with attractive grounds. Since it is old it has some defects—a leaky roof, a damp and musty basement. Because the family has considerable wealth, they have a lot of valuable possessions—ten-speed bikes, a color TV set, a rare coin collection. (Andersen & Pichert, 1978, p. 3)

As a first step in the experiment, the story was broken down into idea units, and raters estimated the importance of the individual elements from three different points of view: that of a prospective burglar,

Table 1
Characteristics That May Distinguish Automatic from Nonautomatic Actions

Automatic	Nonautomatic
unintended	intended
involuntary	voluntary
uncontrolled	controlled
fast	slow
effortless	require effort
unconscious	conscious
do not require attention	require attention
direct	mediated
use no processing capacity	use processing capacity
do not interfere with other activities	interfere with other activities
run to completion, hard to interrupt	easy to interrupt
emotional	cognitive

that of a prospective buyer of the home, or that of a person with no suggested perspective. As the brief passage above shows, some elements, such as the expensive possessions and the fact that no one is home on Thursday, would be important to a burglar. Others, like the leaky roof and spacious grounds, would be important to the prospective purchaser. Finally, separate groups of subjects read the stories and tried to recall them. Some subjects read them from the point of view of a burglar; others read them from the perspective of a home buyer. Following that, the subjects recalled as much of the story as they could.

Before I describe the outcome of this experiment, let me summarize the probable psychological situations of these subjects. The experiment would qualify as an investigation of episodic memory, but different groups are asked to keep certain items from semantic memory in mind as they read and attempt to memorize the story. In one case these items are whatever the subject knows about the habits and preferences of burglars; in the other, the items include information about buying houses. Because the subjects were college students, it seems likely that their knowledge about buying homes would be less than their knowledge—obtained from light reading, one trusts—of the burglar's profession. Certain aspects of the data support such a conclusion. Analysis was confined to 15 items that would be important to a burglar and 15 that would be important to a home buyer. The student subjects recalled a smaller percentage of the home buyer material than of the burglar material.

When presented in the most conventional fashion, this feature of the results makes them seem less impressive than they actually are. In order to produce a clear picture of the outcome of the experiment, in Figure 6 I have presented the data as a percentage above or below average for subjects attempting to recall the story from the point of view of a burglar or a home buyer. The data are broken down into the two sets of items that would be relevant to the interests of one or the other of these viewpoints. Plotted in this way, the perspective effect is quite impressive. The data indicate that what subjects learned from their reading depended upon the perspective they adopted.

Encoding specificity. That the subjects in this experiment remembered more of the material consonant with the perspective from which they read the story than they remembered of material consonant with the alternate perspective can be interpreted as a complex application of the *encoding specificity principle* (Tulving & Thomson, 1973). In its broadest form the principle asserts that people can retrieve only what has been stored and that the way the information can be retrieved depends upon how it was stored. In a narrower sense the principle implies that the context of storage contains the cues that are required to retrieve the stored item.

To support this idea, Tulving and Thomson did an experiment in which subjects studied 24 pairs of words like those in Table 2. They were told to learn the capitalized target words and also told that the

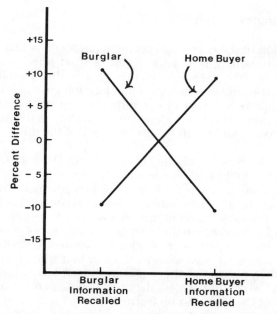

Figure 6. Context effects on memory. The labels on the two curves indicate the subjects' orientations at the time of learning.

other word in each pair (cue word) might be of some help in the process. Later on, Tulving and Thomson showed that although their subjects could produce some 60 to 70 percent of the target words when they were provided with the original cue word, they frequently could not even recognize the target word as a target in another context with different cues. For example, *COLD* was usually produced by the subjects as a response to the cue *ground,* but *COLD* was not recognized when paired with a new cue, *hot.* What makes this result impressive is that *ground* and *COLD* are only weakly associated according to available norms, whereas the association between *hot* and *COLD* is a powerful one.

Table 2
Cues and Target Words

Cue	Target Word	Cue	Target Word
ground	COLD	fruit	FLOWER
head	LIGHT	home	SWEET
bath	NEED	grasp	BABY
cheese	GREEN	butter	SMOOTH

State-Dependent Learning

One implication of the encoding specificity principle is that reinstating the context of learning favors the recall of what was learned in that context. One specific extension of this idea is that learning is state dependent; that is, the psychological and physiological condition of the individual constitutes a part of the stimulus context that controls the process of learning. There is evidence for such state-dependent learning for lower animals and human beings for many of the drugs in common use.

For example, Weingartner and his associates (Weingartner, Aderfis, Eich, & Murphy, 1976) had female subjects learn and later attempt to recall lists of 10 words under the four conditions produced by a crossing of learning and recall when sober or intoxicated—probably quite intoxicated. To produce this condition the women were served a screwdriver cocktail consisting, on the average, of a triple shot of vodka mixed with six ounces of orange juice. Among the various signs that this was enough to produce intoxication was the fact that when sober, the subjects recalled 58 percent of the words in the list learned on an immediate test, and when intoxicated, they recalled 42 percent of the words learned. Half of the words to be learned were high-imagery nouns; the other half were low-imagery nouns. The primary data in the experiment were the percentages of these words still retained in the recall test. The data showed a drug-dependent effect for both types of words. That is, subjects were able to recall words best in a replication of the state in which they originally learned the words (see Figure 7).

Application of the Information Processing Model

In the last 15 years or so, the study of human information processing has matured and contributed important knowledge about real-world learning and memory. In this chapter, I concentrate on applications that relate to the learning of textual materials that might be required of students in a classroom. The most important point of interpretation in this discussion is the extent to which such learning is a constructive process guided by controlling themes or *schemata*.

Some of the most straightforward demonstrations of this last point came from studies that show the remarkable value that just a title can have as an aid to learning. In an early experiment, Dooling and Lachman (1971) allowed subjects to study the following passage. Some subjects were told that the title of this little story was "Columbus Discovering America"; some were not told.

> With hocked gems financing him, our hero bravely defied all scornful laughter that tried to prevent his scheme. "Your eyes de-

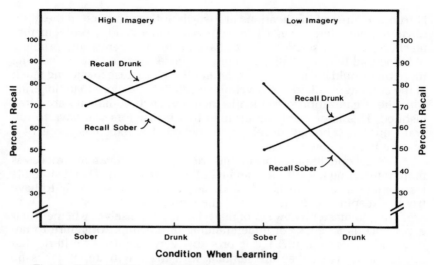

Figure 7. State-dependent learning. Note that the effects obtained were the same for two classes of materials, high-imagery words and low-imagery words.

ceive," he had said, "an egg, not a table, correctly typifies this unexplored planet." Now three sturdy sisters sought proof forging along, sometimes through calm vastness yet more often over turbulent peaks and valleys. Days became weeks as many doubters spread fearful rumors about the edge. At last from nowhere welcome winged creatures appeared signifying momentous success. (p. 217)

Following their study, 65 percent of the subjects who knew the title could write an acceptable version of the story in their own words. In sharp contrast, 97 percent of those who did not know the title failed to produce an acceptable story. This does not mean that the subjects who did not know the title were unable to interpret the story. Rather they were providing their own interpretations.

For many materials, alternate interpretations are available. Consider this example. Most of you know the old tune, "The Sunny Side of the Street." If I asked you what that song is about, I am quite sure that you would tell me that it advocates looking at the world through rose-colored glasses, being optimistic, and in general taking a positive view of things. But suppose I told you that the song means something quite different, that it is a black song, and that the "crossing over" referred to in the lyric "This rover crossed over" is crossing the color line.

I picked "The Sunny Side of the Street" as an example because I think that it reflects what goes on in many educational situations. If this is true, a couple of implications are worth noting. The first is the fairly obvious point that it begins to help one understand a problem that teachers of social science tend to have all too frequently, the problem of being told that it is "all just common sense" or that "there's nothing there that would be news to my grandmother." Because mastering much of the content of a field like psychology entails little more than tinkering with the organization of semantic memory, such comments are often justified. This is probably an attitude that instructors will have to tolerate until psychology develops to the point where it is more of a science than is now the case.

The second implication of this view of the education process is more interesting because it is an invitation to research. If what students learn about a topic is what they already know, they are likely to have trouble keeping accurate track of their progress. When students who are trying to master a new set of materials ask themselves whether their experience is a "click" of understanding or a "clunk" of failure to understand (Anderson, 1979), it is probably very easy to set criteria that are too low. When they are familiar with the raw materials, it is no doubt natural for students to mistake acquaintance with the materials for understanding the organization and to think that they have mastered it when they have not.

These few observations repeat a general theme that appeared in my discussions of conditioning at the beginning of this chapter. In that context, I was able to show that the learning process depends a great deal upon the characteristics that the individual brings to the learning situation. The characteristics I discussed first were biological contributions; in this section on human information processing, they are cognitive. An appealing thought is that all forms of learning, from the simplest to the most complex, may have at least this much in common: All of them represent the strengthening of mental structures within the constraints laid down by the biological and psychological characteristics of the individual.

References

Amsel, A., & Roussel, J. (1952). Motivational properties of frustration: I. Effect on a running response of the addition of frustration to the motivational complex. *Journal of Experimental Psychology, 43,* 363–368.

Anderson, R. C., & Pichert, J. W. (1978). Recall of previously unrecallable information following a shift in perspective. *Journal of Verbal Learning and Verbal Behavior, 17,* 1–12.

Anderson, T. H. (1979). Study skills and learning strategies. In H. F. O'Neil, Jr. & C. D. Spielberger (Eds.), *Cognitive and affective learning strategies* (pp. 77–97). New York: Academic Press.

Bandura, A., Grusek, J. E., & Menlove, F. L. (1966). Observational learning as a function of symbolization and incentive set. *Child Development, 37,* 499–506.

Berstein, I. L., & Sigmundi, R. A. (1980). Tumor anorexia: A learned food aversion? *Science, 209,* 416–418.

Blackwell, H. R., & Schlosberg, H. (1943). Octave generalization, pitch discrimination, and loudness thresholds in the white rat. *Journal of Experimental Psychology, 33,* 407–419.

Bolles, R. C. (1970). Species-specific defense reactions and avoidance learning. *Psychological Review, 77,* 32–48.

Brown, R., & McNeill, D. (1966). The "tip-of-the-tongue" phenomenon. *Journal of Verbal Learning and Verbal Behavior, 5,* 325–337.

Bykov, K. M. (1957). *The cerebral cortex and the internal organs.* (W. H. Gantt, Ed. and Trans.). New York: Chemical Publishing.

Dollard, J., & Miller, N. E. (1950). *Personality and psychotherapy: An analysis in terms of learning, thinking and culture.* New York: McGraw-Hill.

Domjan, M. (1983). Biological constraints on instrumental and classical conditioning: Implications for general process theory. *The Psychology of Learning and Motivation, 17,* 215–277.

Dooling, J. L., & Lachman, R. (1971). Effects of comprehension on retention of prose. *Journal of Experimental Psychology, 88,* 216–222.

Dweck, C. S. (1975). The role of expectations and attributions in the alleviation of learned helplessness. *Journal of Personality and Social Psychology, 31,* 674–685.

Ebbinghaus, H. (1913). *Memory: A contribution to experimental psychology.* (H. A. Ruger & C. E. Bussenius, Trans.). New York: Columbia University Press. (Original work published 1885)

Eikelboom, R., & Stewart, J. (1982). Conditioning of drug-induced physiological responses. *Psychological Review, 89,* 507–528.

Eriksen, C. W. (Ed.) (1962). *Behavior and awareness.* Durham, NC: Duke University Press.

Garcia, J., & Koelling, R. A. (1966). The relation of cue to consequence in avoidance learning. *Psychonomic Science, 4,* 123–124.

Grice, G. R., & Hunter, J. J. (1964). Stimulus intensity effects depend upon the types of experimental design. *Psychological Review, 71,* 247–256.

Guthrie, E. R., & Horton, G. P. (1946). *Cat's in a puzzle box.* New York: Rinehart.

Guttman, N., & Kalish, H. I. (1956). Discriminability and stimulus generalization. *Journal of Experimental Psychology, 51,* 79–88.

Hasher, L., & Zacks, R. T. (1979). Automatic and effortful processing in memory. *Journal of Experimental Psychology: General, 108,* 356–388.

Hirst, W., Spelke, E. S., Reaves, C. C., Caharick, G., & Neisser, U. (1980). Dividing attention without alternation or automaticity. *Journal of Experimental Psychology: General, 109,* 98–117.

Hovland, C. I. (1937). The generalization of conditioned responses: I. The sensory generalization of conditional responses with varying frequencies of tone. *Journal of General Psychology, 17,* 125–148.

Hull, C. L. (1943). *Principles of behavior.* New York: Appleton-Century-Crofts.

Humphreys, L. G. (1939). The effect of random alternation of reinforcement on the acquisition and extinction of conditioned eyelid reactions. *Journal of Experimental Psychology, 25,* 141–158.

Kamin, L. J. (1969). Predictability, surprise, attention, and conditioning. In B. A. Campbell & R. M. Church (Eds.), *Punishment and aversive behavior* (pp. 279–296). New York: Appleton-Century-Crofts.

Kimble, G. A. (1961). *Hilgard and Marquis' conditioning and learning.* New York: Appleton-Century-Crofts.

Kimble, G. A. (Ed.) (1967). *Foundations of conditioning and learning.* New York: Appleton-Century-Crofts.

Kimble, G. A. (1973). Scientific psychology in transition. In J. McGuigan & D. B. Lumsden (Eds.), *Contemporary approaches to conditioning and learning* (pp. 1–19). New York: V. H. Winston.

Kimble, G. A., Garmezy, N., & Zigler, E. (1984). *Principles of psychology* (6th ed.). New York: Wiley.

Maier, S. F., & Seligman, M. E. P. (1976). Learned helplessness: Theory and evidence. *Journal of Experimental Psychology: General, 105,* 3–46.

McGovern, J. B. (1964). Extinction of associations in four transfer paradigms. *Psychological Monographs, 78* (Whole No. 593).

Menzel, E. W. (1973). Chimpanzee spatial memory organization. *Science, 182,* 943–945.

Miller, N. E. (1969). Learning of visceral and glandular responses. *Science, 163,* 434–445.

Miller, N. E., & Brucker, B. S. (1979). A learned visceral response apparently independent of skeletal ones in patients paralyzed by spinal lesions. In N. Birbaumer & H. D. Kimmel (Eds.), *Biofeedback and self-regulation* (pp. 312–331). Hillside, NJ: Erlbaum.

Miller, N. E., & Dworkin, B. R. (1974). Visceral learning: Recent difficulties with curarized rats and significant problems for human research. In P. A. Obrist, A. H. Black, J. Brenner, & L. V. DiCara (Eds.), *Cardiovascular psychophysiology: Current issues in response mechanisms—biofeedback and methodology.* Chicago: Aldine.

Moore, B. R., & Stuttard, S. (1979). Dr. Guthrie and *Felis domesticus* or: Tripping over the cat. *Science, 205,* 1031–1033.

Öhman, A., Fredrikson, M., Hygdahl, K., & Rimmö, P. (1976). The premise of equipotentiality in classical conditioning: Conditioned electrodermal responses to potentially phobic stimuli. *Journal of Experimental Psychology: General, 105,* 313–337.

Pavlov, I. P. (1902). *The work of the digestive glands.* (W. H. Thompson, Trans.). London: Charles Griffin. (Original work published 1897)

Pavlov, I. P. (1927). *Conditioned reflexes.* Oxford, England: Oxford University Press.

Razran, G. (1949). Stimulus generalization of conditioned responses. *Psychological Bulletin, 46,* 337–365.

Rescorla, R. A. (1967). Pavlovian conditioning and its proper control procedures. *Psychological Review, 74,* 71–80.

Rescorla, R. A., & Wagner, A. R. (1972). A theory of Pavlovian conditioning: Variations in the effectiveness of reinforcement and nonreinforcement. In A. H. Black & W. F. Prokasy (Eds.), *Classical conditioning II: Current research theory* (pp. 64–99). New York: Appleton-Century-Crofts.

Rozin, P. (1968). Specific aversions and neophobia as a consequence of vitamin deficiency and/or poisoning in half-wild and domestic rats. *Journal of Comparative and Physiological Psychology, 66,* 82–88.

Rubin, D. C. (1977). Very long-term memory for prose and verse. *Journal of Verbal Learning and Verbal Behavior, 16,* 611–621.

Samelson, F. S. B. (1980). Watson's Little Albert, Cyril Bart's twins and the need for critical science. *American Psychologist, 35,* 619–623.

Schlosberg, H. (1937). The relationship between success and the laws of conditioning. *Psychological Review, 44,* 379–394.

Schwartz, B. (1984). *Psychology of learning and behavior* (2nd ed.). New York: Norton.

Seligman, M. E. P. (1975). *Helplessness—On depression, development and death.* San Francisco: Freeman.

Seligman, M. E. P., & Hager, J. L. (1972). *Biological boundaries of learning.* Englewood Cliffs, NJ: Prentice-Hall.

Sherman, J. E., & Liebeskind, J. C. (1980). An endorphinergic, centrifugal substrate of pain modulation: Recent findings, current concepts, and complexities. In J. J. Bonic (Ed.), *Pain* (pp. 78–99). New York: Raven Press.

Skinner, B. F. (1935). Two types of conditioned reflex and a pseudo type. *Journal of General Psychology, 12,* 66–77.

Skinner, B. F. (1938). *The behavior of organisms: An experimental analysis.* New York: Appleton-Century-Crofts.

Skinner, B. F. (1948). Superstition in the pigeon. *Journal of Experimental Psychology, 38,* 168–172.

Solomon, R. L. (1964). Punishment. *American Psychologist, 19,* 239–253.

Solomon, R. L., & Wynne, L. C. (1954). Traumatic avoidance learning: The principles of anxiety conservation and partial irreversibility. *Psychological Review, 61,* 353–385.

Spence, K. W. (1956). *Behavior theory and conditioning.* New Haven: Yale University Press.

Staddon, J. E. R., & Simmelhag, V. L. (1971). The "superstition" experiment: A reexamination of its implications for the principles of adaptive behavior. *Psychological Review, 78,* 3–43.

Stein, B. S., & Bransford, J. D. (1979). Constraints on effective elaboration: Effects of precision and subject generation. *Journal of Verbal Learning and Verbal Behavior, 18,* 769–777.

Thorndike, E. L. (1898). Animal intelligence: An experimental study of the associative processes in animals. *Psychological Monographs, 2* (Whole No. 8).

Tolman, E. C., & Honzik, C. H. (1930). Introduction and removal of reward and maze performance in rats. *Publications in Psychology, 4,* 257–275. (Discontinued series by University of California Press.)

Tulving, E. (1972). Episodic and semantic memory. In E. Tulving & W. Donaldson (Eds.), *Organization of memory* (pp. 382–403). New York: Academic Press.

Tulving, E., & Thomson, D. (1973). Encoding specificity and retrieval processes in episodic memory. *Psychological Review, 80,* 352–373.

Twitmeyer, E. B. (1974). A study of the knee jerk. *Journal of Experimental Psychology, 103,* 1047–1066.

Valentine, C. W. (1930). The innate base of fear. *Journal of Genetic Psychology, 37,* 394–419.

Watson, J. B., & Rayner, R. (1920). Conditioned emotional reactions. *Journal of Experimental Psychology, 3,* 1–14.

Weingartner, H., Adertis, W., Eich, J. E., & Murphy, D. L. (1976). Encoding imagery specificity in alcohol state-dependent learning. *Journal of Experimental Psychology: Human Learning and Memory, 2,* 83–87.

Weiss, J. M. (1968). Effects of coping responses on stress. *Journal of Comparative and Physiological Psychology, 65,* 251–260.

White, R. W. (1956). *The abnormal personality* (2nd ed.). New York: Ronald.

Wickens, D. D. (1972). Characteristics of word encoding. In A. Melton & E. Martin (Eds.), *Coding processes in human memory* (pp. 191–126). New York: Holt, Rinehart & Winston.

LEONARD KRASNER

LEARNING THEORY APPLICATIONS IN THE ENVIRONMENT

Leonard Krasner is a professor of psychology at the State University of New York at Stony Brook, where he initiated and directed the doctoral training program in clinical psychology. He received his PhD in clinical psychology from Columbia University in 1950.

Krasner is author or coauthor of a number of articles and books that focus on the historical origin, development, ethical implications, and social consequences of behavior modification as a treatment procedure, as a theoretical conception of human nature, and as a revolutionary scientific paradigm. In *Case Studies in Behavior Modification* and *Research in Behavior Modification,* Krasner and Leonard Ullmann brought together virtually all extant research and applications in behavior modifications. In *A Psychological Approach to Abnormal Behavior,* Krasner and Ullmann presented a systematic behavioral model, which Krasner further developed in *Behavior Influence and Personality: The Social Matrix of Human Action.* Recently Krasner and Arthur Houts published the results of their systematic investigation of the value systems of behavioral scientists in the *American Psychologist.*

Krasner has been a member of the Board of Directors of the American Psychological Association and has been involved in various committee and board activities for APA.

LEARNING THEORY APPLICATIONS IN THE ENVIRONMENT

Introduction

The topic of this chapter, learning theory applications in the environment (LTE), presents an exciting challenge. In effect, the three concepts in the title, learning theory, applications, and environment, encompass a major portion of psychology's history, philosophy, theory, and research. In preparing this chapter, I had to choose between attempting to cover the topic broadly and concentrating on a limited aspect of the topic. I must confess that I suffer from a serious mental disorder, listed as are all mental disorders in DSM-III (American Psychiatric Association, 1980), called "compulsive big-picturitis," which compels me to tackle the impossible and to try to cover, at least briefly, the range of research and application implicit in LTE. My aim is to provide a theoretical framework and an historical and philosophical context; to describe the scope of application, the process and complexities of evaluation, and the value implications; and to project future trends. The very scope of this chapter is in itself evidence of the development of LTE and LTE's enormous impact on the broad social environment in which psychologists function. One may, of course, hope that my use of LTE represents the birth of a new sloganistic label that will sweep the country and perhaps culminate in the new "Society for the Advancement of LTE."

Although I use the term LTE, investigators rally around and identify with a series of other somewhat similar labels: behavior modification, ecology, behavioral ecology, ethology, man–environment interaction, environmental psychology, environmental design, operant conditioning, social engineering, systems analysis, applied behavior analysis, and, of course, behavior therapy and its offspring, cognitive-behavior therapy.

A major element in the LTE approach involves placing theoretical and research formulations in the context of the values of, belief systems of, and influences on the investigator as participant-observer. In effect, in this chapter I describe the influence of a variety of labels or slogans around which professional investigators organize their theories, research, and applied interests. In this context, I must begin by listing the labels with which I still identify. I was trained as a clinical psychologist in the period immediately after World War II. Specifically, I was trained as an eclectically oriented psychoanalytic psychotherapist (or was it as a psychoanalytically oriented eclectic psychotherapist?). Psychotherapy and psychoanalysis were important slogans in those days, and to be eclectic was, of course, to hedge bets slightly.

However, a second set of influences affected my clinical behavior. During my graduate training at Columbia University, I was influenced by the then emerging behaviorism of Skinner, as mediated through Keller and Schoenfeld. I evolved into a behavioral clinical psychologist who conceptualized in terminology from learning theory (e.g., consequences of behavioral reinforcement, verbal conditioning, and token economy). I helped develop an approach to changing human behavior called behavior modification (L. Krasner & Ullmann, 1965; Ullmann & Krasner, 1965) and continued to identify with that fine label as it evolved into what is now called environmental design, a term both eloquently simple and sufficiently broad to convey the complexities of the approach (L. Krasner, 1980). For this chapter, I have developed the even simpler, broader, and ultimate label, LTE. Many individuals are involved in LTE. Professionals in the fields of psychology, psychiatry, education, architecture, sociology, economics, law, and related disciplines, by their theoretical conceptualizations, research investigations, and practical applications, are evolving toward the LTE approach in working with people.

In exploring this approach, a fundamental task is to establish the parameters and definitions of the two key concepts, learning theory and environment. To the extent that these two concepts are very broad and are basic to the field of psychology, very little in psychology can be omitted. In discussing learning theory, I touch on the derivation of the term *learning,* types of learning theories, the major theorists, some current issues in the field, and the implications of specific learning theories for changing and influencing the environment. I virtually ignore the various internal processes involved in the learning process, the biochemical, neurological, and physiological correlates of learning, but to do so is a behaviorist's prerogative.

The broader framework of this presentation is the psychology of behavior influence (L. Krasner & Ullmann, 1973), which focuses on the process of change (via learning), the process of creation of concepts, and, in particular, the behavior of the scientist. Whenever possible, I quote the investigators themselves because the learning process cannot be isolated out of social context. I also explore a range of environmental influences that interact with and affect the learning process. The learning process and the environment are inextricably linked, but all models of human behavior can be categorized as focusing on either inner or outer causation. My focus is on outer, or environmental, causation.

The volume of literature generated in the field of LTE is clearly out of control—no individual can keep up with it. Certainly no one summary, even this one, can do more than touch the tip of the iceberg. For example, recently, I was asked by a behavioral journal to write a review of the *International Handbook of Behavior Modification and Therapy* (Bellack, Hersen, & Kazdin, 1982). This book contains more than a thousand double-columned pages. I estimated that at my reading rate, it would take me six 8-hour days of nonstop reading to read the entire volume. Of course, on the seventh day I would rest. This particular handbook represents only a small portion of the literature relevant to LTE.

The first *Annual Review of Psychology* chapter to be devoted to behavior therapy (L. Krasner, 1971) cited 397 references, which was about all there was at that time. Now there are literally thousands of references, which fill a growing number of handbooks and encyclopedias. It is impossible for the individual to keep up with the literature or even to be aware of what to keep up with. This results in specialization and a loss of perspective on what LTE really represents. Annual reviews such as those of behavior therapy (e.g., Franks, Wilson, Kendall, & Brownell, 1984, in press) become useful necessities.

A major issue that I raise, but certainly do not resolve, is whether the LTE model of behavior represents a genuine paradigm shift, in Kuhn's (1962) sense, or merely the culmination in the linkage of a number of streams of influence. A case can be made for either interpretation. Not enough time has passed to achieve the perspective necessary to resolve this issue, but the issue is important not only for understanding the nature of LTE but also for predicting subsequent developments.

Since the original publication of Kuhn's book *The Structure of Scientific Revolutions* in 1962, his concept of *paradigms* has been used to justify a wide range of theories, models, and historical interpretations. Kuhn's own views were affected by a then obscure monograph written by Ludwig Fleck (1935/1979) that studied the impact of the social basis of knowledge ("community thinking") on the scientific study of syphilis. Fleck stressed the dialectic between what was known about a particular problem and the act of knowing it.

Kuhn's approach is that of social historian, placing the behavior and belief systems of scientists in the context of the social, political, and economic developments of their era. Thus, a major element of Kuhn's approach involves analysis of the scientific community at any given time. This analysis considered the education and origins of the members of the community, their professional initiation, and the type of working consensus they brought to bear in approaching their subject matter.

Kuhn came to stress two usages of the term *paradigm*.

> On the one hand, it stands for the entire constellation of beliefs, values, techniques, and so on shared by the members of a given community. On the other, it denotes one sort of element in the constellation, the concrete puzzle solutions which, employed as models or examples, can replace explicit rules as a basis for the solutions of the remaining puzzles of normal science. (p. 23)

These interrelated aspects were encompassed by the term *disciplinary matrix,* which incorporated symbolic generalizations, beliefs in models, shared values (e.g., accuracy and quantification), and *exemplars,* or recognized puzzle solutions. Following Kuhn's approach, LTE should be studied in the context of the belief systems and values of the present and past communities of people involved in LTE.

Historical Context

The obvious reason for placing LTE in historical context is that people can understand what is happening now, and where they are going, only by placing current developments within the context of history. In this historical overview I trace the origins of LTE in the outer-oriented, environmental models of human behavior rather than in the inner-oriented, biological models. LTE did not start with Skinner or even Watson, and probably, like most approaches, it could be traced back to the ancient Greeks, and even perhaps to the Bible. However, I start in a more recent period.

To understand fully the development of LTE, it is necessary to return to the 18th-century philosophical and intellectual *zeitgeist.* John Locke's (1632–1704) doctrine of the child's mind as a *tabula rasa* was widely accepted. Locke had developed his views in opposition to the prevailing Cartesian doctrine that man's ideas, and, therefore, the sources of his behavior, are innate. Locke argued that ideas were not inborn, but came from interaction with the external environment, that is, from experience. Locke expressed his view of learning as follows:

> Let us suppose the mind to be, as we say, white paper, void of all characters, without any ideas; How comes it to be furnished? Whence comes it by the vast store, which the busy and boundless fancy of man has painted on it with almost endless variety? Whence has it all the materials of reason and knowledge? To this I answer, in one word, *experience.* In that all knowledge is founded, and from that it ultimately derives itself. ("Essay Concerning Human Understanding," 1690, cited in Boring, 1929, p. 172).

Although other thinkers, such as Aristotle, also believed that experience determines behavior, it was Locke who made this concept central to philosophy and psychology, and eventually to LTE. Another major philosophical step toward modern viewpoints was the concept of *associationism* originated by David Hartley (1705–1757). The idea of the association of thoughts through temporal contiguity can be found in Aristotle, and others who expressed similar notions included Locke, Berkeley, Hume, and Hobbes. The latter, in fact, even had a chapter entitled "The Association of Ideas" in his seventeenth-century classic, *Leviathan.* Hartley, however, observed a fundamental law of behavior, labeled it "association," elaborated it into a psychological system, created a formal doctrine, and founded a new "school," a process which is prototypical of professional movements such as psychoanalysis, behavior therapy, and, we certainly expect, LTE.

Jeremy Bentham (1748–1832), a philosopher, economist, and lawyer, broadened and amplified Hartley's theory of associationism and made it the central mechanism of psychology. Bentham's theory was deterministic and automatic and did not involve any of the mentalistic concepts then in vogue. (Pavlov's later development of the concept of the conditioned reflex is frequently viewed as based on the same general associationistic concepts). Another of Bentham's principles, that people try to attain the greatest possible happiness and pleasure for themselves, foreshadowed later concepts of positive reinforcement, a basic element in current LTE. Bentham, as might be expected of someone who believed learning to be based on experience, was very concerned with education and had supreme confidence in its limitless power to modify and remedy behavior. Skinner's (1948) utopian society in *Walden Two* is, in part, a modern application of Bentham's theories of associationism and utilitarianism refined by later findings in experimental psychology.

Locke's view had particular influence on the Russian physiologist Sechenov. In his monograph *Reflexes of the Brain* (1863/1965), Sechenov argued that all animal and human behavior, whether physiological or psychical, conscious or unconscious, voluntary or involuntary, simple or complex, was "reflexive" in origin and nature, that is, wholly determined by measurable units and combinations of units of neuromotor (or sensorineuromotor) action. Sechenov said reflexes are learned, the mechanism of learning being association, which in itself is reflexive. Association, and not the innate nature of reflexes, determines "psychic content." To establish "the physiological basis of psychic activity," Sechenov challenged the Cartesian doctrine that body and mind comprise two separate, materially unrelated, parallel systems. Sechenov concluded that psychic activity can be initiated only by stimulation of one or more of the senses. He argued that the real cause of every human activity lies outside the person, in external sensory stimulation. Sechenov tried to account for all the psychic phenomena (e.g., thought, sensation, perception, will, wish, desire, memory, and imagination) within the framework of the reflex arc.

In the same period, also in Russia, another movement that placed emphasis on the connection between human behavior and environmental stimuli was growing. In two centers men with quite different research interests, Pavlov and Bekhterev, were doing work that came to be accepted outside Russia as symbolic of a scientifically based behavioristic movement. The physiologist Ivan Petrovich Pavlov's (1849–1936) early research dealt with circulation and the heart, and he won the Nobel Prize in 1904 for investigations of the physiology of digestion. His work on conditioned reflexes began in 1899 and continued until his death. His basic, and now classic, experimental procedure was simple. He sounded a tuning fork simultaneously with applying a given quantity of powdered meat on a dog's tongue and repeated this procedure at intervals until the tuning fork alone, without the meat, produced a reasonably constant flow of saliva. This was the *conditioned reflex* method; the reflex was conditional upon the fact that a given stimulus had been presented together with one that was originally adequate to elicit the response.

Although many investigators, particularly Russian physiologists, argue that learning and Pavlovian conditioning are synonymous, most psychologists studying learning distinguish between at least two types of conditioning. Pavlovian conditioning is now usually labeled *classical conditioning* to distinguish it from *instrumental,* or *operant, conditioning.*

From the start, the learning theory basis of LTE, particularly its behavior therapy component, was explicit. The following are some of the elements of LTE common to behavior therapy: the statement of concepts so that they can be tested experimentally; the notion of "laboratory" as ranging from animal mazes or shuttle boxes to hospitals, schoolrooms, homes, and the community; the view of research as treatment and treatment as research; an explicit strategy of therapy; and demonstrations that the particular environmental manipulation is indeed responsible for producing specific behavior change. Also, an initial functional analysis or assessment of the problem behaviors in their environmental context usually determines the goals of the modification procedure (L. Krasner, 1971). The unifying factor in early behavior therapy was its derivation from experimentally established procedures and principles. The specific experiments varied widely but had in common all the attributes of scientific investigation, including control of variables, presentation of data, replicability, and a probabilistic view of behavior.

The first use of the term behavior therapy in the literature was in a status report by Lindsley, Skinner, and Solomon (1953) referring to their application of the operant conditioning learning model (of a plunger-pulling response) in research with psychotic patients. Lindsley suggested the term to Skinner, based on its simplicity and linkage to other treatment procedures. Independently of this early usage, Lazarus (1958) used the term to refer to Wolpe's (1958) application of reciprocal inhibition techniques to neurotic patients. Eysenck (1959, 1960) used the term to refer to the application of what he called modern learning theory to changing the behavior of neurotic patients. These applications were based in large part on the procedures of a group of investigators then working at the Maudsley Hospital in London. Franks (1964) brought together the work of investigators of human problems who were influenced by Pavlov and the work of investigators of operant techniques (e.g., Lindsley, Ferster, and Ayllon) under the general rubric of "conditioning techniques." These were also referred to as "behavioral techniques" or "behavior therapy." In the same early period, Wolpe, Salter, and Reyna (1964) edited a series of papers titled *The Conditioning Therapies,* which combined the work of investigators spanning Pavlovian, Hullian, and Skinnerian learning theories. The term *behavior therapy* was used interchangeably with *conditioning therapy.*

The first issues of the journal *Behaviour Research and Therapy,* edited by Eysenck and Rachman, were a landmark in bringing together conceptually the laboratory studies of learning within the behavior therapy framework. Rachman (1963) explained, "Behavior therapy derives its impetus from experimental psychology and is essentially an attempt to apply the findings and methods of this discipline to disorders of human behavior" (p. 3). Combined within this general label of behavior therapy were aspects of learning theory, such as operant conditioning, aversion conditioning, and training in assertive behavior.

In 1969, Franks pointed out that self-identified behavior therapists disagreed on the definition of behavior therapy. He emphasized that "responses alone are the data available to the student of human behavior, and all else is a matter of inference and construct" (p. 2). He noted that at that time most behavior therapists linked their work with what were then called stimulus-response (SR) theories, the learning theories of Pavlov, Skinner, Guthrie, and Hull. Franks attributed theoretical importance to a "common, explicit, systematic and a priori usage of learning principles to achieve well-defined and pre-determined goals" (p. 2).

Perhaps the concept most completely agreed upon by these early investigators was that of learning, although of course there were subtle and sharp differences in the use of the term. Some investigators have consistently defined behavior therapy in terms of learning theory. Wolpe (1969) offered an illustrative definition: "Behavior therapy, or conditioning therapy, is the use of experimentally established principles of learning for the purpose of changing unadaptive behavior. Unadaptive habits are weakened and eliminated; adaptive habits are initiated and strengthened" (p. vii).

A more encompassing framework came from those who viewed behavior therapy in the broader context of social learning (Bandura, 1969) or behavior influence (L. Krasner & Ullmann, 1973). Ullmann and I described behavior therapy as "treatment deducible from the socio-psychological model that aims to alter a person's behavior directly through application of general psychological principles" (Ullmann & Krasner, 1965, p. 244). We contrasted this with *evocative psychotherapy*, which is "treatment deducible from a medical or psychoanalytic model that aims to alter a person's behavior indirectly by first altering intra-psychic organizations." (p. 224).

Although there were many hints that could foreshadow the development of LTE, it was in the early 1970s that the self-identified behaviorists, the progenitors of the LTE of the 1980s, came to embrace a scope broader than the laboratory, the clinic, and the mental hospital. Influenced to some extent by earlier applications of behavioral principles in schoolrooms and hospitals, and affected by the national concerns and debates of the 1960s, a new generation of behaviorists began to view the total natural and human-made environment as the focus for investigation. Social change with a purpose, namely, a better environment for all members of society, became the social rationale for LTE (Rosenbaum, Franks, & Jaffe, 1983).

For example, Nietzel, Winett, McDonald, and Davidson (1977), in a chapter on environmental problems, covered the topics of litter control, recycling, energy conservation, transportation, architectural design, and population change. Of interest here is not so much the specifics of research in these areas but the context in which Nietzel et al. placed the research. They started their chapter with a quote from Fairweather (1972), who in part stated that "population growth. . .environmental degradation. . .and human relations crises face man today. He must solve these problems if he is to survive in a livable environment. He must also find ways of aiding society to adopt the solutions found. Such problem-solving action requires basic social change" (p. 1). Nietzel et al., (1977) used Fairweather's comments to emphasize "the urgency of finding solutions to these problems" and to accentuate the view that "the amelioration of conditions which degrade the environment may have more to do with maintaining and improving the quality of our life and 'mental health' than much of the current work conducted under the rubric of mental health (p. 310)

Thus, in the 1970s, a new theme was emerging from the behaviorists, the future proponents of LTE. They brought attention to the urgent need to solve environmental problems and expressed the belief that the behaviorists might have the skills to contribute to the solutions.

General Principles of LTE

The major theme that integrates LTE investigations is a broad model of human behavior that emphasizes social-environmental causation. The basic theoretical framework of the emerging behavior modification movement of the 1960s was its social learning alternative to the pathology-oriented medical model (Bandura, 1969, 1977; Ullmann & Krasner, 1965). Bandura (1978) amply demonstrated the recycling and reemergence of the medical ideology model in the behavior therapy of the 1970s. Albee (1980, 1982) presented cogent social-humanistic arguments for the replacement of the mental illness, inner defect model by a social learning, competency model.

The issues can be put in the very broad (though perhaps oversimplified) terms of clashing conceptual models of human nature. These models differ in whether they use inner or outer explanations of locus of causation of behavior (the perennial "nature vs. nurture" controversy). There are theorists and investigators who conceptualize in terms of inner concepts, variables, or metaphors, such as disease, pathology, traits, personality, intelligence, mind, and mind–body, health–illness dichotomies. Others, primarily but not exclusively identified as behaviorists or LTE'ers, focus on the outer, environmental, social consequences of behavior; they have a social learning emphasis and a utopian orientation involving planning social environments to elicit and maintain the best of human behavior. This approach to human behavior change, with its emphasis on the individual in social context, is still evolving.

Implicit in the outer-oriented models is, of course, the notion that change in human behavior is possible because human nature is pliable, not fixed and immutable, as implied by the inner-oriented models. Not only is change possible, it is desirable. Each of the two most influential behaviorists of this century, Watson (1929) and Skinner (1948), has offered his version of a utopian society.

In the introduction to his paper "Why I Am Not a Cognitive Psychologist," Skinner (1977) nicely summarized the outer-environmental model with its implicit learning base.

The variables of which behavior is a function lie in the environment. We distinguish between (1) the selective action of that environment during the evolution of the species, (2) its effect in shaping and maintaining the repertoire of behavior which converts each member of the species into a person, and (3) its role as the occasion upon which behavior occurs. Cognitive psychologists study these relations between organism and environment, but they seldom deal with them directly. Instead they invent internal surrogates which become the subject matter of their science. (p. 1)

The behavioral (environmental, social learning) model has broadened within the past decade to the point that it now represents a comprehensive approach to human behavior with major social and political ramifications. LTE may be viewed as a process of training people to conceptualize the environment in which they are living and working in such a way that they can apply the general principles of LTE. Succinctly stated, these principles include the following:

1. A hypothesized model of human behavior is used to conceptualize the locus of influence in the interaction between an individual's behavior and his or her environment.

2. An individual learns by observing and doing.

3. Behavior followed by a rewarding event is likely to be repeated.

4. Any situation can be analyzed to set up specific behavioral goals that are socially desirable, taking into consideration both social and individual needs and desires.

5. Techniques should not be developed in isolation but only in the context of the learning environments with which the individual LTE'er is dealing. The broader influences on behavior, such as social roles and the impact of institutional rituals and restraints, must be considered.

6. The professional influencer is part of the influence process itself, in effect a participant-observer, who should be aware of and in control of the influences on himself or herself, including implicit value systems.

7. Research and application, theory and practice, are mutually interactive and inseparable.

8. The role of the professional behavioral scientist should be placed in the context of history, philosophy, sociology, and psychology of science.

9. Behavior is determined by the influence process, but only in probabilistic terms.

10. Social and personal change are continuous processes.

11. The variables of influence lie in the environment (built, natural, and social), but they may have differential influence as a function of the learning history of the individual.

12. Meaning or truth are not intrinsic but are imposed currently and repeatedly by the observer, investigator, designer, modifier, therapist, or LTE'er.

The role of participant-observer is basic to an understanding of LTE. My usage of the concept has been influenced by the approach of psychiatrist Harry Stack Sullivan toward his clients (Chapman, 1976). In psychotherapy, therapists are engaged in interpersonal relationships with their patients; they are continually observing those relationships, and they are also affecting the nature of those relationships by how they participate in them. Sullivan, in a sense, saw Heisenberg's "uncertainty principle" in the limitations of human beings as observers.

Sarason (1972) clarified the implications of the role of the professional (scientist, therapist, designer, etc.) as participant-observer:

> We are accountable, and that means that we should feel and nurture the bonds of similarity and communality between ourselves and the people we study. It is the difference between *knowing* that you are studying people, like yourself, and not "subjects." Society does not exist for the purposes of scientists. It is arrogance in the extreme to look at society for a *noblesse oblige* stance, expecting that the gifts you give it will be responded to with gratitude, not questions or hesitations. (p. 378)

The participant-observer cannot (and should not) avoid the ethical or value implications of influencing people. I discuss this key issue further in a following section.

Winett offers an "ecobehavioral" approach to the emerging field of health psychology that is equally applicable to LTE in general. His concern, which I share, is that the new field will become "no more than the psychology of individual health behavior without regard to social, economic, environmental, or political context. This is especially true given the field's growth during a time of political conservatism, and a corresponding retrenchment within psychology to the paradigm of the 'contextless individual'" (Sarason, 1981, cited in Winett, 1984, p. 210).

In effect, Winett offers a very sophisticated version of the outer-oriented model, with all its complexities. That is why his approach is pertinent to LTE and a natural complement to and extension of the social learning approach:

> The "true message" of the behavioral paradigm was not that we should narrowly focus on individual behavior and contingencies at the individual level of analysis, but that behavior must be understood and analyzed within interrelationships to broader environmental influences and constraints....The ecobehavioral paradigm does not neglect or discard what is within the person. It is assumed

that any environmental influence is mediated by a range of inter-active, intraindividual, genetic, biological, cognitive, and behav-ioral-skill variables. However, the focus of concern for the ecobe-havioral paradigm is the broader environmental influences and health behaviors of large population segments. (Winett, 1984, p. 1–2)

I will further elaborate on the implications of LTE principles for health psychology in a following section.

Learning Theory

In preparing this lecture, I found it particularly difficult to select a def-inition of learning. I was tempted to go back to early philosophical writers and trace the developments of learning theory to the modern day, with emphasis on the changes and development indicated in the five editions of Hilgard's classic, *Theories of Learning*. Littman (1982), in his review of the fifth edition of Hilgard's text, notes that "by 1948 the most salient feature of experimental psychology in the United States was learning, and there was no comprehensive, authoritarian guide to that sprawling, contentious area. With his first edition of *Theories of Learning,* Hilgard provided it" (p. 95). In fact, that book integrated such materials as Woodworth's 1938 classic, *Experimental Psychology,* and the writings of the then foremost learning theorists, such as Tolman, Guthrie, Hull, Thorndike, Lewin, and Skinner.

However, for the present purposes, I have selected Gagné's (1984) succinct review and definition of learning:

> The question of understanding how human beings learn has been a central theme of psychological research since the time of the English associationist philosophers Hobbes, Locke, and Mill....From that time until the present day, learning has been un-derstood as a change of state of the human being that is remem-bered and that makes possible a corresponding change in the in-dividual's behavior in a given type of situation. This change of state must, of course, be distinguished from others that may be effected by innate forces, by maturation, or by other physiological influ-ences. Instead, learning is brought about by one or more experi-ences that are either the same as or that somehow represent the situation in which the newly acquired behavior is exhibited. (p. 377)

Differences in fundamental approaches to human learning involve such issues as empiricism versus rationalism, contiguity versus reinforcement, gradual increments versus all or none jumps, and cognitive versus behavioral learning. Other issues are whether animal learning can be extrapolated to human learning and whether learning a task in one situation is relevant for other tasks or situations (Bower & Hilgard, 1981). All of these controversies plague the LTE'er seeking to solve the simplest human problems using LTE.

The learning theory that I find most useful is the social learning model of Bandura (1977, 1984). Particularly useful are its emphasis on the impact of models of human nature, the reciprocity between the individual and the environment, and the impact of chance events in the environment; its concept of freedom; and its views on the nature of human nature:

> Social learning theory favors a conception of interaction based on triadic reciprocality...In this model of reciprocal determinism, behavior, cognitive and other personal factors, and environmental influence all operate as interlocking determinants that affect each other bidirectionally...In the transactions of everyday life, behavior alters environmental conditions and is, in turn, altered by the very conditions it creates...Analysis of determinism in terms of triadic reciprocity of influence sheds light on how people are influenced by, and influencers of, the events with which they happen to have contact. (Bandura, 1984, pp. 2–3)

There are, of course, major issues in the various controversies about learning theory that have environmental implications. Fox (1983) describes the debates between those who seek to explain learning primarily in terms of brain machinery and ethologists who emphasize field studies in natural environments. He points out that although learning theory was once conceived as a way to formulate all animal learning behaviors within a simple set of principles, it has become considerably fragmented in recent decades. Optimism has been replaced by disillusionment. Part of the change was caused by growing awareness that learning principles established in one setting, such as the laboratory, could not easily be made to fit another or more natural one, thus forcing theorists to limit generalizations.

Rescorla (1984) points out that interest in conditioning and learning in infrahuman animals has a long and rich heritage going back to its origins in the associationism of British philosophy and in the reflex view of Russian physiology. In the past learning clearly represented the dominant strand of American psychology, and laboratory experimental psychology was virtually identical with the study of learning. Every psychology student knew well the names of Hull, Guthrie, Skinner, and Pavlov.

Yet today much of that is changed. Animal learning is not the "hot" area of experimental psychology, and the names of workers in the field hardly roll off the tongue of students. It is still not entirely clear what happened. Partly graduate students were attracted by competing fields that seemed to offer promise: cognitive psychology and neurobiology. Partly, the study of conditioning did not make good on its overzealous promises of application to all of behavior. Partly the field was perceived as continuing to grapple with old problems without making much progress. The result is that conditioning and learning now represent a relatively small field in psychology, populated by specialists who are disappointingly uncommunicative with their colleagues in allied fields. (Rescorla, 1984, p. 388)

A more optimistic, yet cautious, view of the theoretical linkage between learning theory and the environment comes from Rachlin and Logue (1983), who offer a cogent and comprehensive analysis of current issues in learning theory with their implications for applications in the environment. Some of the major issues they describe involve molar versus molecular approaches, whether one or two kinds of learning exist (classical and instrumental), the way in which reinforcement acts in instrumental conditioning (automatic or maximizing), and biological limits on the laws of learning.

These investigators spell out the implications of applying learning theory to clinical problems and a major issue of interest to LTE'ers, the relationship of systematic change in a clinic or hospital setting to change in the home or office environment of the individual client. They note that there is a strong tendency for clinicians to expect reinforcement and punishment procedures to have more permanent effects in therapy. It is important to realize that the patient returns to environments where the contingencies of reinforcement and punishment that originally generated dysfunctional behavior are reimposed. As the learning theorist would predict, it is the environmental contingencies that are in control of the behavior.

Rachlin and Logue (1983) point to future directions in learning theory that will have major implications for applications in the environment:

Controversial issues that are of recent concern, such as the biological boundaries of learning and the cognitive vs. behavioral approaches to learning, will probably become less clear-cut. There will be fewer adherents of extreme positions on these issues....Psychologists who felt that individual laws of learning would be necessary for every task, and those who felt that cognitive psychology would completely revolutionize animal learning, are examples of scientists whose extreme opinions precipitate theoretical crises and change, but who are probably not representative of future opinions. (p. 118)

Rachlin and Logue foresee that in the future learning theory based on work with animals will increasingly be applied to humans. As they note, the results from studies of taste aversion learning in rats (Logue, 1979) have been used to improve treatments of alcoholism and other clinical conditions involving excessive cravings for or avoidance of specific foods.

Currently researchers are questioning the usefulness of learning theory as the basis for applications, particularly in behavior therapy. Franks, for example, refers to "the increasing dissatisfaction with the unfulfilled promise of learning theory as an adequate foundation of behavior therapy" (Franks et al., in press). He notes that "a small but influential group of research oriented clinicians has become vocal. This past year has seen three such leaders compellingly argue for the failure of learning theory." He cites Wilson, Barlow, and Marks (based on Boulougouris, 1982) as questioning the usefulness of traditional learning theory formulations, particularly in dealing with the neuroses. In his review, Franks observes that "systematically, the various conditioning-based theories of neurosis are examined and found wanting: classical fear theory, including Mowrer's two factor theory; operant conditioning; self-efficacy theory; learned helplessness; Eysenck's revised conditioning theory, and more." But, on the other side, there are those who defend conditioning and modeling as at least temporarily adequate bases for the practice of behavior therapy (e.g., Stampfl, 1983).

Recent evaluations of LTE represent a mixture of skepticism and optimism. For example, Franks and Rosenbaum (1983) note that the current definition or scope of behavior therapy is in effect so broad as to encompass "with ease many diverse positions, different strategies and seemingly disparate techniques" (p. 9). Behavior therapy has grown so broad as to have lost whatever unifying factors may have existed. And because I am presenting an LTE approach which is even broader, this critique may certainly apply to LTE. Further, in noting the remarkable increase in a technology applied to a wide spectrum of fields, Franks and Rosenbaum express concern about this development: "Regretfully, much of this has been accomplished at the expense of time and inclination to reflect about what is going on, a disregard for replication and the consolidation of knowledge, and a failure to develop theoretical models capable of yielding testable predictions. The gap between theoretical development and application is widening" (1983, p. 10).

The Environment

Environment is an English word that is used as a noun, a concept, a theory, a slogan, and a label. In its adjectival form it combines with a host of terms to describe fields, organizations, journals, and, implicitly, theories of human behavior. It is a key term in LTE and a major justification for this paper, but what is this thing called *environment?* My approach will be multidimensional in keeping with big-picturitis.

In utilizing the concept of environment, what are the parameters? The most important is the behavior of others. Thus, aspects of such fields as social psychology, community psychology, environmental psychology, health psychology, behavioral ecology, behavioral economics, environmental design, and communications are relevant. In this section, I explore the environmental influences that interact with and affect the learning process. The learning process and the environment are inextricably linked; as far as behavior is concerned, you cannot have one without the other. The complex interaction between people and their environment is nicely captured by the observation of the architect Lars Lerup: "We design things and things design us" (Lerup, 1977, p. 156). This simple statement represents a clear expression of the LTE approach.

Two of the major characteristics of learning theory applied in the environment are that the applications are oriented toward solving specific problems, and the applications are frequently interdisciplinary in nature. This is particularly so in applications in environmental and ecological psychology. It should be noted that concepts of learning are perhaps more implicit than explicit in the various theoretical offerings of investigators in the environmental field. Certainly most formulations that stress the interaction between the individual's behavior and the environment are based on the previous experiences (learning) in that particular environment.

Environmental psychology (Proshansky, Ittelson, & Rivlin, 1970; Sommer, 1969) and ecological psychology (Barker, 1968) represent major streams of investigation that merge with environmental design and behavior modification or therapy into the LTE approach. Although not synonymous, these fields are concerned with the influence of environmental settings on behavior. The roots of environmental psychology lie in social, experimental, and clinical psychology, and the major influencers, with quite diverse backgrounds, are people such as Wohlwill, Craik, Stokols, Proshansky, Altman, and Sommer. A major impetus to this field was the 1966 issue of the *Journal of Social Issues* on the human response to the physical environment. The paper by Studer and Stea (1966) in that issue linked the notions of environmental design and architectural programming.

As with other fields, environmental psychology may be conceptualized in three aspects: (a) the theoretical, represented by books that offered a label to the field, such as *Environmental Psychology* (Proshansky, et al., 1970; also Ittelson, Proshansky, Rivlin & Winkel, 1974); (b) research; and (c) organizational training, such as the graduate training programs in environmental and ecological psychology at an increasing number of graduate schools (White, 1979). In "Environmental Psychology and the Real World" Proshansky (1976) represented a major linkage to the LTE field by presenting a description of his own personal development and identity as well as specific suggestions for the "methodological requirements" of an environmental psychology that preserves the "integrity of personal/physical-setting events" (p. 306).

A usage of "ecology" as a generic term was offered by Michaels (1974), who attempted to systematically link human ecology with behavior social psychology and behavioral sociology. For Michaels, human ecology involves the study of a population's collective interaction with its environment. The operant conditioner and the human ecologist both recognize the interaction between behavior and environment, the need for quantitative analysis, and the necessity of longitudinal analyses. Concepts of the environment came from a wide range of theorists and researchers who conceptualize in terms of behavior because it is very consistent with and integral to the framework of LTE. Investigators have explored the many problems involved in issues of theoretical framework and methodology (Craik, 1970; Proshansky, 1976; Stokols, 1978).

Schoggen and Schoggen (1980) argue that controversy is to be expected in a field that has attracted

> workers from divergent disciplines such as psychology, sociology, ecology, anthropology, geography, economics, architecture, planning, and engineering. And those workers have attacked a wide range of diverse problems including cognitive and behavioral maps, images of the city, the assessment of college environments, privacy, personal space, crowding, density, time allocation, the effects of noise and temperature, and the analysis of behavior settings. (p. 1)

There are a number of concepts and theories in environmental psychology that focus on the integration of approaches to the environment and the learning process. This is illustrated by the way in which Proshansky et al. (1970) used the concept of learning. They noted that four concepts have been associated with transformations of an organism: growth, maturation, learning, and development. "Learning involves quantitative changes in the reception and retention of information presented to the individual who changes through reacting to it and corrects initial attempts in response to indications about his prior success" (p. 261). Studer (1978) offers operant based formulations linking design and management of environment-behavioral systems.

Schoggen and Schoggen (1980) describe and illustrate several of the principles that underlie and unify the concept of the person in the environment. They emphasize the contrast between those investigators who focus on the content and influence of the specific environmental setting and those who focus on the individual's personality and inner workings. They point out that a major methodological requirement is that the absolute integrity of person/physical setting events be maintained. Thus, behavior should be studied in real-world settings, such as classrooms, living rooms, apartments, hospital wards, playgrounds, or stores, and the relevant social and cultural aspects of the physical settings must be included. The most desirable investigative techniques are those that emphasize observational methods, for example, event sampling, specimen records, and participant observation. Many studies do in fact concern the behavior of the person in an everyday setting, but tend to focus more on the attributes of the person rather than the context and characteristics of the physical setting.

The concept of *learning environments* is a useful integrating approach linking the learning process, the design of environments, and Sommer's (1969) concept of personal space. Porteous (1977) stated this view:

> While the parents are employed in an office or other workplace, children and young adults spend much of their day in learning environments ranging from kindergarten to university graduate school....Most students, and a large number of workers in various fields, are required to spend a considerable amount of time in isolated learning activities. The most familiar settings for such behavior in the university are bedrooms, designated study areas, and libraries. Studying in hall-of-residence quarters becomes a major problem when these rooms are shared. Very frequently desk design and arrangement is such that only one student can study comfortably at any one time. Hence the heavy use of vacant classrooms and other spaces....More frequently, however, students study at high density in libraries and study areas which are far from ideal. (pp. 51–58)

A major aspect of the environment in the LTE framework is the concept of consequences of behavior as influences on behavior. Parsons's (1979) succinct discussion of this principle can serve as a summary of environmental impact:

> The notion that what people do is influenced by what happened to them after what they did earlier is a simple one—as simple and revolutionary as were, in their time, the concepts that the earth was round and circled the sun. How can an event *after* some behavior affect behavior? Yet the apparent simplicity conceals a vast

complexity...contemporary psychologists...use terms to describe it like information feedback, reinforcement (positive or negative), effect, outcome, success, failure, extinction, knowledge of results, incentive, disincentive, utility, disutility, aversive consequence, reward, and punishment. These last two terms are found also in folk wisdom. (p. 1)

Applying LTE

A key part of LTE is the concept of application, and LTE encompasses a large portion of the field of applied psychology. Circa the end of the 19th century and early part of the 20th century, experimental psychology consisted primarily of the learning theories of the day. The originator of the concept of applied psychology was Hugo Münsterberg (Moskowitz, 1977). Between 1907 and 1916, while at the Harvard Psychological Laboratory, Münsterberg wrote a series of papers and books that in effect founded and defined the field of applied psychology.

Currently, learning theory is being applied in virtually every aspect of American society. Münsterberg suggested, advocated, and illustrated these extensions at a time when psychology was still in its infancy. He (1908) argued that

> if experimental psychology is to enter a period of practical service, it can not be a question of simply using the ready-made results for ends which were not in view during the experiments. What is needed is to adjust research to the practical problems themselves....Applied Psychology will then become an independent experimental science which stands related to the ordinary experimental psychology as engineering to physics....those fields of practical life which come first may be said to be education, medicine, art, economics and law. (pp. 8–9)

Thus, he was, at a very early time, offering a prototype of what LTE was to become in American society within the next half century. The next major development was Watson's application of LTE to advertising (Buckley, 1982).

The field of behavior modification itself was a major illustration of LTE. In our introduction to behavior modification, Ullmann and I defined the then emerging field in the framework of applied learning theory:

> In defining behavior modification we follow the work of Robert Watson (1962, p. 19), who noted that behavior modification included many different techniques, all broadly related to the field of

learning, *but learning with a particular intent; namely; clinical treatment and change.* (Ullmann & Krasner, 1965, p.1)

Thus, it follows from this definition that the basis of treatment stems from learning theory, which deals with the effect of experience on behavior at its early stages. Subsequently the basis of behavior modification was a body of experimental work dealing with the relationship between changes in the environment and changes in the subject's responses. The most immediate consequence that distinguished these behavioral approaches was a difference between the methods by which behavioral therapies and evocative therapies were developed. Instead of starting with a treatment procedure and bringing in learning theory after the fact, it seemed much more effective to start with concepts of learning as the basis for developing a program for behavior change.

In the clinical setting, the first step in early behavior modification programs was determining the goals to be accomplished through the application of learning theory. If, for example, the objective were to strengthen the subject's ego, the question would be what the subject would do differently if his or her ego were strengthened. Thus, behavior modification was the application of the results of learning theory and experimental psychology to the problem of altering maladaptive behavior. The focus of attention was overt behavior, and, in terms of both the development and change of behavior, no distinction was made between adaptive and maladaptive responses. This focus was succinctly stated by Eysenck (1959): "Learning theory does not postulate any such 'unconscious causes,' but regards neurotic symptoms as simple learned habits; there is no neurosis underlying the symptom, but merely the symptom itself. *Get rid of the symptom and you have eliminated the neurosis"* (p. 62).

At the time, it seemed that applications of learning theory offered clear-cut implications and that the concept of application was simple and easily understood. But, alas, nothing is simple in life or psychology. Dietz and Baer (1982) discussed the usage of the term *applied:*

> The word "applied" has been used sometimes to label that type of scientific endeavor which seeks to identify the causes of not just any behavior, but socially important behavior. With this definition, it is clearly a form of scientific activity. An *applied* behavior analysis, then, is a form of research which is notably different from any other form of research only by the "interest which society shows in the problems being studied." (p. 4)

Thus, for Dietz and Baer, as for many of the investigators within the LTE framework, the concept of *application* denotes an investigator's behavior that has social consequences. Dietz and Baer (1982) make this linkage even clearer: "But there is a second way the word 'applied' has been used. In this second way 'applied' refers to efforts which may be based on research findings but which are not looking for the same answers (causes) as is basic research" (p. 4). In terms of implications for values and ethics, there is little difference between these two definitions of *applied.* In the next section I discuss the value implications and issues of looking for basic causes of behavior.

The issues of application are extended further by Baer, who offers an analysis of the development of applied behavior analysis, which can be considered a prototype of, and model for, LTE. Baer notes that "the roots of behavior analysis always meant to do more than describe the acquisition and maintenance of new behaviors. Indeed all of them meant to understand the control of behavior in general by the environment in general" (Baer, 1984, p. 2). Baer notes that in using reinforcement, punishment, and extinction contingencies, the behavior analysts were quite similar to other investigators of environmental control. However, the behavior analysts differed in ways that were to make their discipline separate and maintained "that grand conceptual imperialism of the early learning theories: the intention that they would eventually explain everything" (p. 4).

The approach that was to make the behavior analysts unique was that they, in contrast to other learning theorists, began with a theory about behavior and its control by the environment. They began with behavior, any behavior convenient for laboratory research. Their approach was to those elements in the current environments such as reinforcement, punishment, extinction, or discrimination mechanisms that could control the occurrence. Another distinction characteristic of behavior analysis was its concentration on single-subject experimental designs. The aim was to establish control over a single organism at a time. Baer (1984) emphasizes that the most important, although not completely distinctive, characteristic of behavior analysis "is its apparent applicability to a very wide range of behavioral phenomena" (p. 6).

LTE implicitly and explicitly involves a process of translating basic research to applied research. Azrin (1977) offered a most useful strategy for carrying out this procedure:

> As a clinical researcher, I have had two guiding principles. The first was to adhere to the tenets of an objective scientific research methodology. The second principle was to develop an effective treatment. The specific scientific methodology was operant conditioning, and my initial orientation was to take the principles of operant conditioning as developed in laboratory studies and to apply them to practical problems. This orientation has been shared by others in the recently emergent field known as behavior modification, behavior therapy, applied behavior analysis, or the term I use, learning therapies. (p. 141)

Most investigators argue that applied research has different requirements from basic research. Azrin cogently argues that the complex issues involved include considerations of:

> outcome versus conceptual analysis; clinical significance versus response simplicity; situational complexity versus stimulus and laboratory simplicity; population heterogeneity versus subject homogeneity; a systems approach versus single variables; subject preferences versus objective apparatus measures; practicality and cost benefits versus statistical significance; and side effects versus central tendency." (1977, p. 141)

Clinical researchers tend to use correlational rather than real clinical situations, college sophomore volunteers rather than real patients, "studies that have implications rather than applications" (p. 142), and problem-oriented strategies rather than method-oriented strategies.

Baer (1978) tackles this issue in a useful way, consistent with Azrin's strategy and noting the value implications of LTE:

> The experimental analyst made two radical departures from the previous ways of the experimental psychologists. First, the experimental analyst was restricted to the discovery and use of only the powerful, always effective variables, rather than permitted the indiscriminant collecting of any variable that was ever functional to any degree. Second, the experimental analyst focussed on behavior, rather than on theory. . . .Many researchers never meant to validate a general behavior theory, advance the cause of science, or alleviate exams. They meant simply to solve the social problems. (pp. 13–15)

Health Psychology

Can research and applications in the new field of health psychology (behavioral medicine) be considered part of LTE? Health psychology certainly includes learning theory applications, but the focus is on health and internal processes, such as blood pressure, heart function, and development of cancers. However, the basic assumption is that physical health is a function of environmental events. Hence, health psychology belongs within the LTE framework, although I am running a risk of being accused of imperializing and including everything within the LTE framework. But my key point is that as participant-observer I am both observing and, hopefully, influencing this ongoing process. Further, this new field provides some of the best illustrations of the people who have created the LTE field and the basic theoretical learning concepts used, and it presents a view of the environment that encompasses a wide range of human behavior in ordinary everyday life, going well beyond the concern with diseased behavior. Matarazzo (1980) has been most influential in developing this field and offers the following useful definitions of terms:

> It is proposed here, however, that henceforth we use the term *behavioral medicine* for that broad interdisciplinary field of scientific inquiry, education, and practice which concerns itself with health and illness or related dysfunction (e.g., essential hypertension, cholesterolemia, stress disorders, addictive smoking, obesity, etc.); the term *behavioral health* for a new interdisciplinary subspecialty within behavioral medicine specifically concerned with the maintenance of health and the prevention of illness and dysfunction in currently healthy persons; and the term *health psychology* as a more discipline-specific term encompassing psychology's role as a science and profession in both of these domains. (p. 807)

Matarazzo points out that health psychology is based on the outer, social, environmental model of behavior, in contrast to the inner, disease, pathology model. He notes that in the broad field of medicine "physicians have recently echoed the earlier plea that medicine give up its traditional biomedical model and substitute instead a biopsychosocial model" (1980, p. 808). Engel (1977) and Knowles (1977), in particular, argued against the biomedical model in both medicine and psychiatry and for a biopsychosocial model that considers the patient's and the physician's belief systems about health and environmental influences. Thus, a major element in health psychology is a broad model of human behavior that conceptualizes health-related activity in overt behavioral terms.

Some of the general issues involved in applications in health psychology involve broader social and ethical issues. For example, Winett (1983) is critical of Matarazzo (1982) for focusing on the life-style and responsibilities of the individual without focusing sufficient attention on political, social, and economic influences on health and ill health. Winett argues that psychologists should seek to influence the broader legal, political, institutional, and economic influences in the environment that are major factors in developing behaviors detrimental to good health.

In applying LTE to problems of health, the focus might be on adherence to medical regimens, such as exercising, following special diets, and taking medication. Other focuses might be stopping unhealthy behaviors such as smoking, having a high salt intake, and eating high cholesterol foods, or fostering behaviors likely to prevent poor health, such as better nutrition, exercise, early medical check-ups, safer environmental conditions in the home and workplace, and the development of a framework for organizing health promotion that pays equal attention to both the theoretical and technological advances in LTE.

Smoking has all the elements of a prototypical behavior in which the environment clearly has consequences for a major health behavior. There have been many attempts to use LTE to decrease smoking behavior. For example, a series of studies demonstrated the complex interrelationship between psychological and physiological variables that make the smoking habit so resistant to extinction (Schachter, 1977). Educational programs based on research in clinical, social, and educational psychology have been used to reduce the number of new smokers among preteenagers (Evans et al., 1978); studies of ways of influencing compliance to suggestions and influence to stop smoking have been conducted (S. Krasner, 1984; Suedfeld, 1982). Behavior modification principles have been used in anti-smoking clinics; aversive conditioning procedures, such as electric shock, stale smoking air, and nausea pills have also been tried (Yates, 1975); and incentive programs in industrial settings to affect large numbers of people have been developed (Danaher, 1980).

One recent review of current trends in the modification of cigarette dependence (Lichtenstein & Brown, 1982) cites more than 200 studies, including 20 papers reviewing behavioral research on smoking control. Lichtenstein and Brown conclude,

> Like the other substance-abuse problems, cigarette smoking is critically important to health yet difficult to change. Perhaps because smoking is easier to assess than many behavioral problems, we know more about treatment outcomes and so must be cautious in what we can offer clients. While there is a great need for more research, we should not be deterred from implementing our available knowledge. Behavioral approaches still appear to be the most useful, and certainly the most accountable approach now available for the modification of smoking behavior. (p. 604)

Matarazzo (1982) offers a challenge to psychology that highlights the moral and ethical issues involved in LTE. He points out that between 1955 and 1979, following the first U.S. Surgeon General's report on smoking, the percentage of male adult smokers of all ages in this country decreased 16.5 percent. However, during this same period of time the percentage of female smokers increased 4.9%. Matarazzo notes,

> Many experts agree with the American Cancer Society that this increase for females is eloquent testimony to the power of advertisements that were carefully crafted with the help of psychologists who are specialists in the field of subliminal motivational psychology. Examples of these skillfully crafted slogans are "You've

come a long way, baby" with its strong but still subtle appeal to the women's liberation movement. (p. 6)

It is fairly clear that there is a causal connection between smoking and various health disorders, such as lung cancer and emphysema. Thus, it would seem that cigarette advertisements, in effect, encourage behavior that is likely to lead to poor health. I could be very dramatic and state that members of the American Psychological Association (APA), including myself, bear an ethical responsibility for promotion of smoking because APA owns and publishes a commercial magazine called *Psychology Today,* which has in each issue a number of full-page ads for cigarettes. The July 1984 issue has five full-page cigarette ads, in one of which an attractive young woman is smoking and clearly enjoying it. In fact, ads for cigarettes are apparently a major source of revenue for this magazine. What is the ethical responsibility of the individual members of APA in promoting and encouraging smoking behavior?

Matarazzo (1982) goes to the heart of the ethical and value issues involved in LTE when he suggests that psychologists take a more active social role in attempting to affect smoking behavior:

> Should not a greater portion of psychology's currently vast talents and resources be applied to stemming the health and financial costs associated with smoking by children and adults?...As the field which has the longest history in the study of human behavior, and especially individual behavior, psychology has the scientific knowledge base, the practical applied experience, and the institutional supports for individuals within it to begin to make important contributions immediately in preventing smoking among our country's youth and in helping adults who wish to quit to do so successfully. (p. 6)

LTE has been used to tackle a considerable number of additional health problems that plague us all (Brownell, 1982; Lutzker & Martin, 1981; Kazdin, 1984), including alcohol abuse (Marlatt, 1984; Sobell & Sobell, 1978), weight control (Stuart, 1978), hypertension, pain, enuresis, migraine, sexual dysfunction, apprehension about and recovery from surgery, coronary artery disease, seizures, muscle spasms, and stress management. The link between health psychology and the LTE model of behavior is thus increasingly being forged in a variety of contexts (J. M. Michael, 1982; Stachnik, 1980). Among the techniques that have been used in these applications are self-help and self-constraining, counterconditioning, systematic desensitization, aversion therapy, contingency contracting, token economy, development and enhancement of social networks and support systems, biofeedback, relaxation training, incentive systems, and cognitive behavioral strategies.

Education

Through education LTE has had the most impact, or at least has had the greatest potential for impact. It certainly is not necessary to present the case for the obvious impact of educational systems on individuals, families, and American society in general.

In a chapter section entitled "Behavior Modification and the School System," Franks (Franks et al., in press) explained that he used the word *system* deliberately: "Ten years ago, most school behavior modification consisted either of traditional one-to-one procedures carried out in the classroom or psychologist's office or some form of straightforward classroom or school-wide token economy" but as behavioral strategies became increasingly sophisticated, it becomes "virtually impossible to think in terms of one-to-one direct S-R relationships." In education, as in other areas and fields of application, investigators using LTE are increasingly focusing on approaches to systems (Hannafin & Witt, 1983; Piersel & Gutkin, 1983). However, Franks notes that there has not yet emerged a "behaviorally compatible clearly articulated theory of systems" (Franks et al., in press).

M. Krasner (1980) placed current behavioral applications in the classroom within an historical context that traces its origins to Edward L. Thorndike. Thorndike was influenced by taking a course with William James at Harvard in 1897 and switched from literature to psychology as his major (a switch similar to one made by another behaviorist, B. F. Skinner). The law of effect, which developed out of Thorndike's doctoral dissertation, was perhaps the first systematic application of a learning principle in the classroom. Thorndike's *Principles of Teaching* (1906) includes considerable material useful for theories of instruction. It was through his efforts that research in psychology became the basis for classroom application. M. Krasner (1980) notes that she began her historical review

> with Thorndike rather than with more current behavior influencers such as Skinner to emphasize that the relationship between psychological theory of behavior and the classroom is certainly not new or restricted to recent times. With only slight paraphrasing, Thorndike's linkage of learning and instructional theory to the planned environment of the classroom would still apply today. (p. 305)

The literature on the applications of LTE to the classroom, particularly behavior modification, is voluminous. Ruggles and Le Blanc (1982) have classified these studies into those involving ways of maintaining order in the classroom, those analyzing the effects of contingent relationships on the amount and correctness of work produced by the children in the classroom, and those investigating the effects of teachers' instructions and discriminative stimulus materials on children's learning of academic skills.

Other Applications

It is clear that illustrations of the application of LTE in almost all aspects of American society abound. There are now a growing number of fields that by their use of the *behavioral* label (e.g., behavioral medicine, behavioral pediatrics, behavioral geriatrics, behavioral ecology, and behavioral community psychology) indicate their LTE allegiance. LTE has been applied in homes, sports arenas, businesses, supermarkets, industries of every type, transit systems, television, all levels of school systems, and, of course, various mental health settings. I mention additional illustrations in the final section on the future of LTE.

Ethical and Value Issues

It should be clear at this point that ethical and value issues are an integral aspect of LTE. This section presents a brief overview of the major issues. There has been a growing awareness of the complexities, paradoxes, and myths involved and the need to deal with these issues rather than ignore and deny their existence, particularly by insisting that psychology is value free.

One of the contexts within which LTE is presented is, of course, the science of psychology. As I have shown, learning theory derived from and was an integral part of experimental psychology, psychology was indeed a science, and science was value free. Houts and I place our study of the value system of behavioral scientists within the context of the controversy of science as value free or value laden (L. Krasner & Houts, 1984). We note that the traditional conceptualization of science as value free is captured in the phrase "science is about facts, not values" (p. 840). The argument for the value neutrality of science was founded on pivotal assumptions about epistemology and ethics developed in the logical positivist philosophy of science. The history of science was conceived of as a story of progress toward unbiased, objective knowledge. However, this traditional view has been seriously challenged. On the basis of his examination of the history of science, Kuhn (1970) argued that major scientific change was due to changes in the assumptive framework (belief systems, values) of investigators and not to the deliberate logical evaluations of new factual discoveries. Science is not a sacred cow, nor does it have an independent existence. LTE as a scientific discipline represents a social product in a time and place.

The social responsibility of those who use LTE includes placing their own contributions in the social context of their times. They are influencers and are continually being influenced.

Virtually all the early investigators in the applications of learning theory, particularly in behavior modification, considered that there was a very close linkage between their research investigations, social applications, and ethical implications. This view was clearly influenced and promoted by Skinner's writings, particularly *Walden Two*. This novel, from a scientist whose basic research had not yet had its full impact on the field of psychology, raised issues about ethics and morality in social systems. Published in 1948, *Walden Two* anticipated social and ethical issues arising from behavior modification and LTE that have become a focus of concern in the 1980s. Other behavioral investigators also pointed out the social implications of their research (Goldiamond, 1974; Kanfer, 1965; L. Krasner, 1965; Stolz & Associates, 1978).

Ullmann and I linked early behavior modification with concerns about social values, a linkage relevant to LTE today:

> The very effectiveness of behavior modification, the use of terms such as *manipulation, influence, and control of the environment,* and the concept that the therapist has the responsibility to determine the treatment program, all lead to concern with social values. Behavior modification, as an area of social influence, shares this problem with advertising, public relations, and education. These areas have in common individuals who have the interest and the ability to alter the behavior of other people, that is, one person determining what is desirable behavior for another. There are circumstances in which this is beneficial for the individual and society and circumstances in which this is not the case. (L. Krasner & Ullmann, 1965, p. 362)

The person applying LTE must decide what is good or bad behavior for a specific individual, ideally trying to help that individual make these decisions himself or herself. Some people who apply LTE would argue that their major contribution is to reinterpret or operationalize this decision-making process as involving the assessment of the consequences of a given behavior—behavior that leads to positive reinforcement for the individual is good and behavior that leads to aversive consequences is bad. Some would argue that survival is an alternative or a supplement to these goals.

Bandura (1969), in a most influential book that placed "the principles of behavior modification" within the "conceptual framework of social learning," devoted an entire chapter to the discussion of value issues in the modification of behavior. He identified the specification of goals as the major value feature of behavior modification.

The selection of goals involves value choices. To the extent that people assume major responsibility for deciding the direction in which their behavior ought to be modified, the frequently voiced concerns about human manipulation become essentially pseudo issues. The change agent's role in the decision process should be primarily to explore alternative courses of action available, and their probable consequences, on the basis of which clients can make informed choices. However, a change agent's value commitments will inevitably intrude to some degree on the goal selection process. These biases are not necessarily detrimental, provided clients and change agents subscribe to similar values and the change agent identifies his judgments as personal preferences rather than purported scientific prescriptions. (p. 112)

Kanfer (1965) also discussed these problems, arguing that the ethical dilemma of behavior modification procedures consists in

justifying use of subtle influencing techniques in clinical procedures in the face of the popular assumption of integrity, dignity and rights to freedom of the patient. The first step in the resolution of this dilemma is the recognition that a therapeutic effort *by necessity* influences the patient's value system as well as his specific symptoms. (p. 188)

These early statements clearly and unequivocally linked the behavior of those identifying their professional efforts within behavior modification with a deep concern for the ethical implications of their work and their social and value systems and thus set a precedent for the LTE of 1984. In fact, Bandura (1984) cogently observes,

In philosophical discourses, freedom is often considered antithetical to determinism. When viewed from a social learning perspective, there is no incompatibility between freedom and determinism. Freedom is not conceived negatively as the absence of influences or simply the lack of external constraints. Rather, it is defined positively in terms of the exercise of self-influence. . .seen from the social learning perspective, human nature is characterized by a vast potentiality that can be fashioned by direct and observational experience into a variety of forms within biological limits. (p. 5)

An attempt to deal with the values issues, particularly in applied behavior analysis, has been the development of the concept of *social validity* (Baer, 1984). Social validity involves the acceptability of an intervention to those individuals most closely connected to it. According to Baer, social validity methodology involves identifying all relevant persons and groups and asking them, through interviews and questionnaires, about the acceptability of a particular intervention, its means, results, and personnel. If the responses are negative, the intervention must be changed before being used again or the objectors must be educated and then reassessed.

Problems of ethics and values are, of course, not unique to or caused by behavior modification or LTE, but friends and foes alike believed that the development of behavior modification brought with it certain issues and concerns that did not exist before. I once expressed the theme that since behavior modification had arrived on the scene, we must hurry before it's too late:

> Does this mean that we, as psychologists, researchers, or even therapists, at this point could modify somebody's behavior in any way we want? The answer is no, primarily because research into the techniques of control thus far is at the elementary stage. Science moves at a very rapid pace, however, and now is the time to concern ourselves with this problem before basic knowledge about the techniques overwhelms us. (L. Krasner, 1962, p. 201)

Others have, of course, expressed the notion that at long last the complete manipulation of behavior is a possibility, and behavior modification has received the credit (blame). There may even be some who still believe that that state of control is near. Yet the use of any set of procedures, even behavior modification or LTE, in the ultimate control of society (even for the good of society) is still, fortunately, a thing of the indefinite future.

The Future

On a broad level, two related phenomena are currently occurring in American psychology. First, there is an uneasiness, or malaise, about where psychology is going as a science and as a profession (Phillips, 1982). Second, there is a clarion call for change, and for psychologists to explicitly lead in applying basic science, particularly LTE, to broader social and policy issues, in effect to develop a better world. Sarason (1981) cogently argued that psychology as a science and profession has become "misdirected" because of its focus on the individual (personality, dynamics) as an entity without consideration of the social context that influences the individual. Sarason sharply rebukes the direction of postwar mainstream psychology for its avoidance of social issues.

The malaise was nicely expressed in a headline of the April 7, 1981 *New York Times:* "B. F. Skinner Now Sees Little Hope for the World's Salvation." The high hopes and optimism of the post-World War II period, in part generated by the victorious war over an evil enemy and in part generated by the ever-optimistic view of the environmental model of human nature, appear to have faded in frustration. Skinner follows in a direct line from his utopian progenitors by boldly asking, "Why are we not acting to save the world?," the title of his invited address at the 1982 APA Convention.

> Our only hope is to change the behavior of those, mainly in governments, religion, or industry and trade, who control the contingencies under which people live....A much more promising strategy would be to induce people to act to promote a better world. The Utopian literature approaches the problem of the future in that way. But Utopianism which merely portrays a better way of life with no indication of how it is to be achieved is no help. (Skinner, 1982, pp. 22–23)

Although Skinner built Walden Two as an extrapolation of his earlier animal studies to human behavior, a number of other utopia builders have either deliberately or inadvertently incorporated specific procedures based on the experimental laboratory. Perhaps the best example of this comes from Huxley's *Brave New World* (1932), in which he applied satirically his version of Pavlovian conditioning in a society with a value system requiring that certain individuals destined to be workers not be distracted by literature. To be sure that this occurred, Huxley's planners would put a child on the laboratory floor near a few attractive books. As the child moved to the books or touched them, he or she was frightened by loud noises or electrically shocked. This was repeated as often as was necessary, and books remained an aversive object for the rest of the child's life.

The following observations by Manuel and Manuel (1979) offer a context for this utopian revival:

> How do you change a present misery into a future happiness in this world?...Utopias thus became laden with meanings as they moved through time: a literary genre, a constitution for a perfectly restructured policy, a state of mind, the religious or scientific foundations of a universal republic....Although virtually all utopias deal with major aspects of living, such as work, government, love and sexuality, knowledge, religion, beauty, the tone and quality of life, dying, each of these subjects has at one or another time preempted a central position in utopian consciousness and has inspired new forms. (p. 15)

These observations of the Manuels offer a basis for arguing that the developing LTE movement described in this chapter is utopian. The utopian model focuses on helping individuals create a social environment that provides a reasonably satisfactory life for all (or most) individuals.

Morawski (1982) enhances the notion of a utopian framework for psychologists by reporting that several prominent psychologists, including progenitors of LTE, in the early part of the century were also utopiasts:

> Four utopias published between 1915 and 1930 by the hardly obscure psychologists G. Stanley Hall, William McDougall, Hugo Münsterberg, and John B. Watson. These utopias clearly reflect Baconian thinking. . .in their dedication to explaining how psychology, as a science, is instrumental to human welfare. . . .These men were psychologists themselves, and. . .they were unique in their tendentious belief that their own profession was absolutely essential to improving society. The seriousness of this belief is evidenced in the correspondence between their utopian visions and many of their scientific and professional writings. (pp. 1083, 1090)

Several areas of theory, research, and application in the field of psychology are emerging and coalescing into a broad utopian movement. These areas are subsumed under the more generic labels of applied behavior analysis, community psychology, social ecology, health psychology, and preventive psychology. These streams of research and application seem to have as their goal a better life for individuals in American society.

Applied behavior analysis has become the descriptive label for social applications of Skinnerian operant conditioning. The earlier label for this orientation tended to be *behavior modification* (Kazdin, 1978). The history of the behavioral approach included a utopian stream that involved "an ethical concern for the social implications of behavior control, as well as offering blueprints for a better life such as Skinner's *Walden Two.* This stream can, of course, be traced from Plato's *Republic* to the setting up of a token economy on a psychiatric ward or in a community setting" (L. Krasner, 1971, p. 491). A subsequent series of papers emphasizing social inequities as the focus for behavior modification and the comments they engendered are implicit and explicit expressions of utopianism (J. Michael, 1980; Stolz, 1981).

A major stream feeding into the utopian approach is behavioral economics, which developed, in part, from the early token economy programs of the applied behavior analysts (Atthowe & Krasner, 1968; Ayllon & Azrin, 1965, 1968). In effect, these programs emerged from the early operant conditioning studies that used tokens in place of primary reinforcers. Tokens opened up an almost limitless world of reinforcers. Developments in token economy programs in mental hospitals, institutions for retardates and delinquents, schoolrooms, and the community have been exciting, controversial, hopeful, and depressing (Kazdin,

1978, 1982). Winkler (1971) reported a series of studies on token economy programs that tested predictions from economic theory and thus systematically investigated the core of token programs and of society itself. He investigated the complex relationships among prices, wages, and savings and the ways in which these influence individual behavior.

Token economies were found to operate according to principles similar to those economists have identified in national, money-based economies. Token economies not only look like real economies, they function like them, and research in that field has linked the behavioral movement with social planning. A recent development in behavioral economics is the utilization of maximization theory (Rachlin, Battalio, Kagel, & Green, 1981), a concept borrowed from economics as an organizing theory to predict human behavior. The mutual interaction between psychology and economics is basic to the development of utopias because human behavior is intricately linked with economic influences.

Winkler and Winett (1982) call the combination of behavioral interventions and resource conservation a systems approach based on behavioral economics. They put their work in the context of the growing awareness of the need for interdisciplinary conceptualization (Stern & Gardner, 1981), illustrated by the interdisciplinary groups of psychologists, engineers, architects, economists, human factor experts, and media consultants who have recently worked on energy and water conservation (Rohles, 1981; Socolow, 1978; Winett et al., 1981). Winkler and Winett (1982) conclude by noting that

> as the energy level and resource situation in the 1980's becomes progressively more critical, decisions not only affecting resource conservation policy but, without exaggeration, affecting the course of civilization will have to be made. To date, energy policy has been formulated with little input from psychologists, hence, with minimal awareness or focus on effectively modifying human behavior....We have noted the potential contributions of a psychologically based information technology for influencing consumer choice behaviors and have discussed the role of experimental methodology for policy development. On a theoretical and practical level, it is our hope that it may be possible to integrate economic and psychological conceptualizations to develop more effective approaches to resource conservation. (pp. 433–434)

There is another new field that in many ways epitomizes the theme of this chapter—behavioral community psychology. I refer to it as a field because it has the most important characteristic of a field—it has a newsletter, put out by the Behavioral Community Psychology Special Interest Group of the Association for the Advancement of Behavior

Therapy. The newsletter editors contend that the label *behavioral community psychology* reflects their interest in both research and applications concerning the use of behavioral principles and technology in addressing community-based problems.

> Illustrative of the areas and settings in which our members are involved are mental health, physical health, education, criminal justice, environmental preservation, and lifestyle modification. The term "behavioral community psychology" incorporates behavioral approaches which interact with both community mental health (e.g., characterized by an active intervention stance, use of paraprofessionals and natural change agents, consultation by professionals) and community psychology strategies (e.g., prevention orientation; competency and strength building; modification of environmental factors predisposing to behavioral difficulties; interventions aimed at groups, organizations, and communities). (Glenwick, 1982, p. 13)

Heldring (1982) starts her featured paper in this newsletter with Jason's (1981) definition of behavioral community psychology as "the application of behavioral methodology to community based problems" (Heldring, 1982, p. 3). Heldring then notes that this field is a developing discipline "that utilizes behavioral approaches in providing services to individuals and communities" (p. 3). The discipline has dimensions of both active interventions, such as instructional procedures, behavior management methods, and environmental manipulation, and primary or early secondary prevention, such as stress inoculation for children, competency building, and reduction of problematic environmental conditions.

Some of the chapter topics in recent texts on behavioral community psychology and social ecology (Geller, Winett, & Everett, 1982; Glenwick & Jason, 1984; Jeger & Slotnick, 1982; Martin & Osborne, 1980; Nietzel et al., 1977) point out the range and scope of the planned change that is under way. Behavior technology is being applied to: business, industry, and public organizations; litter control; waste reduction and resource recovery; residential energy conservation; transportation; water conservation; population control; community education; social support networks; alternative social systems; an analysis of behavior change in China and Cuba; measurement scales for public housing and urban transportation; helping college students live together; and aging. A marvelously integrating chapter is offered by Fred Keller (1980) on a vision of community development.

Preventive psychology is another aspect of utopianization. At first, the term *prevention* may sound very medical, indicating an inoculation process that is preventing some disease, medical or mental. But the conceptualization of the field by its leading proponents (Albee, 1981;

Bloom, 1984; Cowen, 1980; Felner, Jason, Muritsugu, & Farber, 1983; Rappaport, 1977) makes it clear that what is involved is behavior and environmental change for a better world, developing a way of life that will be more satisfying to the individual. The basic notion pervading much of the literature is the development of ideas for the creation of new settings, an approach ably initiated by Sarason (1972).

Thus I end my discussion of learning theory applications in the environment on an optimistic note. Inherent in the views that the science of psychology is value laden is the view that the scientist-practitioner as participant-observer has a moral responsibility for the social consequences of his or her activities. Most of those involved in LTE are aware of this and seek to develop a better world, aware of the enormous potentialities and untold dangers of such an objective.

References

Albee, G. W. (1980). A competency model to replace the defect model. In M. S. Gibbs, J. R. Lachenmeyer, & J. Sigal (Eds.), *Community psychology: Theoretical and empirical approaches* (pp. 213–238). New York: Gardner Press.

Albee, G. W. (1981). Politics, power, prevention, and social change. In J. M. Joffe & G. W. Albee (Eds.), *Prevention through political action and social change: Vol. 5. Primary prevention of psychopathology* (pp. 5–25). Hanover, NH: University Press of New England.

Albee, G. W. (1982). Preventing psychopathology and promoting human potential. *American Psychologist, 37,* 1043–1050.

American Psychiatric Association (1980). *Diagnostic and statistical manual of mental disorders* (3rd ed.). Washington, DC: Author.

Atthowe, J. M., Jr., & Krasner, L. (1968). A preliminary report on the application of contingent reinforcement procedures: Token economy on a "chronic" psychiatric ward. *Journal of Abnormal Psychology, 73,* 37–43.

Ayllon T., & Azrin, N. H. (1965). The measurement and reinforcement of behavior of psychotics. *Journal of Experimental Analysis of Behavior, 8,* 357–387.

Ayllon, T., & Azrin, N. H. (1968). *Token economy: A motivational system for therapy and rehabilitation.* New York: Appleton-Century-Crofts.

Azrin, N. H. (1977). A strategy for applied research: Learning based but outcome oriented. *American Psychologist, 32,* 140–149.

Baer, D. M. (1978). On the relation between basic and applied research. In A. C. Catania & T. A. Brigham (Eds.), *Handbook of applied behavior analysis* (pp. 11–16). New York: Irvington.

Baer, D. M. (1984, April). *Modern behavior analysis.* Paper presented at the 4th Annual Kansas Students' Conference, Pittsburg State University, KS.

Baer, D. M., Wolf, M. M., & Risley, T. R. (1968). Some current dimensions of applied behavior analysis. *Journal of Applied Behavior Analysis, 1,* 91–97.

Bandura, A. (1969). *Principles of behavior modification.* New York: Holt, Rinehart and Winston.

Bandura, A. (1977). *Social learning theory.* Englewood Cliffs, NJ: Prentice-Hall.

Bandura, A. (1978). On paradigms and recycled ideologies. *Cognitive Therapy and Research, 2,* 79–103.

Bandura, A. (1984). Model of causality in social learning theory. In S. Sukemune (Ed.), *Advances in social learning theory* (pp. 202–227). Tokyo: Kaneko-shoho.

Barker, R. G. (1968). *Ecological psychology: Concepts and methods for studying the environment of human behavior*. Stanford, CA: Stanford University Press.

Bellack, A. S., Hersen, M., & Kazdin, A. E. (Eds.). (1982). *International handbook of behavior modification and therapy*. New York: Plenum.

Bloom, B. L. (1984). *Community mental health: A general introduction* (2nd ed.). Monterey, CA: Brooks/Cole.

Boring, E. G. (1929). *A history of experimental psychology*. New York: Appleton-Century.

Boulougouris, J. C. (1982). *Learning theory approaches to psychiatry*. Chichester, England: Wiley.

Bower, G. H., & Hilgard, E. R. (1981). *Theories of learning* (5th ed.). Englewood Cliffs, NJ: Prentice-Hall.

Brownell, K. D. (1982). Behavioral medicine. In C. M. Franks, G. T. Wilson, P. C. Kendall, & K. D. Brownell (Eds.), *Annual review of behavior therapy: Vol. 8. Theory and practice* (pp. 114–138). New York: Guilford.

Buckley, K. W. (1982). The selling of a psychologist: John Broadus Watson and the application of behavioral techniques to advertising. *Journals of the History of the Behavioral Sciences, 16*, 207–221.

Chapman, A. H. (1976). *Harry Stack Sullivan: The man and his work*. New York: Putnam.

Cowen, E. L. (1980). The wooing of primary prevention. *American Journal of Community Psychology, 8*, 258–284.

Craik, K. H. (1970). Environmental psychology. In R. Brown et al. (Eds.), *New directions in psychology* (Vol. 4, pp. 1–121). New York: Holt, Rinehart and Winston.

Danaher, B. G. (1980). Smoking-cessation programs in occupational settings. *Public Health Reports, 95*, 149–157.

Dietz, S. M., & Baer, D. M. (1982, May). *Is technology a dirty word?* Paper presented at the Annual Meeting of The Association for Behavior Analysis, Milwaukee, WI.

Engel, G. L. (1977). The need for a new medical model: A challenge for bio-medicine. *Science, 196*, 129–136.

Evans, R. I., Rozelle, R. M., Mittlemark, M. B., Hansen, W. B., Bane, A. L., & Havis, J. (1978). Deterring the onset of smoking in children: Knowledge of immediate physiological effects and coping with peer pressure, media pressure and parent modeling. *Journal of Applied Social Psychology, 8*, 126–135.

Eysenck, H. J. (1959). Learning theory and behavior therapy. *Journal of Mental Science, 195*, 61–75.

Eysenck, H. J. (1960). *Behavior therapy and the neuroses*. London: Pergamon Press.

Fairweather, G. W. (1972). *Social change: The challenge to survival*. Morristown, NJ: General Learning Press.

Felner, R. D., Jason, L. A., Muritsugu, J. N., & Farber, S. S. (Eds.). (1983). *Preventive psychology: Theory, research and practice*. Elmsford, NY: Pergamon Press.

Fleck, L. (1979). *Genesis and development of a scientific fact*. Chicago: University of Chicago Press. (Original work published 1935)

Fox, J. L. (1983). Debate on learning theory is shifting. *Science, 222,* 548.

Franks, C. M. (Ed.). (1964). *Conditioning techniques for clinical practice and research.* New York: Springer.

Franks, C. M. (Ed.). (1969). *Behavior therapy: Appraisal and status.* New York: McGraw-Hill.

Franks, C. M. (1984). Foreword to J. L. Matson & T. M. DiLorenzo, *Punishment and its alternatives: A new perspective for behavior modification* (pp. ix–xiv). New York: Springer.

Franks, C. M., & Rosenbaum, M. (1983). Behavior therapy: Overview and personal reflections. In M. Rosenbaum, C. M. Franks, & Y. Jaffe (Eds.), *Perspectives on behavior therapy in the eighties* (pp. 3–14). New York: Springer.

Franks, C. M., Wilson, G. T., Kendall, P. C., & Brownell, K. D. (Eds.). (1984). *Annual review of behavior therapy: Vol. 9. Theory and practice.* New York: Guilford.

Franks, C. M., Wilson, G. T., Kendall, P. C., & Brownell, K. D. (Eds.). (in press). *Annual review of behavior therapy: Vol. 10. Theory and practice.* New York: Guilford.

Gagné, R. M. (1984). Learning outcomes and their effects. *American Psychologist, 39,* 377–385.

Geller, E. S., Winett, R. A., & Everett, P. B. (1982). *Preserving the environment.* Elmsford, NY: Pergamon Press.

Glenwick, D. (1982). Behavioral community psychology special interest group: Why we've changed our name. *Behavioral Community Psychology Newsletter, 1,* 13–14.

Glenwick, D., & Jason, L. (Eds.). (1984). *Behavioral community psychology.* New York: Praeger.

Goldiamond, I. (1974). Toward a constructional approach to social problems: Ethical and constitutional issues raised by applied behavior analysis. *Behaviorism, 2,* 1–84.

Hannafin, M. J., & Witt, J. C. (1983). System intervention and the school psychologist: Maximizing interplay among roles and functions. *Professional Psychology, 14,* 128–136.

Heldring, M. (1982). Defining behavioral community psychology: A survey of content areas. *Behavioral Community Psychology Newsletter, 1,* 3–12.

Hurd, G. S., Pattison, E. M., & Llamas, R. (1981). Models of social network intervention. *International Journal of Family Therapy, 3,* 246–257.

Huxley, A. (1932). *Brave new world.* New York: Harper.

Ittleson, W. H., Proshansky, H. M., Rivlin, L. G., & Winkel, G. H. (1974). *An introduction to environmental psychology.* New York: Holt, Rinehart and Winston.

Jason, L. A. (1981). Call for papers: Journal of Community Psychology. *The Behavior Therapist, 4,* 20.

Jeger, A. M., & Slotnick, R. S. (1982). *Community mental health and behavioral-ecology: A handbook of theory, research, and practice.* New York: Plenum.

Kanfer, F. H. (1965). Issues and ethics in behavior manipulation. *Psychological Reports, 16,* 187–196.

Kazdin, A. E. (1978). *History of behavior modification: Experimental foundations of contemporary research.* Baltimore: University Park Press.

Kazdin, A. E. (1982). The token economy: A decade later. *Journal of Applied Behavior Analysis, 15,* 431–445.

Kazdin, A. E. (1984). *Behavior modification in applied settings* (3rd ed.). Homewood, IL: Dorsey.

Keller, F. S. (1980). A vision of community development. In G. L. Martin & J. S. Osborne (Eds.), *Helping in the community: Behavioral applications* (pp. 401–404). New York: Plenum.

Knowles, J. H. (1977). The responsibility of the individual. In J. H. Knowles (Ed.), *Doing better and feeling worse: Health in the United States* (pp. 57–80). New York: Norton.

Krasner, L. (1962). The therapist as a social reinforcement machine. In H. H. Strupp & L. Luborsky (Eds.), *Research in psychotherapy* (Vol. 2, pp. 61–94). Washington, DC: American Psychological Association.

Krasner, L. (1965). The behavioral scientists and social responsibility: No place to hide. *Journal of Social Issues, 21,* 9–30.

Krasner, L. (1971). Behavior therapy. *Annual Review of Psychology, 22,* 483–532.

Krasner, L. (Ed.). (1980). *Environmental design and human behavior: A psychology of the individual in society.* Elmsford, NY: Pergamon Press.

Krasner, L., & Houts, A. C. (1984). A study of the "value" systems of behavioral scientists. *American Psychologist, 39,* 840–850.

Krasner, L., & Ullmann, L. P. (Eds.). (1965). *Research in behavior modification: New developments and implications.* New York: Holt, Rinehart and Winston.

Krasner, L., & Ullmann, L. P. (1973). *Behavior influence and personality: The social matrix of human action.* New York: Holt, Rinehart and Winston.

Krasner, M. (1980). Environmental design in the classroom. In L. Krasner (Ed.), *Environmental design and human behavior* (pp. 302–319). Elmsford, NY: Pergamon Press.

Krasner, S. (1984). *Abstinence makes the heart grow stronger: An inquiry into personality and behavioral factors related to long-term smoking cessation.* Paper, Stanford Heart Disease Prevention Program, Stanford, CA.

Kuhn, T. S. (1970). *The structure of scientific revolution* (2nd ed.) Chicago: University of Chicago Press.

Lazarus, A. A. (1958). New methods in psychotherapy: A case study. *South African Medical Journal, 33,* 660–664.

Lerup, L. (1977). *Building the unfinished.* Beverly Hills: Sage.

Lichtenstein, E., & Brown, R. A. (1982). Current trends in the modification of cigarette dependence. In A. S. Bellack, M. Hersen, & A. E. Kazdin (Eds.), *International handbook of behavior modification and therapy* (pp. 575–610). New York: Plenum.

Lindsley, O. R., Skinner, B. F., & Solomon, H. C. (1953). *Studies in behavior therapy* (Status Report 1). Waltham, MA: Metropolitan State Hospital.

Littman, R. A. (1982). Excelsior. *Contemporary Psychology, 27,* 95–96.

Logue, A. W. (1979). Taste aversion and the generality of the laws of learning. *Psychological Bulletin, 86,* 276–296.

Lutzker, J. R., & Martin, J. A. (1981). *Behavior change.* Monterey, CA: Brooks/Cole.

Manuel, F. E., & Manuel, F. P. (1979). *Utopian thought in the western world.* Cambridge, MA: Belknap Press.

Marlatt, G. A. (1984). The controlled-drinking controversy. *American Psychologist, 38,* 1097–1110.

Martin, G. L., & Osborne, J. G. (Eds.). (1980). *Helping in the community: Behavioral applications.* New York: Plenum.

Matarazzo, J. M. (1980). Behavioral health and behavioral medicine: Frontiers for a new health psychology. *American Psychologist, 35,* 807–817.

Matarazzo, J. D. (1982). Behavioral health's challenge to academic, scientific, and professional psychology. *American Psychologist, 37,* 1–14.

Michael, J. (1980). Flight from behavior analysis. *The Behavior Analyst, 3,* 1–22.

Michael, J. M. (1982). The second revolution in health: Health promotion and its environmental base. *American Psychologist, 37,* 936–941.

Michaels, J. W. (1974). On the relation between human ecology and behavioral social psychology. *Social Forces, 52,* 313–321.

Morawski, J. G. (1982). Assessing psychology's moral heritage through our neglected utopias. *American Psychologist, 37,* 1082–1095.

Moskowitz, M. J. (1977). Hugo Münsterberg: A study in the history of applied psychology. *American Psychologist, 32,* 824–842.

Münsterberg, H. (1908). *On the witness stand.* New York: Doubleday, Page.

Nietzel, M. T., Winett, R. A., McDonald, M. L., & Davidson, W. S. (1977). *Behavioral approaches to community psychology.* Elmsford, NY: Pergamon Press.

Parsons, H. M. (1979). *Variables in human consequation/feedback* (Technical Report No. 1). Silver Spring, MD: Institute for Behavioral Research.

Phillips, E. L. (1982). *Stress, health and psychological problems in the major professions.* Washington, DC: University Press of America.

Piersel, W. C., & Gutkin, T. B. (1983). Resistance to school-based consultation: A behavioral analysis of the problem. *Psychology in the Schools, 20,* 311–320.

Porteous, J. D. (1977). *Environment and behavior: Planning and everyday urban life.* Reading, MA: Addison-Wesley.

Proshansky, H. M. (1976). Environmental psychology and the real world. *American Psychologist, 31,* 303–310.

Proshansky, H. M., Ittelson, W. M., & Rivlin, L. G. (Eds.). (1970). *Environmental psychology: People and their physical settings.* New York: Holt, Rinehart and Winston.

Rachlin, H., Battalio, R., Kagel, J., & Green, L. (1981). Maximization theory in behavioral psychology. *The Behavioral and Brain Sciences, 4,* 371–417.

Rachlin, H., & Logue, A. W. (1983). Learning. In M. Hersen, A. E. Kazdin, & A. S. Bellack (Eds.), *The clinical psychology handbook.* Elmsford, NY: Pergamon Press.

Rachman, S. D. (1963). Introduction to behavior therapy. *Behaviour Research and Therapy, 1,* 3–15.

Rappaport, J. (1977). *Community psychology: Values, research and action.* New York: Holt.

Rescorla, R. A. (1984). The psychology of learning. *Science, 223,* 388–389.

Rohles, F. H. (1981). Thermal comfort and strategies for energy conservation. *Journal of Social Issues, 37,* 132–149.

Rosenbaum, M., Franks, C. M., & Jaffe, Y. (Eds.). (1983). *Perspectives on behavior therapy in the eighties.* New York: Springer.

Ruggles, T. R., & Le Blanc, J. M. (1982). Behavior analyses procedures in classroom teaching. In A. S. Bellack, M. Hersen, & A. E. Kazdin (Eds.), *International handbook of behavior modification and therapy* (pp. 959–996). New York: Plenum.

Sarason, S. B. (1972). *The creation of settings and the future societies.* San Francisco: Jossey-Bass.

Sarason, S. B. (1981). *Psychology misdirected.* New York: Free Press.

Schachter, S. (1977). Nicotine regulation in heavy and light smokers. *Journal of Experimental Psychology, 106,* 5–12.

Schoggen, P., & Schoggen, M. (1980, September). *Some emerging common themes in behavior-environment research.* Paper presented at the meeting of the American Psychological Association, Montreal, Canada.

Sechenov, J. M. (1965). *Reflexes of the brain* (S. Belsky, Trans., G. Giggons, Ed.). Cambridge, MA: MIT Press. (Original work published 1863)

Skinner, B. F. (1948). *Walden Two.* New York: Macmillan.

Skinner, B. F. (1977). Why I am not a cognitive psychologist. *Behaviorism, 5,* 1–10.

Skinner, B. F. (1982, August). *Why are we not acting to save the world?* Invited address presented at the annual convention of the American Psychological Association, Washington, DC.

B. F. Skinner now sees little hope for the world's salvation. (1981, April 7). *New York Times,* sec. B.

Sobell, M. B., & Sobell, L. C. (1978). *Behavioral treatment of alcohol problems: Individualized therapy and controlled drinking.* New York: Plenum.

Socolow, R. H. (1978). *Saving energy in the home.* Cambridge, MA: Ballinger.

Sommer, R. (1969). *Personal space: The behavioral bases for design.* Englewood Cliffs, NJ: Prentice-Hall.

Stachnik, T. J. (1980). Priorities for psychology in medical education and health care delivery. *American Psychologist, 35,* 8–15.

Stampfl, T. G. (1983). Exposure treatment for psychiatrists [Review of *Learning theory approaches to psychiatry*]. *Contemporary Psychology, 28,* 527–529.

Stern, P. C., & Gardner, G. T. (1981). Psychological research and energy policy. *American Psychologist, 36,* 329–342.

Stokols, D. (1978). Environmental psychology. *Annual Review of Psychology, 29,* 253–295.

Stolz, S. B. (1981). Adoption of innovations from applied behavioral research: "Does anybody care?" *Journal of Applied Behavior Analysis, 14,* 491–506.

Stolz, S. B. & Associates. (1978). *Ethical issues in behavior modification.* San Francisco: Jossey-Bass.

Stuart, R. B. (1978). *Act thin, stay thin.* New York: Norton.

Studer, R. G. (1978). The design and management of environment-behavior systems. In H. Hanloff (Ed.), *Bedingunden des Lebens in des Zukunft und die Folgen für die Erzlehung* (pp. 312–343). Berlin: Technische Universität Berlin.

Studer, R. G., & Stea, D. (1966). Environmental design and human behavior. *Journal of Social Issues, 22,* 127–136.

Suedfeld, P. (1982). Environmental factors influencing maintenance of lifestyle change. In R. B. Stuart (Ed.), *Adherence, compliance and generalization in behavioral medicine* (pp. 125–144). New York: Brunner/Mazel.

Thorndike, E. L. (1906). *Principles of teaching.* New York: Seiler.

Ullmann, L. P., & Krasner, L. (Eds.). (1965). *Case studies in behavior modification.* New York: Holt, Rinehart and Winston.

Ullmann, L. P., & Krasner, L. (1975). *A psychological approach to abnormal behavior* (2nd ed.). New York: Prentice-Hall.

Watson, J. B. (1929, June 29). Should a child have more than one mother? *Liberty,* pp. 31–35.

Watson, R. I. (1962). The experimental tradition and clinical psychology. In A. J. Bachrach (Ed.), *Experimental foundations of clinical psychology* (pp. 3–25). New York: Basic Books.

White, W. P. (Ed.). (1979). *Resources in environment and behavior.* Washington, DC: American Psychological Association.

Winett, R. A. (1983). Comments on Matarazzo's "Behavioral health's challenge. . . ." *American Psychologist, 38,* 120–121.

Winett, R. A. (1984). Ecobehavioral assessment in health lifestyles. In P. Karoly (Ed.), *Measurement strategies in health psychology* (pp. 200–235). New York: Wiley.

Winett, R. A., Neale, M. S., & Grier, A. C. (1981). The effects of self-monitoring and feedback on residential electricity consumption. *Journal of Applied Behavior Analysis, 12,* 173–184.

Winkler, R. C. (1971). Reinforcement schedules for individual patients in a token economy. *Behavior Therapy, 2,* 534–537.

Winkler, R. C., & Winett, R. A. (1982). Behavioral interventions in resource conservation: A systems approach based on behavioral economics. *American Psychologist, 37,* 421–435.

Wolpe, J. (1958). *Psychotherapy by reciprocal inhibition.* Stanford, CA: Stanford University Press.

Wolpe, J. (1969). *The practice of behavior therapy.* New York: Pergamon.

Wolpe, J., Salter, A., & Reyna, L. J. (1964). *The conditioning therapies: The challenge in psychotherapy.* New York: Holt, Rinehart and Winston.

Woodworth, R. (1938). *Experimental psychology.* New York: Holt.

Yates, A. J. (1975). *Theory and practice in behavior therapy.* New York: Wiley.

JACK L. MICHAEL

BEHAVIOR ANALYSIS: A RADICAL PERSPECTIVE

Jack L. Michael, a native of Los Angeles, obtained his BA, MA, and PhD at the University of California, Los Angeles, finishing in 1955. While a student, his main interests were statistics, physiological psychology, and learning. During his first teaching job at Kansas University, he was much influenced by reading B. F. Skinner's text, *Science and Human Behavior*. Since then Michael has been primarily involved in teaching the operant behavioral approach at Kansas University, the University of Houston, Arizona State University, and at Western Michigan University since 1967.

In 1957, largely as a result of his association with Lee Meyerson, he became interested in applying Skinner's behavioral concepts and methods in the areas of mental retardation, mental illness, and physical disability. During the next several years the field of behavior modification was in a period of rapid expansion, and Michael contributed to this growth with his teaching, writing, and public speaking about mental retardation, physical disability, counseling and guidance, mental illness, and education. At Arizona State University as a result of his contacts with Fred Keller, he became interested in a behavioral approach to the field of college instruction. Most recently he has concentrated on the technical terminology of the behavioral approach, basic behavioral theory, and verbal behavior.

In 1971 he received a Distinguished Teaching Award from the American Psychological Foundation. He helped to establish the Association for Behavior Analysis in 1974 and was elected president in 1979. He is currently president of Division 25 of the American Psychological Association. He is the author of *Laboratory Studies in Operant Behavior*, co-editor of *Behavior Modification in Clinical Psychology,* and the author of numerous articles and chapters on basic and applied behavior analysis.

JACK L. MICHAEL

BEHAVIOR ANALYSIS: A RADICAL PERSPECTIVE

A Little Recent History

When he published *The Behavior of Organisms* in 1938, Skinner added the subtitle "An Experimental Analysis." *Experimental* had its ordinary meaning, but *analysis* would appear to have been an affirmation of his analytic approach in spite of the widely known criticism of analysis by Gestalt psychologists (Skinner, 1979, p. 203). By 1946 there was a small group of experimental psychologists working with Skinner at the University of Indiana and with Fred Keller and W.N. Schoenfeld at Columbia University. Because of their unconventional methodology (discussed in detail later), these psychologists were having trouble getting their work published in experimental psychology journals, and at meetings their papers were presented in sessions that were not related to this group's interests.

As a temporary solution Skinner, Keller, and Schoenfeld organized their own conference at Indiana University on the *experimental analysis of behavior,* a name derived from the subtitle of *The Behavior of Organisms.* Before long members of this group were using this term to refer to their work. *Experimental analysis* now meant research on operant functional relations employing the rather unique methodology that characterized Skinner's approach. *Behavior* was an affirmation of their behavioristic orientation in considering behavior to be a proper subject matter in its own right, rather than simply a manifestation of underlying inner causes.

Others have considered this work to be a subclass of learning theory research, but *learning* in the sense of the acquisition of new behavior is too narrow, especially because a large number of the studies were concerned with factors that influenced the maintenance of behavior after it had been learned—the effects of schedules of intermittent reinforcement. And the fact that the research was rather specifically *not* the testing of theories and *not* an application of the hypothetico-deductive approach to science made *theory* quite inappropriate as well. The field is often referred to as *operant psychology,* which is all right if reference is being made to the general research interests of this group. But this label is not good if it carries the implication that the adherents deny the existence or importance of unconditioned behavior or of respondent relations and processes, which they clearly do not.

By 1958 the research output from this orientation had become large enough that the group could establish their own journal, the *Journal of the Experimental Analysis of Behavior* (*JEAB*), now in its 25th year of publication, and in 1964 they formed a division of the American Psychological Association, the Division for the Experimental Analysis of Behavior. During the late fifties and early sixties the number of practical applications of operant behavioral procedures in the areas of mental illness, mental retardation, education, child development, rehabilitation, and so forth increased rapidly, justifying the establishment of the *Journal of Applied Behavior Analysis* (*JABA*) in 1968.

The term *experimental* was now being contrasted with *applied* (although *basic* is a better contrast with *applied* because the applied researchers also rely on experimentation). A considerable body of literature was also developing that stemmed from Skinner's more theoretical and philosophical writings but was closely related to the basic and applied operant research. So the behavior analysis enterprise was no longer solely experimental as opposed to applied, and not even experimental as opposed to theory and philosophy. Therefore, in 1975, when a group of people with these diverse interests formed the Midwest Association for Behavior Analysis, soon to become simply the Association for Behavior Analysis, *experimental* was dropped. In 1978 this association established another journal, *The Behavior Analyst.* So *behavior analysis* is what first- and second-generation (and now third, fourth, etc.) Skinnerians call their substantive and methodological activities and interests.

Now, what about the word *radical?* Among the common synonyms, *thoroughgoing* is probably the most appropriate for the radical behaviorism of John B. Watson, and likewise for Skinner's use of the term in 1945 to refer to his own approach (p. 277). In that article he was clarifying the status of private stimuli and responses, which, from the logical positivism viewpoint held by many behaviorists at that time, could not be included as a part of science because science depended upon public or consensual validation. For reasons discussed later in this chapter, Skinner wished to include private events, "... feelings, consciousness, states of mind" (1974, p. 4) within his field, even if only by inference, and he thus contrasted his radical or all-inclusive behaviorism with what he called "methodological behaviorism," the more conventional view that insisted on consensual validation. *Radical* in the sense of *thoroughgoing* or *all inclusive* became even more appropriate for Skinner later as he "behavioralized" several other topics usually considered to belong to other disciplines, such as human language (1957, the entire book), the philosophy of science (1957, chap. 18), and the area of values or ethics (1953, chaps. 27, 28, 29; 1971, chaps. 6, 7, and 8).

So "Behavior Analysis: A Radical Perspective" refers to the substantive and methodological approach derived from the experimental research of B. F. Skinner and from his interpretive extensions to human behavior. What this consists of in more specific terms is the subject of the sections that follow.

Concepts and Principles

Unlearned Relations Between Environment and Behavior

Behaviorism, and especially radical behaviorism, is widely thought to be committed to the proposition that all human behavior is learned. This is a serious misconception. Watson did not hold this view and neither does Skinner, but the truth is somewhat complex, and it is not difficult to see how the misconception arises.

It is quite clear that some important behavioral differences between species are due to genetic factors and, ultimately, to the action of the environment in natural selection. In some cases it is even possible to identify the chromosomal region that carries a behavioral trait. Most of the available information relates to the behavior of invertebrates (mollusks, insects, worms, etc.) or of nonmammal vertebrates (fish, birds, amphibians, reptiles), but there is also some such information regarding mammals. (For an excellent introduction to this general area see Fantino and Logan, 1979, chap. 9.)

In terms of just what *is* inherited in any particular species, it is convenient to consider three kinds of behavioral relations. First, all organisms inherit some fairly specific stimulus–response relations called unconditioned reflexes, for example, the reflex whereby an increase in light striking the retina leads to pupillary constriction. In addition, some organisms inherit more complex environment–behavior relations, previously referred to as *instinctive* and now more likely to be called *released* behavior. In many species mating behavior and nest building illustrate this type of inherited functional relation. It is an empirical matter in each case whether these kinds of behavior are built-in response patterns triggered by specific though complex stimuli or the effect of special kinds of reinforcement that develop and maintain the specific form of behavior. Finally, it is also quite clear that organisms inherit certain capacities to be changed behaviorally by the environment; thus the capacity for reflex responses to be conditioned to novel stimuli (respondent conditioning) and the capacity for some environmental occurrences to increase the future frequency of the type of behavior they follow (operant conditioning). In fact, all principles of behavior are descriptions of built-in capacities in this sense. There are a number of complex interrelations among these three kinds of phylogenic provenance, but roughly speaking this is what is generally considered to be inherited within the field of behavior analysis.

So, between-species differences are often explained in terms of phylogenic provenance; that is, behavior analysts readily attribute to innate endowment many behavioral characteristics that are shared by all members of a species and that distinguish one species from others. So why is it so often claimed that behaviorism denies the importance of innate endowment? There are several reasons. For one thing, there is very little research being done at present on unlearned behavior by psychologists or zoologists operating from a behavior analysis perspective. Also, most of the current efforts at theoretical integration in this area—by ethologists—make extensive use of mentalistic or cognitive explanatory concepts, which makes such theory (but not necessarily the data) unattractive to behavioral psychologists.

But the main problem is that laymen and professionals in various fields are not really interested in the kind of innate endowment that is constant within a species and that explains differences between species. The important innate endowment for most people is the one that might help to explain behavioral differences among different people. The behavioral position regarding this type of inheritance follows from the general view, but typically does not go far enough to suit most nonbehaviorists. Certainly people must inherit physiological characteristics that make them behave differently from other people. It is completely unreasonable to assume that we are all exactly alike in all behavioral characteristics—in rate of learning new stimulus–response relations, for example. This admission is easily obtained from most behavior analysts, but they are likely to become reluctant to attribute any specific difference to inheritance.

There seems to be two reasons. Often such attribution is simply based on ignorance of any other relevant variables, and in this sense inheritance is an explanatory fiction. But in addition, the basic issue is really a matter of degree. The behaviorist is very likely to argue that there is already strong evidence for large environmental effects, which

must be well understood before one attributes much to innate deter-
mination.

Take athletic ability, for example. It would be quite unreasonable
to assume that we are all born exactly equal with respect to the ability
to run a fast mile. There must be many relevant inherited characteristics, such as height, body proportions, lung capacity, and certainly more
complex neuromuscular characteristics. However, it would certainly be
wrong to attribute the large differences in running speed of members
of a randomly sampled group of humans to innate endowment. It seems
quite reasonable to expect that the range of such differences would be
greatly reduced if all members of the sample had been trained from
birth to be mile runners. Even after such training there would, of course,
still be differences, but they might not be very great. And in terms of
practical matters, a training program would clearly guarantee large effects in a relatively short time as compared with a selective breeding
program. Likewise with so-called personality characteristics, before a
large genetic explanation of individual differences is accepted, obviously relevant environmental factors must be better understood.

So, the behavior analyst readily acknowledges innate determina-
tion, but then when it comes to the only kind that most people are
really interested in, becomes increasingly resistant. The behaviorist is
then quite justifiably credited with a preference—but not an unreasonable one—for environmental explanations.

Respondent Functional Relations

In *The Behavior of Organisms* (1938) Skinner began with a description
of functional relations involving reflexes (unlearned behavior), largely
based on the work of Sherrington (1906). Skinner next considered conditioned reflexes (respondent or classical conditioning) based on Pavlov's work (1927), and finally he described behavioral functional relations involving behavioral consequences (operant conditioning). Likewise in *Science and Human Behavior* (1953) and *About Behaviorism*
(1974), the systemic treatment of behavior begins with reflexes and
respondent conditioning. He has never questioned the existence or the
importance of respondent behavioral relations. Specific conditioned reflexes such as salivation to taste stimuli or pupillary constriction or
dilation to light changes are not of great importance in human affairs,
but the functional relations revealed by studying such responses are
important for understanding emotional variables and effects. It is also
very important to understand the respondent type of stimulus control
so as not to confuse it with operant stimulus control.

Briefly stated, Pavlov studied the way in which stimuli that did not
elicit reflex responses could be brought to do so by being paired with
the unconditioned stimuli for such responses. The former stimuli are

then called conditioned stimuli, and Skinner systematically used *elicitation* to refer to the effects of both unconditioned and conditioned stimuli. Presentation of the conditioned elicitor by itself leads to a decrease in its effectiveness as an elicitor, and this procedure is called respondent *extinction.*

Respondent relations most commonly involve smooth muscles and glands, as opposed to the striped muscle effectors most commonly subject to operant conditioning, as described next. The expression *respondent behavior* and its contrasting *operant behavior* might imply that one could classify a response as respondent or operant solely on the basis of a careful inspection of the behavior itself. There are a number of exceptions, however, to this rough correlation between type of effector and type of effective conditioning procedure, which is why I use the term *respondent functional relation* in this paper. It is only the controlling relation between independent variable and behavior that can be identified as respondent or operant, not the behavior alone.

Most of Skinner's *Behavior of Organisms* is concerned with operant functional relations. It was the effect of behavioral consequences that had been previously neglected or confused with respondent or classical conditioning and needed extensive exploration, and it is the human operant repertoire that is the most important to other humans. Likewise, the researchers working in the experimental analysis of behavior who followed up Skinner's work have been primarily extending our knowledge of operant relations. Also, when the field of behavior modification or applied behavior analysis was started in the late fifties, the manipulation of behavioral consequences quickly became the standard technique of that movement.

As a result of this emphasis on the operant relation, Skinner's approach is often called an *operant conditioning approach,* or *operant psychology,* or *operant behaviorism,* especially by those who wish to contrast it with some supposedly broader orientation. This is clearly a mistake. Irrespective of a justifiable emphasis on operant relations, behavior analysts (radical behaviorists, Skinnerians, etc.) acknowledge the importance of unlearned behavior and of respondent conditioning as a form of learning, in addition to the importance of operant conditioning. In fact, recent work in the area of respondent conditioning (Rescorla & Wagner, 1972) has revealed some general features of compound stimulus control, blocking and overshadowing, that are the subject of much current research in the experimental analysis of operant stimulus control.

It should be noted that *respondent conditioning* does not refer solely to the procedure of pairing stimuli, but also to the pairing of specific kinds of stimuli, one of which elicits a reflex response and one of which does not, with the result that the neutral one acquires an eliciting function. This is reconsidered in the following discussion of conditioned reinforcement.

Operant Functional Relations

Operant conditioning. Operant conditioning is typically explained without reference to prior stimuli, that is, solely in terms of the response and the reinforcing consequence. Operant stimulus control is then introduced later in connection with generalization and discrimination. Motivative relations are also not discussed in the primary definition of operant conditioning. However, these postponements can cause conceptual trouble, so my discussion will be more complex at the beginning but (I hope) conceptually clearer in the long run.

The basic operant functional relation can be stated in terms of four kinds of events, as follows. In a particular (1) stimulus situation, some (but not all) kinds of (2) behavior, when followed by certain (3) environmental consequences (reinforcement) show an increased future frequency of occurrence in the same or in a similar stimulus situation. For the environmental consequences to have functioned as reinforcement, some (4) motivative variable must have been in effect, and the increased frequency of response occurrence is only seen when that motivative variable is again in effect. This relation is often referred to as the three-term contingency of (1) stimulus, (2) response, and (3) reinforcement, but the (4) motivative variable responsible for an environmental event functioning as reinforcement must also be specified. A food-deprived rat reinforced with food for pressing a lever in a particular type of experimental chamber will have an increased tendency to press the lever when it is next in that chamber or one resembling it, but only if it is food deprived at that time.

Motivation in behavior analysis usually refers to one or both of two effects produced by variables like food deprivation: (a) a change in what functions as effective reinforcement and (b) a change in the relative strengths of different parts of the organism's repertoire. The food-deprived organism is reinforceable by food, in that any behavior that immediately preceded food delivery would increase in strength; and the behavior that had previously been reinforced by food is momentarily strong in the food-deprived organism's repertoire at the expense of other behavior. Another way of looking at the basic operant relation is to say that reinforcement produces in the organism's repertoire a lasting increase in the strength of a relation that involves a particular type of behavior, a particular stimulus situation, and a particular motivative variable.

Stimulus control is actually somewhat more complex than implied above. It is true that a single instance of reinforcement will result in some control of the response by the stimulus situation present during reinforcement, but more commonly the organism will make the same response and not be reinforced in a stimulus situation that differs in some way from the original one. Responding without reinforcement is called *operant extinction,* and operant stimulus control generally involves continued reinforcement in the presence of a particular stimulus condition and extinction in the absence of that stimulus condition. Skinner introduced the term *discriminative stimulus* (1938, p. 177) for the stimulus condition in which the response is reinforced, abbreviated it as S^D, and referred to the condition in which reinforcement is not provided as S^Δ. An S^D, then, is a stimulus condition in the presence of which a response has occurred and been reinforced, and in the absence of which the response has occurred and not been reinforced.

It is essential to emphasize the importance of the immediacy of reinforcement. Events that are delayed more than a few seconds after the response do not directly increase the future frequency of that response. When human behavior is apparently affected by long-delayed consequences, the change is accomplished by virtue of the human's complex social and verbal history, and this change should not be thought of as an instance of the simple strengthening of behavior by reinforcement. When, for example, industrial work behavior is increased by public posting of daily productivity, this effect could not possibly be the direct result of reinforcement, because the posting occurs hours (sometimes days) after the relevant behavior. This is not to say that such procedures don't actually alter the relevant behavior, but rather that they do it in a much more complex way, which is only just beginning to be understood. This point will become important when rule-governed behavior is considered later in this chapter in connection with extensions of these basic concepts to more complex human behavior.

It is unfortunate that the term *extinction* is used for both respondent and operant relations, because the procedures are quite different. In respondent extinction the conditioned stimulus is presented without being paired with the unconditioned stimulus, but no aspect of the procedure requires any responding. In operant extinction, however, the response that was reinforced earlier must occur again in the relevant stimulus situation and must not be reinforced.

Some events function as reinforcement, given the proper motivative operation, irrespective of any learning history on the part of the organism: People do not have to learn to be reinforced by food when they are food-deprived, or by water when they are water-deprived, and so forth. Such events are referred to as *unconditioned* reinforcers. Other stimulus changes acquire their capacity to reinforce behavior by being systematically related to certain other reinforcing events, and these stimulus changes function as *conditioned* reinforcers. In a common laboratory demonstration a food-deprived rat is trained to press a lever in the presence of an overhead light through the use of food reinforcement. Typically the light-on condition is alternated with a light-off condition where pressing can occur but is not reinforced. When good stimulus control is developed, the light onset will function as reinforcement for any new response that turns the light on, such as pulling a chain that is suspended from the ceiling.

The procedure for developing conditioned reinforcers is sometimes called respondent conditioning because it involves the pairing of stimuli, but this is not good usage because it is not a future elicitation effect that is important, but rather the future effectiveness of a stimulus as a reinforcing consequence. That a stimulus elicits respondent behavior is neither necessary nor sufficient for it to be considered a conditioned reinforcer: It must increase future response frequency when it is used as the consequence of a response.

In addition to being classified as unconditioned or conditioned (*primary* and *secondary* are sometimes used, but easily imply more than just the relevance of a learning history, and are thus less precise), reinforcers are often called *positive* if they strengthen by being immediately presented and *negative* if they strengthen by being immediately removed following the response. The term *negative reinforcement* has caused considerable confusion, however, because it is so easily equated with punishment (described later in this chapter). The distinction between positive and negative reinforcement may be unnecessary and seems to be made less often now than a few years ago, but in any case, a possible way to avoid the confusion is to note that negative reinforcement is highly desirable. If offered negative reinforcement, one should accept the offer. It is always good to have bad things terminated or removed. It may also help to reflect on the fact that one should not be able easily to choose between an offer of positive and negative reinforcement.

In *The Behavior of Organisms* Skinner described the detailed results of what he called *periodic* reconditioning, later referred to as a *fixed interval* schedule of reinforcement. This is an arrangement where the first response following a fixed time period from the last reinforced response is reinforced, and also starts another time period, and so on. It is one of the large variety of intermittent reinforcement schedules falling between the extremes of reinforcement for every response and reinforcement for no responses. Work on intermittent reinforcement has constituted a large proportion of the research in the experimental analysis of behavior, starting with the extensive results reported in Ferster and Skinner's *Schedules of Reinforcement* in 1957 and continuing to occupy much of the content of the early volumes of *JEAB*.

This work has been important for several reasons. Some schedules of reinforcement have become standard research tools and techniques that are used to study a wide variety of other phenomena in the science of behavior. Understanding how a particular schedule produces its characteristic pattern of performance has been an intriguing research area in its own right and has led to much new knowledge about behavior. The knowledge gained from studying various schedules of reinforcement has also greatly improved the technology of behavioral control. But probably the most important effect has been the enrichment of the behavioral independent variable.

Prior to Skinner's discovery of interval and ratio schedules, the basic behavioral independent variables were the variables of respondent conditioning and reinforcement (also punishment) of varying magnitudes and qualities, either given or withheld. Yet behavior seemed to be a very complex dependent variable, a situation that encouraged the invention of inner determiners to account for unexplained behavioral variation. The study of the effects of intermittent reinforcement has shown that behavior is not only sensitive to whether it is reinforced or not, but also sensitive to the arrangement of reinforcement in combination with requirements or contingencies involving time, number of responses, and the presence of stimuli. Adding time, number, and stimulus requirements to the ordinary four-term contingency now yields an independent variable that is more than sufficiently complex to be considered as the prime determiner of variations in the dependent variable, behavior.

The study of intermittent reinforcement has also revealed the role of consequences in maintaining behavior after it has been acquired. Historically, differences or fluctuations in response frequency after learning have been assigned to the topic of motivation. Removing from this topic differences that are due to different schedules of intermittent reinforcement leaves for motivation only the differences due to variables, like deprivation, that alter response frequency while altering the effectiveness of various events as reinforcement. Reinforcement is thus seen to be a much more important variable than was previously realized and the topic of motivation much more restricted and manageable.

Operant weakening by punishment. Some, but not all, kinds of behavior, when followed by certain environmental changes (punishment), decrease in future frequency of occurrence in the same or in a similar stimulus situation and when similar environmental events are effective as punishment. As with reinforcement, punishment must be immediate to have much of an effect, and as with reinforcement, punishing events can be classified as unconditioned and conditioned, dependent upon the necessity of a learning history.

It now seems reasonable to describe this basic operant weakening relation as the opposite of the basic relation of operant conditioning, but the issue has had a long and complex history, and many behavior analysts, especially those in the applied field, may still contest the correctness of this approach. Punishment has been more difficult to study than reinforcement, largely because it cannot be studied easily by itself. One must have some behavior to punish, which means behavior that has been or is still being reinforced. Thus punishment has always been superimposed on a recent or a continuing schedule of reinforcement for the same behavior.

Early experiments by Skinner (1938) and by Estes (1944) seemed to show that punishment did not actually weaken behavior directly, but rather only constituted an arrangement that favored the development of behavior that was incompatible with the punished behavior. On the basis of these experiments and possibly other less formal kinds of evidence, Skinner provided an extensive treatment of the topic in *Science and Human Behavior* (1953), which for a time was the generally accepted view. In a series of experiments begun in the late fifties, Azrin and his colleagues corrected flaws in previous experiments and provided a comprehensive picture of the effects of electric shock punishment on the operant behavior of pigeons. A detailed treatment of the topic of punishment, including the results of the previous ten years of research, appeared as a chapter (Azrin and Holz, 1966) in the first handbook of operant behavior (Honig, 1966), which is the basis for the currently accepted interpretation as stated at the beginning of this section.

Another common form of operant conditioning consists of the reinforcement of behavior by the termination of environmental events, which when presented would function as punishment. Such stimuli have been called *aversive,* and their termination is the negative reinforcement referred to earlier. When the response terminates an unconditioned aversive stimulus, the procedure is called *escape;* when it terminates a warning stimulus that has become a conditioned aversive stimulus due to its relation to the onset of the unconditioned aversive stimulus, the procedure is called *avoidance.* The interpretation of avoidance behavior is currently somewhat controversial, especially with respect to nondiscriminative avoidance, that is, avoidance without a warning signal. Rats, monkeys, and humans readily learn to press levers that do not actually terminate any form of exteroceptive stimulus, but rather only postpone the onset of the next (typically brief) aversive stimulus. In the *molar* interpretation the reinforcement for the lever pressing behavior is simply the decreased frequency of aversive stimuli that results, even if there is no immediate reinforcement (Sidman, 1962; Herrnstein & Hineline, 1966). In the *molecular* interpretation the stimuli resulting from the lever pressing behavior itself (kinesthetic, tactile, etc.) are the reinforcement, in that they are never followed immediately by shock as contrasted with the stimuli they replace (Dinsmoor, 1977).

The molar–molecular controversy is not restricted to the interpretation of avoidance, but is in fact a major current topic of research and theorizing. The basic issue is whether reinforcing or punishing consequences alter behavior primarily by being temporally contiguous with it—the molecular view, which was Skinner's interpretation when he first focused on the importance of behavioral consequences—or by being dependent upon the behavior, even if temporally remote from it—the molar view (for example, Herrnstein, 1969; Baum, 1973; Hineline, 1977).

At present temporal contiguity is seen as quite important, but whether it is strictly necessary or strictly sufficient is still controversial, as are many issues within the field of behavior analysis. Although the general outline seems quite clear, the field should not be thought of as being committed to any existing principle. Behavioral knowledge is constantly being refined and in some cases, drastically revised. In spite of the unfinished nature of the field, however, I think the general view can be safely described as highly deterministic. Although the details are not completely known, it is assumed that human behavior will be completely accounted for by specifying the relevant unlearned and learned functional relations.

Methodology

Skinner's research in the thirties and forties and the work of those who followed him differed in the following ways from other research in the psychology of learning.
* The main dependent variable was rate of response, typically portrayed as the cumulative curve of responding produced by a single animal
* Each subject was exposed to all values of the independent variable and only a few subjects were studied in any one experiment
* No use was made of statistical inference (significance tests)
* The research was not construed as a test of a theory.

Because large numbers of subjects, complex statistical treatment (typically the analysis of variance), and explicit theory testing were used increasingly to evaluate research on learning during that period, the experimental analysis of behavior was very different in ways that were often interpreted as deficiencies. Because these four methodological idiosyncrasies still characterize much of behavior analysis research and are seen as distinguishing features by many, it is not inappropriate to consider them in some detail.

Rate of Response

For Skinner, rate of response was more than just a convenient dependent variable; it was the only direct reflection of response probability that was the basic concern of a science of behavior. "A natural datum in a science of behavior is the probability that a given bit of behavior will occur at a given time. An experimental analysis deals with that probability in terms of frequency or rate of responding" (1966, p. 213). Other measures commonly used in experimental psychology—latency, reaction time, time to complete a task (to traverse a runway, for example), number of errors made, number of trials to a criterion—were all criticized as "not related in any simple way to probability of response" (p. 214). And again, "Rate of responding is a basic dimension, not simply because responses can be accurately counted, but because rate is relevant to the central concern of a science of behavior" (p. 214).

The appropriate use or meaning of the concept of probability is presently very controversial in the physical sciences and in the philosophy of science (Fine, 1973). Skinner acknowledges the difficulty with the concept (1953, pp. 62–63; 1957, p. 22, p. 28) but doesn't deal with it, and any justification of rate in terms of its relation to probability remains problematic. Response rate is much easier to justify empirically, because the way its study has led to the accumulation of increasingly precise information about the principles of behavior. It is also easy to justify in the applied areas where frequency of occurrence (too high or too low) is the essential feature of most behavioral problems.

Within-Subject Comparisons

Behavior analysis is often said to favor single-subject rather than the more generally common group-statistical experimental designs. The essence of this distinction concerns the way in which the different values of the independent variable are compared with each other in terms of their effects on the same subject at different times (a within-subject comparison) or in terms of their effects on different subjects (a between-subject comparison). When the within-subject comparison is made, the reliability of the differences between the effects of the different values of the independent variable is assessed by observing the performance of a single subject at each of these values, often repeatedly introduced and removed. Several experimental subjects (seldom more than three of four) are used to assess the generality of the findings. If the performances of the small number of subjects differ very much from one another, one solution is to increase the number of subjects and average their results to reveal the general functional relation; another is to try to isolate the sources of uncontrolled variation and then perform the experiment again under better conditions of experimental control. It is this latter approach that has typified behavior analysis research.

Skinner's early research on conditioning and extinction using rate of response in a free responding (as contrasted with discrete trial) situation required prolonged study of the same organism, and the similarity of the cumulative curves across subjects made it unnecessary to study more than three or four animals in any given experiment. The later research on intermittent reinforcement resulted in interesting behavioral changes even after many hours of exposure to the independent variable, which made the careful study of a few organisms the only practical option. Most of the research published in *JEAB* similarly involves prolonged exposure to independent variables and an emphasis on stable performances prior to changing conditions, factors that work against the use of the between-subject comparisons.

Although it is the within-subject feature of this research that is methodologically somewhat unique, not the actual number of subjects used, between-subject comparisons typically require quite a few more subjects. When the different values of the independent variable are applied to different subjects, individual differences are confounded with those values and typically can only be unconfounded by averaging the results of several subjects, and several usually means five or more. Thus within-subject experiments typically use three or four subjects; between-group experiments are likely to involve a group of five or more for each value of the independent variable, although with extremely stable and well-understood individual performances, a between-subject comparison could involve only a few subjects.

Statistical Inference

Skinner and subsequent basic and applied researchers have had no reluctance to use ordinary descriptive statistics such as frequency distributions, means, medians, percentages, scatter diagrams, correlation coefficients, and so forth when the statistics facilitate effective reaction to data. They have made little use, however, of the significance tests of statistical inference. The reasons are probably quite complex. Highly effective experimental control makes such techniques superfluous. When repeated application of the different values of the independent variable leads to obvious changes in the dependent variable, the assessment of the probability of such differences occurring by chance is uninteresting. It is also true that the language of statistical hypothesis testing seems most appropriate when the experiment is itself formulated within a hypothetico-deductive or theory testing approach to research, and much of the early behavior analytic work explicitly disavowed this general orientation. It is also not entirely irrelevant that there were no easily applicable significance tests (and still aren't) for the type of within-subject comparisons most commonly made in the analysis of behavior.

Theory as a Basis for Research

During the late thirties and throughout the forties much research in learning was an explicit application of the hypothetico-deductive approach. This was especially true of research generated by Hull's postulate system (Hull, 1943), aimed either at refining the postulates and theorems or at refuting them. Skinner's orientation was by contrast much more descriptive. He had discovered a sensitive dependent variable and had developed a methodology for studying its relation to obvious and important independent variables. With the further discovery of the area of intermittent reinforcement, research questions were easily formulated and easily investigated, in the sense that one study led to another, and there was plenty of work for anyone who was interested.

In the context of the learning psychologists' "love affair" with theory testing, however, the work of Skinner and his followers was often criticized as a sort of purposeless data gathering. Skinner reacted by writing the widely quoted paper, "Are Theories of Learning Necessary?" (1950), which was an emphatic negative answer to the question posed, and which earned him the antitheory reputation that he now holds. It was only certain types of theories that he opposed, however. These were "any explanation of an observed fact which appeals to events taking place somewhere else, at some other level of observation, described in different terms, and measured, if at all, in different dimensions" (1950, p. 193). He specifically criticized the explanatory use of inferred physiological entities or relations, mental events, and the hypothetical constructs of the Hullian and similar theory builders (pp. 193–194).

This orientation still characterizes the behavior analysis approach, with inferred cognitive processes being the current opposition party. However, a good deal of the research recently published in JEAB is considerably more theory oriented than was considered appropriate 20 years ago. This is especially true of efforts at quantification (see, for example Commons and Nevin, 1981). These last three methodological features, within- versus between-subject comparisons, visual inspection versus significance tests, and description versus a theory-testing basis for research are logically quite independent of each other. Currently all possible combinations are found in JEAB and JABA, although the largest proportion still resembles the earlier work in the experimental analysis of behavior.

It is in connection with theory that Skinner's orientation has sometimes been called antiphysiological; however his opposition is only to inferred physiological processes as explanations of behavior. He has never expressed any opposition to actual physiological independent or dependent variables, and he has been quite enthusiastic about the possible cooperative roles of the experimental analysis of behavior and the physiology of behavior. It is true that he sees the direction of usefulness, at least in the near future, to be moving from the experimental analysis of behavior to physiology. Valid behavioral relations cannot be refuted by any physiological discoveries, but physiologists must know principles of behavior in order to know what to look for (Skinner, 1966, pp. 282–284).

It is important to point out that only by comparison with other work in the experimental psychology of learning did Skinner's methodology seem unusual. It was not at all unlike the methodology practiced in physiological psychology, psychophysics, and, for that matter, in much of biology, chemistry, and physics. Sidman's *Tactics of Scientific Research* that described and justified this methodology was published in 1960, and it quickly became the standard reference for researchers in behavior analysis. Several other books describing various aspects of this approach have become available recently (Johnston & Pennypacker, 1981; Bailey & Bostow, 1979; Hersen & Barlow, 1977), and the approach appears to be accepted increasingly within experimental psychology.

Extensions

Behavior Modification or Applied Behavior Analysis

There are undoubtedly many antecedents to the applied branch of behavior analysis, but Skinner's *Science and Human Behavior* (1953) is probably the most relevant. There, for the first time, respondent and operant functional relations were used to interpret many aspects of human individual and social behavior. Contingencies of reinforcement, ubiquitous but often quite subtle, played the leading role in this sensitive and highly sophisticated look at the human condition. Mastery of this text prepared the behaviorist to approach almost any human problem with some chance of success, and further, to have a behavioral interest in almost any aspect of human behavior.

By the late fifties and early sixties descriptions of specific research projects in the areas of mental illness, education, and mental retardation began to appear in the literature, and in 1968 the *Journal of Applied Behavior Analysis* was founded. In these early applications behavior problems were interpreted in terms of the concepts and principles of the operant (and to some extent, respondent) conditioning laboratory, and treatment procedures followed from these interpretations. More recently many applications have used the methodology of behavior analysis, but with an outcome orientation that does not seem to require interpretation in terms of conditioning concepts and principles.

At first behavior modification was applied mainly to institutionalized clients and to children, but its use has expanded to many other phases of human behavior. This can be nicely appreciated by considering the chapter headings of a typical recent text in behavioral applications, *Behavior Change* by Lutzker and Martin (1981):
1. Behavior Change: History, Principles, and Processes
2. Assessment and Evaluation
3. The Community and the Environment
4. The Working World: Business, Industry, and Government
5. Health Care: Adults
6. Health Care: Children
7. Children
8. Classrooms

9. Severe Problems: Institution and Community Intervention
10. Personal Problems: Obesity, Smoking, Chemical Dependency
11. Personal Problems: Anxiety and Depression
12. Relationships and Sexual Behavior
13. Training, Ethics, and the Future

As can be seen from this list, applied behavior analysis includes all the traditional areas of applied psychology (clinical, industrial, educational) as well as more recent developments, such as behavioral medicine, rehabilitation, and environmental psychology. Several other areas not covered in the Lutzker and Martin text that are being dealt with by behavioral psychologists include problems of aging (note Skinner's and Vaughan's 1983 *Enjoy Old Age*), legal jurisprudence and criminal justice, the analysis and design of instructional materials (as with programmed instruction), and sports psychology.

Four Interpretive Analyses by Skinner

Even with the preceding description of basic concepts and principles, of the distinctive methodology, and of the applied branch of the field, the character of behavior analysis is not accurately portrayed without mention of some of Skinner's unique theoretical contributions. They represent interpretive analyses of complex human behavior, and four of the most important are presented next.

Verbal behavior. Even before *The Behavior of Organisms* was published in 1938, Skinner began the analysis of human language that was ultimately published as the book *Verbal Behavior* in 1957. Although Skinner considers this to be the contribution that will ultimately be seen as his most important (personal communication, 1981), it has only recently begun to have a noticeable impact on the field. However, this book represents a completely behavioral treatment of human language that is not only unique, but also incompatible with both common sense and professional (linguistic, psycholinguistic) treatments. Not only that, but it is also very complex, as it must be to do justice to the topic; and the basic notions presented in the first part of the book must be mastered in order for the later sections to make sense. The journal *Behaviorism* began publication in 1972, and has had a steady stream of contributions related to *Verbal Behavior.* The Association for Behavior Analysis began annual conventions in 1974, and the conventions have had a verbal behavior specialty area since 1978. Perhaps it simply took 20 years or so even for behaviorists to appreciate this very revolutionary way of thinking about language.

In his book, Skinner began by defining *verbal behavior* as behavior that achieves its effect on the world through the mediation of someone else's behavior. Its reinforcement is thus indirect, as compared with the reinforcement of nonverbal behavior. The nonverbal behavior of reaching for an object is reinforced by tactile contact with the object; the verbal behavior of asking for the object is only reinforced with the object if there is someone available who responds to the request. The implications of the indirectness of the reinforcement for verbal behavior are far reaching and, in fact, are responsible for many of the unique and powerful features of human language (Skinner, 1957, pp. 203–206).

Next Skinner identified several elementary verbal units (mand, echoic, textual, intraverbal, and tact) that are distinguished from each other by the relation between the form of the response (what is said or written) and the nature of the controlling variable. He then considered the extension of these elementary verbal operants to novel conditions on the basis of stimulus generalization (generic extension, metaphor, metonymy, etc.); the effects of multiple controlling variables; and finally the role of ongoing verbal behavior as a controlling variable for further verbal responses (autoclitic verbal behavior).

This basic approach is enriched with hundreds of examples that illustrate the interpretive power of the small number of completely behavioral concepts. Unfortunately, but unavoidably, the book assumed a good deal of familiarity with topics considered in traditional treatments of language, and this added to its general difficulty, but also contributed to the persuasiveness of the argument. Skinner essentially demonstrated that there are no aspects of human language that cannot be understood, at least in this interpretive sense, in completely behavioral terms.

As mentioned before it seems that increasing use is being made of Skinner's analysis, in philosophical and theoretical activity and also in research. The effect of the book has not been seen in some areas where it might have been expected (for example, the recent efforts to develop human language in apes, unfortunately for that enterprise, show no detectable influence by *Verbal Behavior*), but it has influenced many in the field of behavior analysis and is being taught about and written about now more than ever before.

Private events. In "The Operational Analysis of Psychological Terms" in the 1945 *Psychological Review,* Skinner first presented his analysis of verbal behavior under the control of private stimuli. Rather than attempt to provide operational definitions for terms like *ache, itch, hunger pangs, anger,* and so forth, he asked how the verbal community could develop in the speaker a verbal repertoire under the control of such private stimuli. He concluded that the development is accomplished indirectly, in one of two ways. The community can base its feedback (reinforcement, extinction, punishment, etc.) to the learner on common public accompaniments of the private stimuli (including those resulting from behavior already controlled by the private stimuli, such as scratching, crying, etc.). For example, an adult can use the language of pain in comforting a child who has been cut by a sharp object. The child is affected primarily by the private stimuli generated by the injury, which are completely unavailable to the adult. The adult can, nevertheless, react to the public visual features of the damaged tissue and the public features of the child's crying.

Second, control by private stimuli also comes about as the result of stimulus generalization, where a response learned with respect to public stimuli simply occurs because a private stimulus has something in common with the public one. For example, *sudden* may be acquired under the control of public visual or auditory events and be at some strength by stimulus generalization when a private stimulus such as a stomach pain shows the same temporal property.

This brief treatment cannot do justice to the thoroughness of Skinner's derivation of this basically simple notion, nor is there space for considering its significance for understanding many long-standing psychological and philosophical problems. One implication, however, is that the language of feelings can never be precise, and another is that introspection is not a way of making contact with basic causal variables, but is only verbal behavior controlled—and not well—by stimuli. Skinner's analysis of the role of private stimuli and responses as just more stimuli and responses to be accounted for, rather than essential causal variables underlying all behavior, is in fact the defining feature of radical behaviorism, and it has been the subject of much discussion and debate. For example, every volume of *Behaviorism* contains several articles directly related to Skinner's analysis of private events.

Chapter 17, "The Role of Private Events in a Natural Science," in *Science and Human Behavior* (Skinner, 1953) is an expanded version of his 1945 article; the same topic is considered in the chapter on the tact in *Verbal Behavior* and was the basis for his 1963 *Science* article, "Behaviorism at Fifty." Most recently the role of private events was systematically considered in chapters 1 and 2 of *About Behaviorism* (1974). Although Skinner's analysis of private events is considered by many to be one of his most valuable contributions, it would be a mistake to assume that for him, private stimuli are of great importance in human life. For Skinner, the main reason for dealing with private stimuli is to put them in proper perspective, which represents a considerable reduction in their significance from the essential causal role they are thought to play in traditional and common sense accounts.

Rule-governed behavior. In Chapter 6 of *Contingencies of Reinforcement* (1969), "An Operant Analysis of Problem Solving," Skinner introduced the distinction between rule-governed and contingency-shaped behavior. Contingency-shaped behavior refers to a repertoire developed as a result of exposure to reinforcement contingencies (involving stimuli, responses, motivative variables, and effective consequences). Rule-governed behavior refers to a repertoire developed as a result of exposure to a verbal description of contingencies (involving stimuli, etc.) but not to the contingencies themselves. Speaking one's native language is an example of the former; the early phases of learning a second language in school—composing sentences by using a grammar book and bilingual dictionary—is an example of the latter.

Skinner originally emphasized the distinction in order to offset the increasingly common practice (among cognitive psychologists) of interpreting contingency-shaped behavior as the following of rules. This point is especially clear in the chapter "Causes and Reasons" in *About Behaviorism.* "We do not need to describe contingencies of reinforcement in order to be affected by them. Lower organisms presumably do not do so, nor did the human species before it acquired verbal behavior" (1974, p. 141). The chapters of *Contingencies of Reinforcement* were published or given as talks prior to being published in that book, and at the end of each chapter, notes were added supplementing or updating the original material. The four notes added to the chapter on problem solving take up half as many pages as the chapter itself, and they are mostly concerned with rule-governed behavior: "Why are rules formulated?", "The objectivity of rules", "Some kinds of rules", and "Differences between rule-governed and contingency-shaped behavior" (1969, pp. 157–171).

Within the last ten years it has become increasingly clear that much human behavior is rule governed rather than contingency shaped. Whenever our behavior is affected by consequences that occur more than a few seconds after the behavior and where bridging stimuli are not present, the effect cannot generally be interpreted as the direct result of the consequence, but is probably related to our ability to generate and to be affected by descriptions of contingencies. It thus becomes incumbent upon psychologists to deal more specifically with such behavior and to understand how it works in terms of elementary behavioral principles. Skinner's earlier analysis of instruction in *Verbal Behavior* (1957, pp. 357–367) was a good beginning, and his treatment of rule-governed behavior in *Contingencies of Reinforcement* more explicitly acknowledged the importance of the issue and provided a technical term for this type of behavior control.

Others have begun to deal with the issue (for example, Hayes, Zettle, & Rosenfarb, 1982) and there is now an active area referred to as human operant research that is also much concerned with the effects of rules (provided by others or by the behaver) on nonverbal behavior (for example, see Lowe, 1979). In many respects this area, initiated or at least emphasized by Skinner's distinction, is the behavior analysis version of the cognitive behaviorist's concern for such topics as modeling and observational learning. It can also be seen as an inevitable extension of basic behavioral concepts and principles to increasingly complex human behavior.

Design of a culture. Skinner's attempts at cultural redesign are probably better known than most of his other contributions. *Walden Two,* his utopian novel, was published in 1948 and *Beyond Freedom and Dignity,* a nonfiction argument for the design of a culture along behavioral lines, was published in 1971. Both received extensive popular press coverage. Less well known are the last three chapters in *Science and Human Behavior* (1953) and numerous separate articles on the same general issue, namely that it is time to abandon the traditional view of human nature and to deliberately design cultural practices on the basis of the science of behavior.

Although these writings are full of intriguing suggestions for new and more effective cultural practices, they are really most important as a critique of existing practices and especially of the traditional view of human nature that is used to justify these practices. A scientific approach that views human behavior as the completely determined product of innate endowment plus environmental events is contrasted by Skinner with a traditional view of people as self-determining autonomous agents. Freedom of choice is seen as an illusion, based on failure to appreciate the nature of control by positive reinforcement—people tend to recognize control only when aversive events are the responsible variables. Most importantly, our continuing failure to accept the scientific view is responsible for the majority of our current problems, and unless we begin to design the culture in order to achieve long range effectiveness or survival, it may soon perish. These points are, of course, not simply asserted, but rather argued in meticulous and persuasive behavioral detail.

In the process of making his general point about the necessity of deliberate cultural design, not impeded by the traditional notion of freedom, Skinner attacks the long-standing philosophical practice of distinguishing sharply between facts and values. Contrary to the view that science is concerned with facts, but that value judgments are the province of some other kind of knowledge, he identifies the value judgment as a particular type of behavior and thus a proper topic within the science of behavior. This particular analysis is clearly made in *Science and Human Behavior,* pages 428–436, and in *Beyond Freedom and Dignity,* chapters 6, 7, and 8. Like Skinner's analysis of language, his behavioral value theory is not easy to understand on first contact, because it is so different from the consideration of values that is implied in everyday language and that is a part of our religious and legal heritage. But the argument is logically tight, and the implication for survival of the human species is quite clear.

The approach to the prediction, control, and understanding of human behavior that has been described in this chapter should not be thought of as a static set of concepts, principles, and methods. Behavior analysis is constantly changing in little ways, and every once in a while a big change—a breakthrough—occurs. It is a deterministic view that sees human behavior as the inevitable product of innate endowment and environmental events that take place during the person's life time, and nothing else. In many respects it is just scientific method applied to behavior in all its manifestations.

This view is *not* concerned only with operant conditioning. It does *not* exclude private stimuli and covert behavior from scientific consideration. It does *not* insist that behavior can change only as a result of direct exposure to contingencies, but readily acknowledges behavior change by instruction and by the description of contingencies. It is not antiphysiological, antigenetic, or antitheoretical (except in the sense of inferred inner explanations). It is, in short, the science and technology of behavior.

References

Azrin, N. H., & Holz, W. C. (1966). Punishment. In W. K. Honig (Ed.), *Operant behavior* (pp. 380–447). New York: Appleton-Century-Crofts.

Bailey, J. S., & Bostow, D. E. (1979). *Research methods in applied behavior analysis.* Tallahassee: Copygrafix.

Baum, W. M. (1973). The correlation-based law of effect. *Journal of the Experimental Analysis of Behavior, 20,* 137–153.

Commons, M. L., & Nevin, J. A. (Eds.). (1981). *Quantitative analyses of behavior: Vol. 1. Discriminative properties of reinforcement schedules.* Cambridge, MA: Ballinger.

Dinsmoor, J. A. (1977). Escape, avoidance, and punishment: Where do we stand? *Journal of the Experimental Analysis of Behavior, 28,* 83–95.

Estes, W. K. (1944). An experimental study of punishment. *Psychological Monographs, 57,* (Whole number 263).

Fantino, E., & Logan, C. A. (1979). *The experimental analysis of behavior.* San Francisco: Freeman.

Ferster, C. B., & Skinner, B. F. (1957). *Schedules of reinforcement.* New York: Appleton-Century-Crofts.

Fine, T. L. (1973). *Theory of probability.* New York: Wiley.

Hayes, S. C., Zettle, R. D., & Rosenfarb, I. (1982, May). *An empirical taxonomy of rule-governed behavior.* Paper presented at the meeting of the Association for Behavior Analysis, Milwaukee, WI.

Herrnstein, R. J. (1969). Method and theory in the study of avoidance. *Psychological Review, 76,* 49–69.

Herrnstein, R. J., & Hineline, P. N. (1966). Negative reinforcement as shock-frequency reduction. *Journal of the Experimental Analysis of Behavior, 9,* 421–430.

Hersen, M., & Barlow, D. (1977). *Single case experimental designs.* New York: Pergamon Press.

Hineline, P. N. (1977). Negative reinforcement and avoidance. In W. K. Honig & J. E. R. Staddon (Eds.), *Handbook of operant behavior.* Englewood Cliffs, NJ: Prentice-Hall.

Honig, W. K. (Ed.). (1966). *Operant behavior.* New York: Appleton-Century-Crofts.

Honig, W. K., & Staddon, J. E. R. (Eds.). (1977). *Handbook of operant behavior.* Englewood Cliffs, NJ: Prentice-Hall.

Hull, C. L. (1943). *Principles of behavior.* New York: Appleton-Century-Crofts.

Johnston, J. M., & Pennypacker, H. S. (1981). *Strategies and tactics of human behavioral research.* Hillsdale, NJ: Erlbaum.

Lowe, F. (1979). Determinants of human operant behavior. In M. D. Zeiler & P. Harzem (Eds.), *Reinforcement and the organization of behavior.* New York: Wiley.

Lutzker, J. R., & Martin, J. A. (1981). *Behavior change.* Monterey, CA: Brooks/Cole.

Pavlov, I. P. (1927). *Conditioned reflexes.* (G. V. Anrep, Trans.) London: Oxford University Press.

Rescorla, R. A., & Wagner, A. R. (1972). A theory of Pavlovian conditioning: Variations in the effectiveness of reinforcement and nonreinforcement. In A. H. Black & W. F. Prokasy (Eds.), *Classical conditioning II: Current research and theory.* New York: Appleton-Century-Crofts.

Sherrington, C. (1906). *The integrative action of the nervous system.* New York: Scribner's.

Sidman, M. (1960). *Tactics of scientific research.* New York: Basic Books.

Sidman, M. (1962). Reduction of shock frequency as reinforcement for avoidance behavior. *Journal of the Experimental Analysis of Behavior, 5,* 247–257.

Skinner, B. F. (1938). *The behavior of organisms.* New York: Appleton-Century-Crofts.

Skinner, B. F. (1945). The operational analysis of psychological terms. *Psychological Review, 52,* 270–277.

Skinner, B. F. (1948). *Walden Two.* New York: Macmillan.

Skinner, B. F. (1950). Are theories of learning necessary? *Psychological Review. 57,* 193–216.

Skinner, B. F. (1953). *Science and human behavior.* New York: Macmillan.

Skinner, B. F. (1957). *Verbal behavior.* New York: Appleton-Century-Crofts.

Skinner, B. F. (1966). What is the experimental analysis of behavior? *Journal of the Experimental Analysis of Behavior, 9,* 213–218.

Skinner, B. F. (1969). *Contingencies of reinforcement.* New York: Appleton-Century-Crofts.

Skinner, B. F. (1971). *Beyond freedom and dignity.* New York: Bantam/Vintage.

Skinner, B. F. (1974). *About behaviorism.* New York: Vintage.

Skinner, B. F. (1979). *The shaping of a behaviorist.* New York: Knopf.

Skinner, B. F., & Vaughan, M. E. *Enjoy old age.* New York: Norton.

LAUREN B. RESNICK

COGNITION AND INSTRUCTION: RECENT THEORIES OF HUMAN COMPETENCE

Following receipt of her undergraduate degree from Radcliffe College, Lauren B. Resnick earned a master's in Teaching and an EdD in Research in Instruction from the Harvard Graduate School of Education. Resnick is currently a Director of the Learning Research and Development Center and Professor of Psychology and Education at the University of Pittsburgh. She is past president of the Division of Educational Psychology of the American Psychological Association (APA), and a fellow in the APA's Divisions of Experimental Psychology, Developmental Psychology, Educational Psychology, and the Experimental Analysis of Behavior. She also has served as vice president of the American Educational Research Association's Division of Learning and Instruction, is a fellow of the American Association for the Advancement of Science, and is a member of the National Academy of Education.

Resnick's primary interest is the emerging field of the cognitive psychology of instruction, and she is playing an active role in its development. Her major current research focuses on the learning of mathematics and science. She has also studied reading and other subject-matter domains. In addition to her research efforts, Resnick is founder and editor of *Cognition and Instruction,* the major new journal in the field.

COGNITION AND INSTRUCTION: RECENT THEORIES OF HUMAN COMPETENCE

Introduction

My goal in this essay is to sketch the current state of knowledge about how intellectual competence is acquired and to suggest directions for future research, especially research that promises to improve instruction. My task is more complex and more exciting than it would have been 10 years ago because the psychology of learning and development has in that time undergone a profound change. In the past decade, a number of the assumptions that had guided research on learning have been called into question, and a vigorous new "cognitive science" has taken hold. The implications of this change for conceptions of human mental functioning are vast and the possibilities for a revitalized science of learning and instruction are just beginning to be realized.

Until 10 or 15 years ago, psychologists interested in the nature and acquisition of intellectual competence were faced with some unpalatable choices. One set of psychological theories—those in the associa-

The research reported herein was supported by the Learning Research and Development Center, funded in part as a research and development center by the National Institute of Education (NIE), Department of Education. The opinions expressed do not necessarily reflect the position or policy of NIE, and no official endorsement should be inferred.

tionist and behaviorist traditions—offered a rigorous experimental approach and an active concern not only for the nature of changes in performance but also for the means to influence change. These theories provided a strong basis for studying and prescribing interventions and were attractive to those who wanted to have an impact on instruction and education. But the associationists and behaviorists had little to say about the nature of thought processes or the questions of structure, organization, and meaning in learning. In their insistence that overt behavior was the only proper object of scientific study and their attempt to reduce thought to collections of associations, these psychologists offered no theoretically sensible way of dealing with questions of understanding and provided little wisdom concerning the nature of intellectual competence or the role of structure and meaning in learning.

On the other hand, structuralist theories (those of Piaget and the Gestalt psychologists, for example), which did treat mental life as real and important, and which offered strong theories about the role of structured knowledge and meaning in intellectual competence, had very weak theories of acquisition. And they had even less guidance to offer on how to intervene in acquisition. Despite elegant examples of the kinds of instructional goals that might be promoted, neither Piagetian nor Gestaltist analyses proceeded very far in specifying goals for instruction in anything like the rigorous detail that learning theorists offered for the associations or behaviors to be fostered by instruction. Furthermore, the relative silence, at least for Piagetians, on questions of instruction was further heightened by a kind of mistrust of intervention that was inherent in biologically oriented developmental theories (cf. Resnick, 1981a). Psychologists thus were faced with a choice between (a) theories that were centrally concerned with changes and how to promote them, but fundamentally unconcerned with thinking and meaning and (b) theories that were centrally concerned with structures of thinking and with understanding, but very vague about mechanisms of acquisition and disinterested in or even mistrustful of instruction.

Recent developments in cognitive psychology offer a new set of perspectives on this troubling dichotomy. The heart of cognitive psychology is the centrality given to the human mind and the treatment of thinking processes as concrete phenomena that can be studied scientifically. Researchers in various branches of psychology have found common ground in the study of cognition, and they have been joined by computer scientists, linguists, and philosophers to form a new cognitive science research community. This new interest in cognition has resulted in (a) a flourishing of research on complex forms of knowledge and skill, (b) a convergence on some key points between experimental and structuralist tradition in psychology, and (c) the development of a variety of new methods of research and forms of theorizing that are gradually developing a new scientific method specifically suited to the study of human mental functioning.

One of the most important developments in cognitive science has been the gradual construction of new ways of linking knowledge and performance. Process theories of cognitive functioning provide precise statements of how the knowledge that people possess permits them to perform in certain ways on certain kinds of tasks. The interest in processes of thought has led to the refinement of methods that trace sequential steps in thinking. These methods include recording patterns of reaction times for stimuli or tasks of different complexity, tracking eye movements as subjects read texts or solve visually presented problems, and using "think-aloud" protocols in which subjects solve problems while verbalizing what is going through their minds as they work. Because think-aloud methods seem to share features of the long-discredited introspective methods of psychology, they have evoked a certain degree of skepticism. Careful methodological work (e.g., Ericsson & Simon, 1984) has established the limits and powers of these methods.

Study of the relations between processes and content of thought is further stimulated and strengthened by the active enagagement of psychologists with computer scientists, especially those interested in the study and development of artificial intelligence. Viewing the computer as a metaphor for the human mind has stimulated cognitive psychology, allowing for more intentional and goal-driven processes than the older image of the mind as a switchboard, which was so neatly compatible with associationist theories. However, the real power has come not from the general metaphor, but rather from the use of computer programs as detailed simulations of human thinking and, thus, as a way of both energizing and disciplining cognitive theory. When computer programs behave as humans do—making similar mistakes, pausing at similar points, expressing confusion over the same issues— it is reasonable to assume that the internal processes of the human and the computer are similar, and researchers can treat the programs' visible processes as a theory of the invisible processes of humans.

Initially applied to limited forms of problem-solving task performance (Newell & Simon, 1972), computer simulation as a form of psychological theory has subsequently been extended to a wide variety of tasks and domains, and more recent work provides complex models of how knowledge is structured and accessed in addition to the procedures and heuristics used in manipulating it. This use of computer programs as models of human thinking has been enhanced by important shifts within artificial intelligence itself (Dehn & Schank, 1982). Artificial intelligence researchers, finding that truly complex forms of thinking depend on optimally structured knowledge and heuristic rather than exhaustive forms of searching this knowledge, are turning more and more to studies of human intelligence to inform their efforts to build intelligent machines. In this emerging field of cognitive science, it is not always easy to tell who is a psychologist and who is an artificial intelligence specialist.

In addition to having an interest in thinking and recognizing the central role of structured knowledge in the process of thought, the modern cognitive science converges with structuralist traditions in psychology in rejecting the long-held *tabula rasa* assumptions of American psychology in favor of what can best be called a *constructivist* assumption. In associationism there was no way to imagine knowledge entering a human's mind except from the outside. Objects could be perceived, associations between events noted, and mental bonds gradually built. These bonds were, it was assumed although often not directly discussed, direct reflections of the external information to which one was exposed. To learn was to build up more and more of these records and to make them more quickly accessible. But to learn was not to construct new associations and relationships through purely mental activity.

Today's cognitive science, by contrast, gives a central place to organizing structures and thus provides the terms in which theories of how individuals build new relationships can be developed. Knowledge is no longer viewed as a reflection of what has been given from the outside; it is a personal construction in which the individual imposes meaning by relating bits of knowledge and experience to some organizing schemata. This constructivist view in cognitive science is not identical to Piagetian constructivism, but it is close enough in spirit that psychologists who a decade ago could find little ground for serious debate can now successfully respond to and build upon each others' work. One result has been a rejoining of forces by certain groups of developmental and experimental psychologists who had for some decades diverged in their interests.

I will illustrate and elaborate all of these trends and the research methods on which they are based in the course of this chapter. I will also stress another important characteristic of recent cognitive research—that is the extent to which it is both relevant to and driven by questions concerning instruction and the deliberate modification of human competence. Partly because cognitive scientists are seeking complex and "ecologically valid" domains of human intellectual functioning in which to develop their theories, and partly because of a drive toward socially relevant applications of their work, cognitive psychologists are devoting substantial effort to research on the kinds of tasks that are studied in school or other educational institutions.

Both the nature of competence in such domains and its acquisition are increasingly central questions in today's research. Instructional experiments, when conducted so as to reveal details of the learning process, are a valuable tool in research on processes of acquisition, and these experiments further tighten the links between fundamental research on learning and thinking and potential applications to a science of instruction. To illustrate all of this, I will build my chapter around four broad topics: understanding written and spoken language; learning to read; developing mathematical competence; and the nature of problem solving, intelligence, and learning abilities. These are all domains in which the convergence of basic and applied research on human cognition is highly evident and in which many of the methodological tools and theoretical issues of current cognitive science can be displayed.

Understanding Natural Language

I will focus first on how people understand that most complex of human intellectual productions, language. This question has captured the attention of some of the world's best psychologists, linguists, and computer scientists over the last 15 years, and the result of their work is a rich body of knowledge and theory about how people understand what they read or what other people tell them.

Contrary to certain older views, cognitive scientists now agree that the process of understanding language is not one of absorbing and recording what is written or said. Rather, in this process the message is used to build up a representation in one's mind of the situation to which the message refers. This representation is simultaneously selective and elaborative with respect to the message. It does not exactly match the message. Rather, some things that the message says are left out, and some other information that the message left out is put in. The mental representation is elaborated by the reader or listener to include things not stated explicitly but necessary to make sense of the message. Information that the receiver construes as not being crucial to the meaning is left out of the receiver's mental representation. This process of constructing representations based on messages highlights a central feature of natural language understanding: Except in special circumstances, it is not the message itself that is represented, but its reference. People use language to refer to something external to the language itself, and the processes of language interpretation are all aimed at understanding that external situation. Knowledge of linguistic conventions as such, while crucial to the process of understanding, is normally employed to aid understanding of the reference situation rather than as an end in itself.

The processes by which the referential meaning of a message is constructed by a reader or listener have been a central concern of cognitive scientists interested in natural language understanding. Two major themes emerge from this work. First, prior knowledge is essential in constructing meaning for a new text. Second, the construction of meaning is one that centrally involves inference.

The Role of Prior Knowledge in Constructing Representations: Schemata in Language Processing

An example from a now classic experiment in cognitive psychology is the best way to demonstrate the importance of prior knowledge in understanding a text. Read the text in the following paragraph, but do not look ahead to Figure 1 as you do so.

> If the balloons popped the sound wouldn't be able to carry since everything would be too far away from the correct floor. A closed window would also prevent the sound from carrying, since most buildings tend to be well insulated. Since the whole operation depends upon a steady flow of electricity, a break in the middle of the wire would also cause problems. Of course, the fellow could shout, but the human voice is not loud enough to carry that far. An additional problem is that a string could break the instrument. Then there could be no accompaniment to the message. It is clear that the best situation would involve less distance. Then there would be fewer potential problems. With face to face contact, the least number of things could go wrong. (Bransford & Johnson, 1972, p. 719)

Unless readers know of the Bransford and Johnson (1972) experiment and thus remember what the text is about, virtually everyone reading this text has the experience of not understanding. The text seems garbled and senseless. Now look at Figure 1; it tells you, via a pictorial illustration, what the text is about. After seeing this serenade picture, most people experience a sense of insight concerning the text. They are ready to say, "Now I understand." The framework provided by the picture provides a "scaffolding" for interpreting the text.

The text in this study was a particularly ambiguous one, deliberately chosen to show that prior knowledge about the reference situation is crucial in understanding a text. Yet the same phenomenon has been observed in far less extreme situations as well. Hints provided in advance by the experimenter or the reader's own background have been shown to make a difference in what the reader understands in a text. For example, one study (Anderson, Reynolds, Schallert, & Goetz, 1977) shows that music students interpret the following passage as a description of an evening of playing chamber music, whereas physical education students interpret it as a story about an evening of card playing. This kind of study shows clearly that the background knowledge and interpretive schemata that readers bring with them to a text make a difference in what they understand the text to be saying.

> Every Saturday night, four good friends get together. When Jerry, Mike, and Pat arrived, Karen was sitting in her living room writing some notes. She quickly gathered the cards and stood up to greet her friends at the door. They followed her into the living-room, but as usual they couldn't agree on exactly what to play. Jerry eventually took a stand and set things up. Finally, they began to play. Karen's recorder filled the room with soft and pleasant

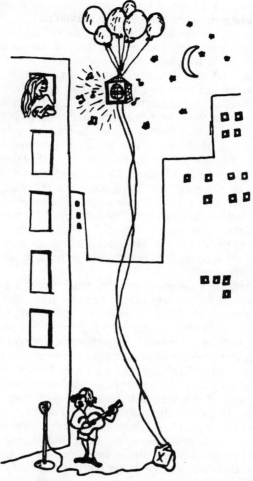

Figure 1. Appropriate context for ambiguous textual passage. Reprinted from Bransford and Johnson (1972) by permission.

music. Early in the evening, Mike noticed Pat's hand and the many diamonds. As the night progressed, the tempo of play increased. Finally, a lull in the activities occurred. Taking advantage of this, Jerry pondered the arrangement in front of him. Mike interrupted Jerry's reverie and said, "Let's hear the score." They listened carefully and commented on their performance. When the comments were all heard, exhausted but happy, Karen's friends went home. (Anderson, Reynolds, Schallert, & Goetz, 1977, p. 372)

Demonstrations of these kinds, together with many more formal experiments, underlie what has become known as the *schema theoretic* view of language comprehension. The theory holds that *schemata,* which are prototypical versions of a situation, are stored in people's minds and are used to interpret new instances and events in those situations. The schemata describe classes of situations and specify the relations between objects and events. The specific events and objects vary according to the particular case, but the relations specified in a more general schema still hold and are used to interpret the case at hand. Schemata result from a cumulation of prior learning and experience. They are necessary if one is to comprehend new verbal material, and thus they are important to all learning that depends on verbal presentations. This schema-based view of understanding goes back to early work in experimental psychology by Bartlett (1932), which showed that when a text was recalled, elements were deleted or highlighted according to a directing interpretive schema. Schemata of this kind, given various labels (such as "scripts," "frames," "memory organization packets"), are at the core of all artificial intelligence models of language understanding (see Dehn & Schank, 1982; Schank & Abelson, 1977, for discussion of these points).

In the serenade example, consider what might have happened to produce the initial failure to understand and the subsequent sense of understanding without difficulty. It is not the words of the text itself that produce the difficulty; English language readers can attach meaning to each word, and every sentence is grammatically correct. In fact, read by itself, each sentence is understandable. The problem occurs when the reader tries to make the sentences fit together in a coherent whole. Pairs of adjacent sentences seem to have no connection to one another. Once the context of the serenade is known, however, the reader can infer the connections and the passage makes sense.

With this simple analysis, I have already identified several elements of the process of understanding: Readers and listeners must access previously stored knowledge about the meaning of individual words; they must use their knowledge of syntactic rules and conventions and of the world to sensibly convert phrases and sentences in the text into propositions about a situation; and they must link the propositions into a coherent representation of a single situation. An excellent description of the various kinds of processing activity used to comprehend a text is given by Perfetti (in press). Perfetti shows that even in assigning meaning to individual words and analyzing sentences into sensible propositions about the world (both processes that proceed largely automatically without conscious effort or attention), prior knowledge about the reference situation and the conventions of language play a powerful role. After the propositions are developed, other processes and knowledge are used to link them into a coherent representation of the reference situation for a text.

Inference and Coherence-Building in Understanding Language

All natural language communications are incomplete because they do not specify everything about the reference situation that is needed for a complete and coherent representation. To build a coherent representation, readers or listeners must use their knowledge to infer links between individual propositions in a text and to provide a framework in which to interpret specific information supplied in the text. The work of Kintsch and vanDijk (1978) and their colleagues is the most extensively developed theory of the process of building coherence. I use an example based on Kintsch (1979) to illustrate.

The brief text passage that follows this paragraph is broken down into numerous propositions. These propositions are the elementary pieces of information conveyed. Sentences may contain one or more propositions. A text is said to be locally coherent to the extent that each new proposition makes explicit reference to recently stated prior propositions. Proposition sequences 1–4 and 5–11 are fully coherent because the actor in each proposition has already been named. This means that these segments are coherent within themselves. However, the two parts are not coherent if the sequences are joined, because proposition 5 is not explicitly linked to its predecessors. To understand this text the reader must infer a proposition that will link proposition 5 to its predecessors. Such a proposition might be: "The Swazi tribe had warriors."

Text:

The Swazi tribe was at war with a neighboring tribe because of a dispute over some cattle. Among the warriors were two unmarried men named Kakra and his younger brother Gum. Kakra was killed in battle.

Propositional analysis of text:

1. The Swazi tribe was at war.

2. The war was with a neighboring tribe.

3. The war had a cause.

4. The cause was a dispute over some cattle.

5. There were warriors.

6. The warriors were two men.

7. The men were unmarried.

8. The men were named Kakra and Gum.

9. Gum was the younger brother of Kakra.

10. Kakra was killed.

11. The killing was in a battle. (see Kintsch, 1979)

In extensive research on the processes of building local coherence, Kintsch and vanDijk and their colleagues have shown that features of the text, such as the number of missing propositions and the distance in the text that must be traversed to find explicit links, affect how long it takes to read the text and how easy it is to understand the text. Kintsch and vanDijk's theory accounts for a large body of such findings. This theory assumes—as do other modern information processing models—that human capacity for holding information in *immediate* (working) memory and for operating on this information is limited. For this reason, one cannot imagine that in the process of building a representation of a text, all propositions that have been read are brought into working memory every time a search for coherence is made. Instead, the theory assumes that reading and representation-building occur in cycles, where each cycle represents an attempt to link one or more new (just read) propositions to the representation already built. Because of working memory limitations, not all of the representation can be held in working memory—and therefore be searched—on a given cycle.

The ease or difficulty of comprehending and the time that comprehension takes depends, therefore, on whether the particular part of the representation retained in working memory or in a given cycle contains a reference to which the next proposition can be linked. If not, a new choice of propositions will have to be made, which produces time delays and at least temporary hesitation and confusion. Immediately preceding propositions from the text are always likely to be in working memory, and this accounts in part for the fact that when links can be created between adjacent propositions, comprehension proceeds more smoothly than when links must be created with propositions stated some time earlier. For more distant (earlier) propositions, ease of comprehension will depend on whether the choice of propositions to retain in working memory has been felicitous. This depends, in turn, on the extent to which the text provides clues as to what information is most important and the extent to which the reader or listener is adept at using these clues. This brings me to the important question of how people know, and how texts signal, what is most important in a verbal message.

Macrostructures and Frameworks for Interpretation

For most written texts, readers tend to agree fairly well on which statements are important or central and which ones are subordinate, perhaps functioning only as elaborations. Meyer (1975) has used this regularity to develop a method of coding the statements in a passage for their relative centrality; other less systematic ways of judging centrality have also been developed. Using measures of this kind, it has been possible to show that the material most likely to be forgotten or left out of a summary is the material lowest in the hierarchy of importance. Conversely, if material high in the hierarchy is not specified in the text, people will have trouble interpreting the text at all, will tend to insert missing high-level propositions in their summaries, and will spend a long time studying the portion of the passage where the high-level organizing material is expected to be (Kieras, 1977). Also, when asked whether a given statement was or was not present in the text, people are likely to assert with great confidence that highly central material that is consonant with the main theme of the text was there—even when it was not.

Voss and his colleagues (Chiesi, Spilich, & Voss, 1979; Spilich, Vesonder, Chiesi, & Voss, 1979) have shown that readers' ability to make inferences depends upon what they already know about the topic of the text. Finally, several studies have shown that more competent readers are better able than weaker readers to detect the hierarchy of importance in a text, picking out not only the main idea but also layers of supporting argument and detail (Meyer, 1984). I have already shown that knowing what a text is about plays a role in understanding it. However, in ordinary reading—unlike the serenade example—the necessary information about the theme of a text is not provided externally by a picture, but rather must itself be inferred in the course of reading.

In the process of successful comprehension, readers not only build up local coherences between propositions but also develop a representation of the *gist* of the message. A gist representation includes only the most important information given in the text; details are dropped out. But the gist representation is not just a string of important individual elements. It is itself organized so that these elements make sense with respect to one another. Kintsch and vanDijk have called these gist structures "macrostructures," to distinguish them from the "microstructures" that are constructed as individual propositions that are related to one another. They have elaborated a theory of how macrostructures are created by the reader, who uses special operators to pick out and combine elements of microstructure. This can successfully be done only when appropriate schemata already in the readers' (or listeners') long-term memories are found and applied.

Macrostructure representations are built up gradually in the course of reading or listening. If the initial macrostructure provides a sensible framework for the entire text, then the macrostructure will be elaborated and refined but not essentially modified in the course of understanding. Sometimes, however, the framework that has been guiding text interpretation turns out to be inappropriate as more of the text is read or heard. The tribal war story allows me to illustrate this point and also to emphasize again the central and multiple roles that prior knowledge plays in understanding any verbal communication. For the part of the story analyzed thus far (propositions 1–11), the macrostructure that is constructed concerns tribal war. The initial sentence would surely evoke such a theme and subsequent sentences do not disturb such an interpretation. However, the actual text from which the excerpt is drawn in fact goes off in another direction. The next sentence is: "According to tribal custom, Kakra was married subsequently to the woman Ami." A propositional breakdown of this sentence would include the propositions shown in the following paragraph.

Propositional analysis of text:

12. Kakra was married.
13. The marriage was after Kakra was killed.
14. The marriage was to a woman.
15. The woman was named Ami.
16. The marriage was in accord with tribal custom. (see Kintsch, 1979)

It is easy to find the links that make these propositions coherent at a microlevel. It is not even difficult, if only microlevel coherence were in question, to link it to the preceding representation. Only a couple of propositions back there is reference to the actor in the first new proposition, Kakra. This, however, cannot be a full model of how humans understand a text, for all readers immediately recognize an anomaly and refuse the simple linkage at the propositional level. How can Kakra, who has been killed, now be married? Theories of understanding must be able to explain how such anomalies are recognized. All such theories base the recognition on prior schema-like knowledge: People have a schema for killing that produces an automatic inference that Kakra is dead; people have a schema for marriage that requires that husbands be alive. This means that Kakra cannot fill the *husband* slot in the marriage schema, so a fully coherent representation of the text cannot be built without further information.

There is in fact another schema that, if available, would solve the problem. The schema concerns ghost marriage, a tribal custom in which the oldest son of a family who dies without heirs is subsequently married with his younger brother taking his place until an heir is produced. A ghost marriage schema would provide a slot, not for a live husband, but for a dead man and a younger brother. Kakra can fill the dead man's slot, Gum the younger brother's, and now a representation coherent at a macrolevel of interpretation can be constructed. This new representation will also contain a new candidate for the organizing theme of the story: It now appears that a summary of the story ought to include a ghost marriage, and it might well be that as the text continued, the theme of tribal war would disappear at the macrostructure level in favor of the custom of ghost marriage.

I have focused here on a particular example and on one theory of how text representations are built. Many other investigators have explored how high-level organizing information—that is, macrostructures—controls and supports the process of comprehending a text. A particularly well-developed domain for this research has been story understanding. Several investigations (see Stein & Trabasso, 1983) have shown that there is a prototypical structure of narratives that is used by people to interpret stories. The idealized story, in effect a schema of a story, organizes and directs peoples' interaction with the particular story they are reading or hearing. The story schema specifies the types of information that should be presented and the types of logical relationships that should link the story elements. Several categories of information must occur in order: a setting, an initiating event, an internal response, an attempt to obtain a goal, an outcome or consequence, and a reaction.

Some of the categories in this structure are more central than others. This is shown by substantial regularities in the portions of stories that people omit and the portions they add when asked to retell stories they have heard. Initiating events, attempts to achieve a goal, and consequences are nearly always included, but other categories, especially internal cognitive responses of the characters, are likely to be omitted (Mandler, 1978; Mandler & Johnson, 1977; Stein & Glenn, 1979; Thorndyke, 1977). Story comprehension and recall are also sensitive to the order in which categories of information are presented. People have difficulty recalling stories when information is given in an order other than that specified in the idealized story schema, and they tend to recall story information in the order predicted by the schema even when the text from which they learn the story uses a nonstandard order.

Recent research (see Flammer & Kintsch, 1982) suggests that the semantic content, rather than just form or placement of the information within the story, may be determining recall. Attempts to enlarge research on story understanding beyond the simple demonstration of story schemata (sometimes called "story grammars") have been leading psychologists increasingly to study the specific kinds of social knowledge held by children of different ages and stages of development. The newest research on story understanding suggests that widely shared knowledge about goals, plans, actions, outcomes, and motives (e.g.,

Voss, 1984) is at the heart of story understanding. Trabasso, Secco, and van den Broek (1984), for example, present evidence that knowledge about physical and psychological causality plays a central role in understanding stories. The relative weights and possible interactions between this kind of general knowledge of the world and knowledge of rhetorical structures such as story grammars is a topic of much debate in the field today.

One of the features of the Kintsch and vanDijk theory just outlined is that the processing of texts is assumed to be more or less sequential; that is, people build up their representation of the reference situation of the text bit by bit, as they go along. This means that the process of interpretation is continuous. People do not hold pieces of uninterpreted text in mind for a period of time and then later reflect on its meaning. Another important line of research on reading that has used quite different methods of study confirms this sequentiality. Just and Carpenter have for a number of years been studying reading, using eye-movement records as their basic data. They have constructed a model (a computer simulation program) of the reading process (Thibadeau, Just, & Carpenter, in press) that accounts for the patterns of eye movements observed in subjects while reading. This model, READER, processes the text in a largely word-by-word fashion. As it encounters each new word, it finds the meaning of the word and more or less simultaneously uses schemata and related semantic processing mechanisms to build up a representation to that point. It does not, in other words, delay interpretation until a whole phrase or sentence has been read. Furthermore, it builds its representation using a combination of expectations for what *should* appear next based on the context and the information actually in the printed text.

There is a striking degree of convergence between the different kinds of available evidence for how people understand written texts. It appears first that what is done automatically can also be done consciously; that is, some portions of think-aloud protocols produce sequences of steps that are not very different from those of automatic processing, in which people make successive links between sentences and store up partial interpretations as they go. However, when difficulties are encountered in the course of reading, skilled readers seem to use conscious processes to resolve the problem. In the time-course studies of reading, these are the points at which very long delays occur, and the protocol analysis studies provide a good sense of what is happening at those points of delay. At these times, there is a considerable amount of looking back, of reconstructing, and of forming or accessing new schemas for interpretation. Thus, the studies that focus on automatic processing and those that focus on conscious processing reveal similarities that seem to create a plausible account of the reading process.

Learning to Read

Research on reading, construed as a process of interpreting printed symbols, has a relatively long history in psychology. Scientific research on the psychology of reading began at least a century ago with the work of Cattell (1886). Other early scholars included Huey (1908/1968) and Buswell (1920). Fueled in part by its obvious relevance to a central educational task of schools, research on reading has continued in an almost unbroken line. Much of this research was stimulated by and played a role in a long-standing debate over ways to teach reading: a word recognition emphasis versus a contextual meaning emphasis; direct instruction in the grapheme–phoneme mappings of alphabetic languages (i.e., on phonics) versus focusing on words as visual wholes.

In this chapter, I consider these pedagogical debates only indirectly, concentrating instead on a body of cognitive research that sets the debates in a somewhat new light. I develop two main themes: (a) the active interplay between expectations for what will appear in a text and the visual stimuli of printed words—that is the interaction of *top-down* and *bottom-up* processes in reading; and (b) the central role of automatic—that is, very fast and nonconscious—processes of word recognition. Both the top-down/bottom-up interaction and the automaticity of processing are also important aspects of many other cognitive skills. Thus, in considering the process of learning to read, I am in fact addressing issues that are central in much research on the nature of cognitive skill.

Interaction of Top-Down and Bottom-Up Processes in Reading

The description of Just and Carpenter's READER model of text processing has already introduced the notion that there is an interaction between expectations for what will appear in a text—expectations based on the representation of the text's meaning built to date—and the actual words that appear in the text. Similar interactions between expectations and actual stimuli occur in the act of recognizing words as well as in interpreting them. To the extent that expectations for what ought to appear drive the process of word recognition, reading is considered to be a top-down process. To the extent that the printed symbols drive the word recognition process, cognitive scientists speak of reading as a bottom-up process.

In a purely bottom-up view of reading, lower level processes (i.e., detecting features of letters, combining features into letters, and combining letters into words) are assumed to occur prior to and independent of higher level processes. First words are recognized, then a syntactic processing occurs, and finally a semantic interpretation is made based on the sentence syntax. Furthermore, these processes are controlled entirely by the printed input: Word recognition precedes comprehension of meaning. By contrast, in a purely top-down conception of reading, higher level processes, such as making inferences about meaning, are assumed to control the system, and lower level processes are called into play only as they are needed. Hypotheses about the meaning of the text are generated from prior knowledge of the topic, knowledge of the specific textual context, and a minimal syntactic parsing and sampling of visual cues. Then the printed text is used to confirm or disconfirm the hypotheses. According to an extreme top-down view, comprehension of meaning precedes recognition of words, and complete encoding of separate words may not occur at all (cf. Frederiksen, 1979).

There is ample evidence that both top-down and bottom-up processes are involved in reading. Evidence of the influence of semantic context and prior knowledge—top-down effects—includes the following kinds of phenomena: Oral reading errors, even in young readers, tend to be semantically and syntactically appropriate to the context; long hesitations or misreadings occur at points in texts where there are syntactic or semantic anomalies; people are faster at pronouncing a word in context than when the same word appears in isolation, and they are faster at pronouncing words when the preceding context is congruous with the word than when it is incongruous; word recognition is also faster when the semantic category to which the word belongs has been presented in advance (e.g., *parakeet* is recognized faster after the word *bird* than after the word *mammal*). Finally, letters can be discriminated more quickly in the context of a word than in isolation or in an arbitrary string of letters. (Resnick, 1981b). There has been less effort experimentally to establish the reality of bottom-up effects in word recognition, because it seems self-evident that people must be paying some attention to actual features of the printed stimulus as they read, else the process could not properly be called reading.

Recent research on the nature of reading has focused not on whether bottom-up or top-down processing predominates, but rather, on how the two kinds of processes interact to produce both word recognition and comprehension of a written text. Rumelhart and McClelland (1981) have developed an influential interactive model of word recognition. In this model, both features of the written words and expectations about meaning cause "activation" in the brain. The two sources of activation together, through a complex system of interaction, eventually determine what word will be "seen" by the reader.

Automaticity

The interactive model of word recognition offers an explanation of how the automatic processing of printed words might occur. It is not an accident that psychologists have been seeking to account for complex cognition in terms of processes that do not depend entirely on conscious, planned mental activity. One must assume that much processing is automatic not only because people cannot always correctly report their processing, but also because there must be compensation for humans' limited active memory capacity.

The limited capacity of human working memory is probably the earliest fact that emerged from the beginnings of cognitive psychology. In a seminal work, Miller (1956) suggested that adults have only seven "slots" (plus or minus two) for holding information in working memory, which is where active, planned processing must occur. This notion of a limited capacity for information processing is central to all cognitive science. Psychologists are no longer certain that slots in memory is the best way to describe capacity limitations, or that there is any reality to the number 7 ± 2 as the capacity of working memory. Nevertheless, all cognitive scientists agree that there is some computing work that has to go on for thought to proceed, that the capacity for doing this is limited, and that this can create a bottleneck. That is, if too much capacity is devoted to any one component of a complex learning task, then other components will suffer.

Despite this limited processing capacity, people are able to perform complicated tasks. How? There are two major mechanisms that allow people to overcome memory capacity limitations: (a) Certain components of a task become automated so that they require very little direct attention and therefore use up little working capacity, and (b) information is "chunked" so that each slot in working memory is filled with a cluster of related knowledge. The role of automatic processing in facilitating complex performances has been investigated most heavily in the context of acquiring basic reading skills. A growing research literature that contrasts good and poor readers at various stages of development is identifying particular components of reading skill that distinguish the contrasting skill groups. A consistent finding in this research is that people who read poorly (i.e., who score poorly on standardized reading comprehension tests) also are generally slower at recognizing words. It is speed, rather than accuracy of word recognition, that seems to be important. Some individuals apparently have large recognition vocabularies and adequate word recognition skills as long as they are permitted indefinite amounts of time to process each word, but they seem to proceed so slowly that they cannot effectively understand what they are trying to read.

In the interactive theories of reading such as those just examined, timing is often crucial, for several sources of information must be integrated and thus must be present in working memory at the same time. Memory capacity is also crucial. Processes that take up too much working memory capacity or too much direct attention may drive out the other processes that are needed to provide all of the necessary information simultaneously to the system. Automation of the word recognition component of reading may be necessary both for quick and timely processing of meaning and for reducing the working memory demands that allow reading to proceed smoothly.

Establishing a correlation between automatic word recognition and comprehension skill does not of itself explain how automaticity is acquired, nor does it necessarily mean that automatic recognition causes the development of comprehension skill. To the contrary, practice in reading and comprehending texts might be the cause of improved automaticity, or automaticity and comprehension skill might both depend on some other, as yet unidentified, process. A recent longitudinal study helps to limit the possibilities. Lesgold and Resnick (1983) found that children in the first grade who have large automaticity problems are very likely to have difficulties in comprehension a year or two later. Early comprehension difficulty, however, does not predict later automaticity difficulties. This asymmetric relationship allows researchers to reject the possibility that comprehension skill causes automaticity and suggests that automaticity difficulties may indeed be helping to cause difficulties in learning to comprehend written texts.

If automaticity is a prerequisite for acquiring comprehension skill, then it should be the case that training in automaticity of word recognition would produce improved comprehension. Does it? In one study (Fleisher & Jenkins, 1978) it was found that even though speeded practice can significantly increase speed of recognizing isolated words, there is no immediate transfer to comprehension. This means that comprehension skill is not ready and waiting to be "released" by improved word recognition automaticity. However, the processes of acquiring comprehension skill may nevertheless be enhanced by increased recognition speed. If that is the case, the effects on comprehension performance would be visible only after some delay, during which time reading comprehension was practiced. Psychologists do not yet know the long-term effects of training in fast word recognition. Furthermore, training that focuses only on speed, rather than on aspects of word analysis believed to function in highly skilled reading performance, may deflect learners' attention from the very features of words that allow for automated access to meaning. A current research program (Frederiksen, Warren, & Rosebery, in press) is pursuing the hypothesis that training adolescents with very poor reading skills to quickly recognize frequently recurring spelling patterns will improve their general reading performance. These patterns are the building blocks of words and according to some theorists (e.g., Venezky & Massaro, 1979) are the units in reading that correspond directly to meaning.

Developing Mathematical Competence

When we turn to other domains of intellectual competence, many of the same themes as have been noted for natural language understanding again emerge as central. Consider mathematics. Understanding mathematics, like understanding natural language, requires that people have a certain number of particularly powerful schemata that are used as prototypes to interpret specific expressions and situations. Further, inference processes are central in both learning mathematics and in solving mathematical problems, just as they are in reading and writing natural language texts.

In the case of mathematics, however, there is a special problem of linking symbols to their referents. Like natural language texts, mathematical expressions and mathematical procedures have both a syntax and a semantics. That is, they obey rules of "well-formedness" that are equivalent to the grammar of sentences or the rhetorical structures that constrain the more global forms of texts. In mathematics, as in formal logic, there are complex rule systems for manipulating expressions that ensure that new expressions constructed in the course of solving problems or performing algorithms will be syntactically correct. So much attention is paid to these syntactic properties of mathematics in the ordinary course of teaching and learning mathematics that people sometimes treat mathematical expressions as if they were nothing but strings of syntactically well-formed symbols.

But mathematical expressions also have a semantics—they refer to something external to themselves. These mathematical referents are quantities and relations, and it is these quantities and relations that are in fact manipulated when one performs operations with mathematical symbols. People rarely, if ever, think about natural language sentences as if they were simply sets of syntactically well-structured character strings. Instead, people treat language automatically as a way of referring to an external situation. In mathematics, by contrast, people sometimes treat mathematical expressions as if they were divorced from any referent, and this causes difficulty in learning mathematics for many people. At the same time, to be skilled in mathematical thinking requires that the person be able to manipulate the symbol system fluently. There is thus a special set of problems that arise when one analyzes mathematics as a domain of cognition and learning.

Implicit Understanding of Mathematical Principles

I begin with evidence of the role that organizing schemata have in mathematics learning. There is growing evidence that children, and uneducated adults as well, possess considerably more knowledge of certain mathematical principles than is habitually ascribed to them. This understanding is evident most typically in the kinds of informal arithmetic methods that they use. When such methods have not been taught, either formally in school or informally in the culture, they can be used to infer the kind of underlying understanding that people have of mathematical principles. Herbert Ginsburg and his colleagues (Ginsburg, 1977, 1983; Houlihan & Ginsburg, 1981) used a variety of interview methods to document a wide range of numerical problem-solving procedures that are used by young children and by adults in unschooled cultures who have not had formal instruction in specific arithmetic routines. Similar kinds of invented procedures have also been documented by other investigators using laboratory methods of research.

Invented counting procedures. The earliest and apparently most frequent way that young children solve arithmetic problems if they have not memorized the answer is to use some form of counting. This may be "counting in the head," rather than overt counting of physical objects, as has been demonstrated in a number of studies of mental addition and subtraction. Groen and Parkman's (1972) research is the point of reference for work on simple mental calculation. They tested a family of process models for single-digit addition. All of the models assumed that a "counter in the head" could be set initially at any number, then incremented a given number of times, and finally "read out" (see Figure 2). The specific models differed in where the counter was set initially and in the number of increments-by-one required to calculate the sum. For example, the counter can be set initially at zero, the first addend counted in by increments of one, and then the second addend counted in by increments of one. If one assumes that each increment needs about the same amount of time to count, then someone doing mental calculation this way ought to show a pattern of reaction times in which time varies as a function of the sum of the two addends. This has become known as the *sum* model of mental addition.

A somewhat more efficient procedure begins by setting the counter at the first addend and then counting in the second addend by increments of one. In this case—assuming that the time for setting the counter is the same regardless of where it is set—reaction times would be a function of the size of the second addend. A still more efficient procedure starts by setting the counter at the larger of the two addends,

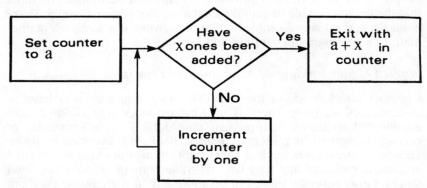

Figure 2. Schematic model for mental counting in arithmetic. Adapted from Groen and Parkman (1972) by permission.

regardless of whether it is the first or the second, and then incrementing by the smaller. Obviously, this requires fewer increments. Because this procedure produces reaction times that are a function of the size of the minimum addend, it has become known as the *min* model.

Groen and Parkman evaluated these models (along with some others that were logically possible but psychologically implausible) by comparing the predicted and observed patterns of reaction times for each model. They found that the reaction times of children as young as first-graders fit the predictions for the min procedure. Figure 3 shows a characteristic data plot. Note that problems with a minimum addend of 4 cluster together and take longer than problems with a minimum addend of 3, and so on. Subsequently, the prevalence of the min model has been confirmed in studies that have extended both the range of problems and the children studied from those aged 4½ or so to those aged 9 or 10 (Groen & Resnick, 1977; Svenson & Broquist, 1975; Svenson & Hedenborg, 1979; Svenson, Hedenborg, & Lingman, 1976).

Counting models have also been applied to other simple arithmetic tasks, especially subtraction (Svenson et al., 1976; Woods, Resnick, &

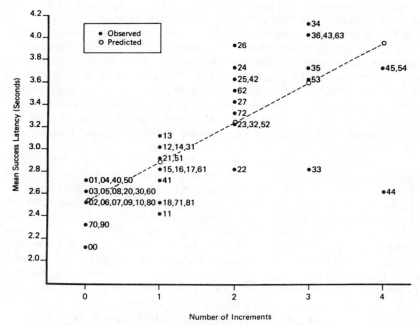

Figure 3. Reaction times for first graders solving addition problems. Pairs of numbers listed beside dots stand for single-digit addition problems. For example: 70,90 means 7 + 0, 9 + 0. Dots indicate average reaction times for adding each pair of numbers.

Groen, 1975) and addition with one of the addends unknown (Groen & Poll, 1973). In the case of subtraction, at least three mental counting procedures are mathematically correct. One procedure, *decrementing,* would involve initializing the counter in the head at the larger number (the minuend) and then decrementing by one as many times as indicated by the smaller number (the subtrahend). In the decrementing model, reaction times would be a function of the smaller number. In the second procedure, *incrementing,* the counter would be initialized at the smaller of the two numbers and be incremented until the larger number is reached. The number of increments then would be read as the answer. Reaction times for this incrementing model would be a function of the remainder, the number representing the difference between the minuend and subtrahend. In a particularly efficient procedure, *choice,* either the decrementing or the incrementing process is used for subtraction, depending upon which required fewer steps on the counter. Reaction times would be a function of the smaller of the subtrahend or the remainder. This choice model is what most primary school children use, although a few second-graders use the straight decrementing model.

It is always risky to attribute complex processes such as min and choice to people entirely on the basis of their reaction time patterns. For this reason, it is important to ask if any converging evidence exists that points to the reality of mental counting procedures. Observations of overt counting-on strategies for addition by several investigators (e.g., Carpenter, Hiebert, & Moser, 1981; Fuson, 1982; Steffe, Thompson, & Richards, 1982) suggest that the counting presumed in these models is real. Furthermore, Svenson and Broquist (1975) interviewed their subjects after each timed trial and found that on about half of the problems children reported counting-up from the larger number (by ones or in larger units).

Invented regrouping procedures. The existence of privileged, particularly well-learned number *facts* is the basis for another class of invented procedures that emphasize the regrouping of quantities. Typically, among young children and unschooled adults, not all number facts are equally well known. Those involving smaller numbers are better known than those involving larger ones, people tend to know addition facts better than subtraction facts, and more people know certain privileged types of facts: doubles, those involving the addition of 1 or 2, possibly those involving the addition or subtraction of 5, and, for older children and certain cultures, those facts involving 10 and multiples of 10. A person who cannot easily retrieve $3 + 5 = 8$ as an addition fact might regroup the problem to take advantage of a known doubles fact and would solve instead $(3 + 3) + 2$. In cultures that use a decimal notation and counting system, regrouping patterns often take special advantage of the decimal structure. Here is an example, complete with a characteristic error, from an interview study of the development of decimal number understanding:

E: Can you subtract 27 from 53?

S (an 8-year-old): 34.

E: How did you figure it out?

S: Well, 50 minus 20 is 30. Then take away 3 is 27 and plus 7 is 34.[1]
(Resnick, 1983, p. 131)

Sometimes regrouping around privileged number facts and counting are combined. For example, Resnick and Omanson (in press) have used reaction-time methods to document a procedure that some children use to add a one-digit number to a two-digit number. The procedure is called *min of the units* because when people use it, their pattern of reaction times is a function of the smaller of the two units digits[2] in the numbers to be added. The person using this method decomposes the two-digit number into a tens component and a units component, then recombines the tens component with whichever of the two units digits is larger. The mental counter is set to this reconstituted number and the smaller units digit is counted in increments of one. For example, for 23 + 9, the counter would be set at 29 and then incremented 3 times to a sum of 32. The regrouping of numbers to take advantage of well-known number facts is also characteristic of people who are exceptionally good at complicated mental arithmetic (e.g., multiplying); however, such individuals have a much wider store of well-learned, privileged facts and show much more flexibility in regrouping to use the facts than do young children or unschooled adults.

Understanding implicit in invented procedures. Research of the kinds just described has now established that people use a considerable variety of invented arithmetic strategies. A concomitant step has been to show, through appropriate analyses, the kinds of understanding of mathematical principles that underlie these inventions. The first systematic effort along these lines appeared in Gelman and Gallistel's (1978) work on the nature of counting competence in very young children. They used a number of aspects of preschool children's performance to establish the fact that the children know implicitly—although they are unable to verbalize—five principles.

- The one-to-one principle: Each item in an array must be tagged with one and only one unique tag
- The stable-order principle: The tags used must be drawn from a stably ordered list

---

[1] The error is in the confusion about which of the right-hand digits is to be added and which is to be subtracted.

[2] In decimal notation, the digit to the far right represents "units;" one multiplies it by 1 to obtain its value. The next digit represents "tens;" one multiplies it by 10 to obtain its value. Subsequent digits represent "hundreds," "thousands," and so forth.

- The cardinal principle: The last tag used for a particular count represents the cardinal number of the array
- The abstraction principle: Any set of items may be collected together for a count
- The order-irrelevance principle: The order in which items in a set are tagged is irrelevant.

Greeno, Riley, and Gelman (1984) have described the counting principles as a form of *conceptual competence* that can be inferred from the *performance competence* that children exhibit on a range of counting tasks. Performance competencies are granted when a child can assemble a set of procedures that produce a performance that adheres to the conceptual principles. Conceptual competence is most clearly revealed when a new variant of a procedure must be invented. For example, when the children in Gelman's study were given an array of objects to count and told to "make this one (an object in the middle of a straight-line array) number one" or "make this one (the object in the normally first-counted position in the array) number three," the children adjusted the order in which they touched the objects but not the order in which they said the numbers, and they still touched each object only once. These children thus clearly demonstrated command of the order-irrelevance principle, the stable-order principle, and the one-to-one principle.

Data and analyses of this kind make it possible to articulate the presence of implicit knowledge and hence circumvent the need to have people state their knowledge before granting them an understanding of principles. The role of conceptual understanding that is implicit in invented procedures is also revealed in work done by Neches (1981; also Resnick & Neches, 1984). In this work Neches attempted to provide a formal account of the way that children invent the min addition procedure (described earlier) of counting on from the larger of the two addends. Neches has constructed a computer simulation program that begins by counting up both addends (essentially the sum procedure); it then modifies itself so that after a number of trials, it performs the min procedure of counting on from the larger number. To do this, the program must "discover" that setting the counter to a number will always yield the same thing as counting the objects specified by a number (a form of quantity conservation), and that it does not matter which number is set in the counter and which is added in (a form of commutativity).

Neches's program makes these discoveries by continually inspecting its own performance and applying a small set of procedure-changing heuristics. Although the final version of the program cannot be said to "know" about commutativity in the sense of explaining it, it behaves as if it understood commutativity, and it does so on the basis of its own knowledge construction without having been "told" about commutativity. Neches's program is a plausible theory—but not the only possible one (cf. Baroody & Gannon, 1984; Resnick, 1983)—that explains how children might invent the min procedure and what understanding it is appropriate to grant them on the basis of that invention.

Schemata in mathematical problem solving. Another source of evidence demonstrating the role of implicit knowledge in children's early mathematical performances comes from research on how children solve simple arithmetic problems given in story form. Research in several countries has demonstrated great regularity in the kinds of addition and subtraction problems that are hardest to solve (Carpenter & Moser, 1982; Nesher, 1982; Vergnaud, 1982). Several analyses of this cumulative body of data have converged on an explanation of these regularities that attributes to children an understanding of the principle that mathematicians call the "additive composition of number." This principle maintains that numbers are composed of other numbers, that the number 7, for example, is not only the cardinality of the set that one can count by tagging objects up to 7, but also a composition of 1 and 6, 2 and 5, and so forth (Resnick, 1983). In the analyses of story problems, additive composition is attributed to children in the form of a *part–whole schema* (Figure 4). The schema specifies that any quantity (the whole) can be partitioned into the parts as long as the combined parts neither exceed nor fall short of the whole. By implication, the parts make up or are included in the whole. The part–whole schema thus provides an interpretation of number that is quite similar to Piaget's (1941/1965) definition of an operational number concept.

Figure 4 shows how the fundamental part–whole relation underlies several classes of story problems as well as number sentences. In each problem the whole is coded as a dot-filled bar, whether it is a given quantity or the unknown quantity. Similarly, each part is uniquely coded. The relation between parts and whole for all the problems, including the number sentences, is shown in the center display. Any bar can be omitted and thus become the unknown. Although number sentences and the given words of story problems cannot be mapped directly onto one another (Nesher & Teubal, 1975), each can be mapped directly onto a more abstract part–whole representation such as the bars shown here. The part–whole schema thus provides an interpretive structure that can permit the child either to solve certain more difficult problems directly by the methods of informal arithmetic or to convert them into number sentences that can then be solved through procedures taught in school.

Riley, Greeno, and Heller (1983) have developed a set of computational models that explain differences in the difficulty of solving certain kinds of addition and subtraction story problems. These models suggest that it is the application of the part–whole schema that makes it possible to solve difficult classes of story problems that children usually cannot solve until their second or third school year. These include set-change problems with the starting set unknown (e.g., "John

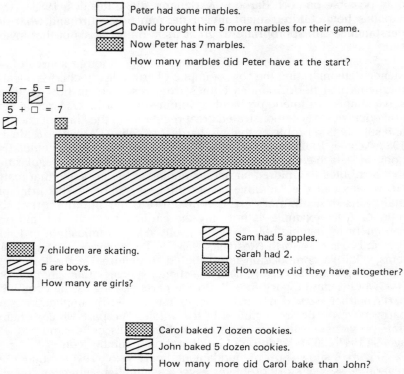

Figure 4. Mapping of stories and number sentences to a concrete model of Part–Whole. Reprinted from Resnick (1983) by permission.

had some marbles. Michael gave him 4 more. Now he has 7. How many did he have to start?") and various kinds of comparison problems (e.g., "John has 4 marbles. Michael has 7. How many more does Michael have than John?"). For these problems, solution proceeds by mapping the statements in the problem to the slots of the part–whole schema. The numbers in the problem are assigned to either *part* or *whole* status, and this permits the unknown to be clearly identified as a part or a whole.

An alternative story problem model by Briars and Larkin (1984) solves some of the more difficult problems by constructing a mental script that reflects real-world knowledge about combining and separating objects, rather than abstract part–whole relations. The script describes the actions in the story and allows the system to keep track of the sets and subsets involved. Yet in Briars and Larkin's model, too, it is possible to solve unknown-first problems only by using a part–whole schema. Both theories show that schematic knowledge about the reference situations for mathematical problems is essential at even the simplest level of problem solving.

The Pervasiveness of Inference: Invented Errors

Side-by-side with the accumulating evidence of implicit understanding shown in informal arithmetic performances, there is equally compelling evidence of the presence of persistent and systematic errors. In fact, documenting systematic errors exhibited in the course of learning procedures is a major and pervasive feature of recent research on learning. These systematic errorful procedures are also invented by learners, but unlike those procedures described in the preceding section, these do not reflect understanding of mathematical principles. Although systematic errors in arithmetic procedures have been documented for several different parts of the school mathematics curriculum, the two that have received the most careful analysis by cognitive scientists are subtraction with borrowing and algebra. These two example domains provide contrast in detail, but they support each other with respect to the fundamental processes that seem to be involved.

In their analysis of subtraction, J. S. Brown and R. R. Burton (1978; Burton, 1982) have constructed an extensive catalog of incorrect procedures that are used by children for written subtraction with borrowing. These incorrect procedures are variants of the correct ones; they are analogous to computer algorithms with "bugs" in them and have therefore been christened "buggy algorithms." A finite number of bugs, which in various combinations make up several dozen buggy algorithms, have been identified for subtraction. Figure 5 shows a few of the most common buggy algorithms identified in this research.

These examples show that the results of buggy calculations tend to "look right": Everything is organized into columns, there is only one digit in each column, there are numbers crossed out and small digits handwritten in the conventional places, and so forth. Buggy algorithms thus look rather sensible and often contain only small departures from the correct algorithms. It appears that the buggy procedures are constructed by children when they encounter an arithmetic problem for which they have an approximate, but incomplete, rule. Rather than giving up, these children try to patch and repair the rule so that it appears to work.

J. S. Brown and K. VanLehn (1982) have developed a formal theory, in the form of a computer simulation, of the origin of bugs in arithmetic. The program invents the same bugs that children do, but not a large number of other logically possible ones. It thus constitutes a theory of the kinds of knowledge and processes that children use when they

1. **Smaller-From-Larger.** The student subtracts the smaller digit in a column from the larger digit regardless of which one is on top.

$$
\begin{array}{r} 326 \\ -\,1\,1\,7 \\ \hline 2\,1\,1 \end{array}
\qquad
\begin{array}{r} 542 \\ -\,389 \\ \hline 247 \end{array}
$$

2. **Borrow-From-Zero.** When borrowing from a column whose top digit is 0, the student writes 9 but does not continue borrowing from the column to the left of the 0.

$$
\begin{array}{r} 6\,\cancel{0}{,}2 \\ -\,4\,3\,7 \\ \hline 265 \end{array}
\qquad
\begin{array}{r} 8\,\cancel{0}{,}2 \\ -\,396 \\ \hline 506 \end{array}
$$

3. **Borrow-Across-Zero.** When the student needs to borrow from a column whose top digit is 0, he skips that column and borrows from the next one. (Note: This bug must be combined with either bug 5 or bug 6.)

$$
\begin{array}{r} \overset{7}{\cancel{8}}\,0{,}2 \\ -\,327 \\ \hline 225 \end{array}
\qquad
\begin{array}{r} \overset{7}{\cancel{8}}\,0{,}4 \\ -\,456 \\ \hline 308 \end{array}
$$

4. **Stops-Borrow-At-Zero.** The student fails to decrement 0, although he adds 10 correctly to the top digit of the active column. (Note: This bug must be combined with either bug 5 or bug 6.)

$$
\begin{array}{r} 7\,0{,}3 \\ -\,678 \\ \hline 175 \end{array}
\qquad
\begin{array}{r} 6\,0{,}4 \\ -\,387 \\ \hline 307 \end{array}
$$

5. **0 − N = N.** Whenever there is 0 on top, the digit on the bottom is written as the answer.

$$
\begin{array}{r} 709 \\ -\,352 \\ \hline 457 \end{array}
\qquad
\begin{array}{r} 6008 \\ -\;\;327 \\ \hline 6321 \end{array}
$$

6. **0 − N = 0.** Whenever there is 0 on top, 0 is written as the answer.

$$
\begin{array}{r} 804 \\ -\,462 \\ \hline 402 \end{array}
\qquad
\begin{array}{r} 3050 \\ -\;\;621 \\ \hline 3030 \end{array}
$$

7. **N − 0 = 0.** Whenever there is 0 on the bottom, 0 is written as the answer.

$$
\begin{array}{r} 976 \\ -\,302 \\ \hline 604 \end{array}
\qquad
\begin{array}{r} 8\,\cancel{5}{,}6 \\ -\,409 \\ \hline 407 \end{array}
$$

8. **Don't-Decrement-Zero.** When borrowing from a column in which the top digit is 0, the student rewrites the 0 as 10, but does not change the 10 to 9 when incrementing the active column.

$$
\begin{array}{r} \overset{6}{\cancel{7}}\,0{,}2 \\ -\,368 \\ \hline 344 \end{array}
\qquad
\begin{array}{r} \overset{1}{\cancel{2}}\,0{,}5 \\ -\;\;\;9 \\ \hline 1106 \end{array}
$$

9. **Zero-Instead-Of-Borrow.** The student writes 0 as the answer in any column in which the bottom digit is larger than the top.

$$
\begin{array}{r} 326 \\ -\,117 \\ \hline 210 \end{array}
\qquad
\begin{array}{r} 542 \\ -\,389 \\ \hline 200 \end{array}
$$

10. **Borrow-From-Bottom-Instead-Of-Zero.** If the top digit in the column being borrowed from is 0, the student borrows from the bottom digit instead. (Note: This bug must be combined with either bug 5 or bug 6.)

$$
\begin{array}{r} 7\,0{,}2 \\ -\,3\,\cancel{6}8 \\ \hline 454 \end{array}
\qquad
\begin{array}{r} 5\,0{,}8 \\ -\,4\,\cancel{5}9 \\ \hline 109 \end{array}
$$

Figure 5. Descriptions and examples of Brown and Burton's (1978) common subtraction bugs. Adapted from Resnick (1982) by permission.

invent buggy subtraction algorithms. The repair theory program is a "generate and test" problem-solving routine of the kind that characterizes many successful performances in other domains (cf. Simon, 1976).

According to the theory, buggy algorithms arise when the child encounters an arithmetic problem for which his or her current algorithms are incomplete or inappropriate. The child, trying to respond, eventually reaches an impasse, a situation for which no action is available. At this point, the child generates a candidate *repair* by calling on a list of actions to try when a standard action cannot be used. The repair list includes strategies such as performing the action in a different column, skipping the action, swapping top and bottom numbers in a column, and substituting an operation (such as incrementing for decrementing).

The outcome generated through this repair process is then checked by a set of *critics*. The critics inspect the resulting solution for conformity to some basic criteria such as no empty columns, only one digit per column in the answer, only one decrement per column, and the like. Note that the generate-and-test problem solution calls on no knowledge about the quantities that the numerical symbols represent. This is a crucial characteristic of buggy arithmetic, and one that I will return to.

Several researchers (Carry, Lewis, & Bernard, 1980; Davis, 1983; Greeno, 1983; Sleeman, 1982) have studied the errors (often called *malrules*) that students make in algebra. When students apply the rules of transformation that are the basic tools of algebraic problem solving, these investigators have shown (a) that many errors are made by beginners as a result of either incorrect rules or incorrect applications of correct rules; (b) that these errors persist for a long time, showing up occasionally even among expert algebra performers; (c) that there is great systematicity in which errors appear in different students (i.e., only a small number of the logically possible algebra errors actually tend to be made); and (d) that there is, nevertheless, a lack of stability in the performance of any given individual (i.e., learners do not always apply the same algebra malrule even in what is, to the experimenter at any rate, the same situation).

The best developed theory to date that explains how these malrules are invented is one by Matz (1982). Matz's theory, like the Brown and VanLehn theory of subtraction bugs, is expressed as a simulation program that invents the malrules that were observed in algebra solutions; other possible malrules are not invented. Matz proposes that children learning algebra construct prototype rules from which they extrapolate new rules. Although the results are malrules, both the construction of the prototypes and the extrapolation follow regular principles. An example appears in Figure 6.

The initial rule is the distribution law that is typically taught in a beginning algebra course. From this correct and specific rule, a prototype is created by generalizing over the operator signs. That is, the prototype specifies not that multiplication (×) can be distributed over addition (+), but that any operator (□) can be distributed over any other operator (△). From this prototype, new but incorrect distribution

1. The correct rule as taught:

$$a \times (b + c) = (a \times b) + (a \times c)$$

2. Prototype created by generalizing over operator signs:

$$a \,\square\, (b \,\triangle\, c) = (a \,\square\, b) \,\triangle\, (a \,\square\, c)$$

3. Incorrect rules created from the prototype.

$$a + (b \times c) = (a + b) \times (a + c)$$

$$\sqrt{b + c} = \sqrt{b} + \sqrt{c}$$

Figure 6. Example of the formation of an algebra malrule. Based on Matz's (1982) theory.

rules can be constructed by substituting specific operations for the generalized operators in the prototype. The elegance of Matz's model does not prove that it is a correct theory of the origin of algebra malrules in human learners, but it does establish the conditions for an ongoing discussion of the nature of malrule invention (see, e.g., Sleeman, 1982) that is specific about the knowledge and processes likely to be involved. Such a discussion is therefore useful both for understanding difficulties in mathematics learning and for explicating general principles of cognitive acquisition.

The prevalence of buggy algorithms and malrules in mathematical learning points to a pervasive feature of human cognitive functioning. It is natural to seek meaning and to draw inferences. People will do this on the basis of whatever knowledge they have available—even if it is incomplete or incorrect. For this reason, perfectly good inferential and reasoning processes will sometimes produce errors.

Linking Symbols and Their Referents

Buggy algorithms and algebra malrules also point to a special difficulty that must be overcome whenever formal representational and rule systems are part of the subject matter to be learned. This relation between formal systems and intuitive or informal ones is most evident in mathematics, where specialized notational systems and rules for manipulating them amount to a new language, complete with grammatical rules, that must be mastered. The difficulty is that for a language to function appropriately, its grammar and formal rules must work in concert with its referential system. In technical terms, the syntax and the semantics of a language system must function together so that sentences are "well-formed" (i.e., they obey the grammar of the language) and at the same time the referents of the sentences are clear (i.e., they maintain the semantics of the language). In natural languages, this coordination of syntax and semantics seems to occur without any special work or attention on a human learner's part. In an earlier section of this chapter, I discussed models of text comprehension that show that people reading or listening to a natural language text naturally and quite automatically build up a representation of what the text refers to. In mathematics, syntax and semantics sometimes become separated.

A reconsideration of buggy subtraction can make this point more clearly. I have already noted that subtraction bugs seem not only to respect the syntax of written arithmetic, but also to disobey constraints that would be apparent if the quantity referents were being kept in mind. For example, consider the second bug, borrow-from-zero, in Figure 5. At a strictly symbolic level, this procedure seems a reasonable response to encountering a zero in the course of borrowing. The zero is changed to 9, which is a familiar result of borrowing when zeros are present. However, the bug violates the fundamental principle that the total quantity in the minuend must be conserved during a borrow. Interpreted semantically—that is, in terms of quantities rather than simply manipulations of symbols—a total of 100 has been added to the minuend, 10 in the units column, and 90 in the tens column, with no compensating decrement in the hundreds column. The next bug, borrow-across-zero, shows a similar disregard for the need to conserve the minuend quantity. The bug respects the syntactic rules for symbol manipulation that require that a small "1" be written in the active column and that some other (nonzero) column be decremented. The bug violates the conservation principle, however, by removing 100 from the hundreds column but returning only 10 to the units column.

This informal analysis is supported by reexamining Brown's and VanLehn's repair theory of the origin of subtraction bugs. The repair theory program produces bugs by generating repairs and checking them against critics. All of the critics in the program are syntactic in nature; that is, they reflect rules for symbol manipulation, but they do not embody any knowledge of principles of quantity. The fact that repair theory matches human performance by inventing only the bugs that children do and not other logically possible bugs suggests that children represent subtraction to themselves as sets of rules for transforming symbols without reference to the quantities that these symbols in fact are meant to represent.

Further evidence that symbols take on a life of their own, apart from the quantities that they represent, comes from a training study (Resnick & Omanson, in press) in which children who had been diagnosed as using buggy algorithms were taught the correct principles of subtraction just described (e.g., conserving the minuend quantity). This teaching was done in a form that insured that the children's knowledge of the principles was in fact linked by them to the steps in the algorithm they were being taught. Detailed interviews established with considerable certainty that some of the children had fully understood the principles and their application to written subtraction algorithms. Nevertheless, as soon as they returned to a situation of routine calculation performance, half of those children who understood and could apply the principles returned to their buggy algorithms. That is, they did subtraction in a way that violated principles they clearly knew. This is further evidence of a tendency within mathematics for the syntactic system to become separated from its semantic referents even when the necessary knowledge of principles is in fact present in the individual. Similar evidence of this tendency can be found in symbolic logic and algebra problem solving. When this major problem in human cognitive functioning is better understood, cognitive scientists may be able to eliminate it through changed forms of instruction and teaching.

Problem Solving, Intelligence, and Learning Abilities

Problem solving is in a very real sense the birthplace of cognitive science. Efforts that began in the late 1950s and culminated in 1972 with the publication of *Human Problem Solving* by Newell and Simon showed how intelligent computer programs could reason and solve problems, not by doing the kind of dumb, exhaustive searching of a very large memory that was assumed to be the principal capability of computers, but by using strategies to analyze a problem situation and to select actions most likely to advance toward a specified goal. What is more, evidence was developed in the course of these efforts to show that the behavior of the programs using these methods matched in significant ways the behavior of humans working on similar problems. That is, when humans solved the problems, "thinking aloud" as they worked, they showed particular points of hesitation, backtracking, and insight, and they made typical kinds of errors. The computer programs often showed the same kinds of hesitation, backtracking, and errors. The processes built into the programs could therefore be supposed to be functioning in humans as well, although they could not be directly observed in humans.

Of course, programs never matched human performance exactly, and investigators were careful to specify what parts of human performance were not well explained by the computer-expressed theories. Clear identification of these nonmatches was a powerful spur to successive stages of research and theory development. I have already provided an example of how a nonmatch between a theory and human performance reveals the need for a different level of theory in the Kakra and Gum story. The microcoherence-building model of Kintsch and VanDijk would have accepted Kakra's marriage after his death without hesitation, but human readers (who are not thinking about ghost marriages) immediately reject it as impossible. This kind of mismatch made it clear that the microcoherence model alone could not account for how people understood texts, and suggested that a macrocoherence model was needed as well. Noting mismatches and using them to direct further research is characteristic of all of the work that uses computer simulation as a form of theorizing about human thinking.

General Heuristics in Problem Solving

The early research on problem-solving focused on a set of puzzle-like tasks well-suited to initial efforts. The tasks studied included theorem proving in symbolic logic (a task in which all legal expressions and all allowable transformations are specified and the problem-solver must show how it is possible to derive a target expression from a given expression), cryptarithmetic (a decoding puzzle in which letters of the alphabet stand for digits, and a solved arithmetic problem sets constraints on which letters can have which digit values), a variety of artificial problems (such as the Tower of Hanoi, or Missionaries and Cannibals), and, finally, chess. With the exception of chess, which has been shown to depend heavily on extensive knowledge of chess positions, chess moves, and their likely effects, all of the problems studied depended only minimally on knowledge beyond what could be supplied in the experimental situation itself. In these knowledge-poor task environments, cognitive scientists focused their efforts on identifying general processes of problem solving.

Several strategies of problem solving that could be properly called general methods were identified and elaborated in the course of this work. I have already mentioned some of them: For example, the generate-and-test method is usable whenever there is a limited set of possible operators or objects that can be tested to see whether they meet a current goal. Another general method, recurring in many problem-solving models, is means–ends analysis, a kind of general heuristic that reduces the length of search through long-term memory. In means–ends analysis, the problem solver compares the current situation with the goal situation and identifies specific differences between them. A subgoal is then set to reduce a difference that has been identified. (A special set of heuristics governs which subgoal to work on first.) Then a search is conducted to find the operator that will reduce the identified difference. This is a very abbreviated search, because operators are assumed to be organized in memory according to the goals they can serve. It is important to note that means–ends analysis assumes a system that has intentions (goals) and acts on them: It is capable of analyzing its situation and planning its actions on the basis of goals, albeit in a very restricted domain. The General Problem Solver (GPS) was one of the first programs to instantiate all of these general methods in a system that solved symbolic logic problems (see Ernst & Newell, 1969; Newell & Simon, 1972).

More recent work in problem solving has, along with the rest of cognitive psychology, become much more focused on performance in information-rich domains. Many of the basic strategies of heuristic search, subgoal formation, and the like turned out to be relevant for these domains as well. But it has also proved necessary to attribute to the problem-solver, whether human or artificial, specific and organized knowledge about the domain in which problem solving is to take place. Some of the best demonstrations of the role of organized knowledge in problem solving have come in recent research that compares novices and experts in physics as they solve the kinds of problems that are characteristically given as exercises in college-level physics textbooks. In these studies, good beginning students have been compared with advanced students or teachers. The studies show that one's initial understanding, even of a simple textbook problem, depends upon one's level of knowledge in the field.

In one study (Chi, Feltovich, & Glaser, 1981), novices and experts were asked to sort physics textbook problems on any basis they wished. Novices grouped problems on the basis of the kind of apparatus involved (lever, inclined plane, balance beam, etc.), the words used in the problem statement, or the visual features of the diagram presented with the problem. Experts classified the same problems on the basis of the underlying physics principle that was needed to solve the problem (e.g., energy laws, Newton's Second Law). Some typical novice classifications are shown in Figure 7; the contrasting expert classifications are shown in Figure 8. Clearly, novices are affected more by the way the problem is presented, whereas experts bring their own knowledge of important principles to bear in a way that reshapes the problem, usually into a more solvable form. This is much like the way in which good readers use their past knowledge about the topic or the form of discourse to impose a useful structure on a text, while beginning readers are much more victimized by poorly written material or indirect forms of expression.

Initial differences in the ways that experts and novices sort and classify problems are only the beginning, however; the process of solution is also different. What novices usually do is to translate the given information directly into formulas. They then work on the formulas

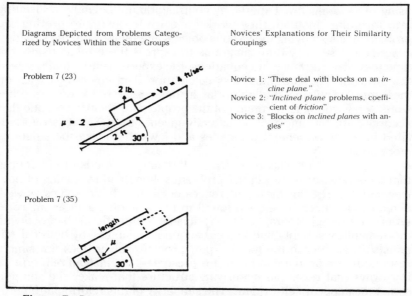

Figure 7. Diagrams of physics problems categorized by novices as similar, and samples of three novices' explanations for their similarity. Reprinted from Chi, Feltovich, and Glaser (1981) by permission.

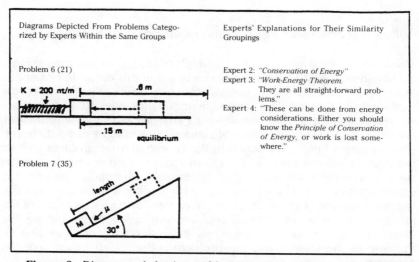

Figure 8. Diagrams of physics problems categorized by experts as similar, and samples of three experts' explanations for their similarity. Reprinted from Chi, Feltovich, and Glaser (1981) by permission.

using rules of algebra. Experts, by contrast, do not begin by translating into formulas. Instead, they work for a while on reinterpreting the problem and specifying the various objects and relations in the situation described. They may draw diagrams to express these relations. By the time they are ready to write equations, the experts have virtually solved the problem. They do much less calculation than novices, at least on the simple problems studied so far in this research. Experts, in other words, construct a new version of the problem for themselves, one that accords with the information actually given, but one that is reformulated in terms of general principles and laws that make the solutions more apparent.

I have used physics research to illustrate the kinds of differences that have been observed in the problem solving and reasoning of novices and experts. But these differences occur in other domains as well. Similar differences have been found in tasks as divergent as interpretation of x-ray photographs by physicians, arithmetic problem solving by elementary school children, and economic planning by political scientists. In each case the more expert problem solver does not simply respond to the problem in the terms presented, but instead reinterprets it in ways that reveal an underlying structure that makes the solution sometimes appear self-evident. The similarity of this reformulation process to the processes involved in reading comprehension described earlier is not an accident. It is a fundamental reflection of the nature of human reasoning and of the constructive character of learning and thinking.

Bottom-Up Processes in Reasoning and Problem Solving

There are other ways, as well, in which research on problem solving echoes themes that I have already discussed in this essay. For example, both top-down and bottom-up processes play a role in problem solving as they do in reading. The various heuristic strategies that I have considered up to now, such as means–ends analysis and subgoal formation, are essentially top-down kinds of processes. A system using them imposes a general plan, developed in the course of prior problem-solving experience, on the specific stimuli of the problem at hand, and the stimuli presented are interpreted in terms of this plan. Similarly, the expert physics problem solvers use their prior knowledge to reorganize the problem that is given. They are more top-down solvers than are the novices. The focus on general problem-solving methods and on the directing role of prior knowledge has led research attention away from the role of the stimuli and the problem setting itself in the solution process.

Research carried out some years ago in my own laboratory (Magone, 1977) helps to clarify the role of bottom-up or stimulus-driven processing in problem solving. In one study, subjects were asked to solve one of the classic Gestalt problems. Two strings were suspended some distance apart in a room, and the subject was asked to tie them together—a simple assignment, except that the strings were deliberately made so short that it was not possible to reach both of them at the same time. Three classes of solutions to this problem were possible: extension (tying another long object to the string or extending the arm by using some rigid, long object to hook the string in); anchoring (holding one string down in the middle, while walking over to reach the other one); and pendulum (putting a weight on one string and swinging it toward the other). There were six objects available that could be used to help solve the problem. They were chosen so that each one tended to suggest a particular class of solution, but some could be used for more than one class. All subjects had to try to solve the problem using each of the six objects in succession.

There was an important difference in the way in which the task instructions were given that tended to evoke either top-down or bottom-up patterns of solution. Some of the subjects in the study were asked by the experimenter to use the first object to solve the problem and to use a specific class of solution. These subjects tended to use the same class of solution over and over on successive objects, sometimes even using the objects in quite unusual and difficult ways in order to stay with their preferred solution type. Another group of subjects were simply told to use all of the objects. These subjects typically picked up the objects in the order in which they fell to hand and used each object in its most characteristic way. They were, in other words, object-driven, and thus bottom-up solvers. It is of interest to note that the bottom-up solvers succeeded in solving the problem in essentially 100 percent of their tries: That is, they found a way to use every object to tie the two strings together. The top-down solvers, by contrast, had a somewhat lower rate of success: They sometimes failed to see an obvious way of using an object because they were intent on trying to make it fit into their top-down solution strategy.

Intelligence and Learning Abilities

Over the decades, one of the most provocative and difficult questions faced by psychologists is the nature of intelligence and the extent to which it can be modified through teaching or other environmental interventions. The previous descriptions of research on reasoning and problem solving lead quite naturally to the question of whether general reasoning skills can be taught and whether this might improve people's general ability to learn. These questions are by no means new ones. In one form or another, they have motivated major branches of psychological research and divided both psychologists and the public at large (see Curtis & Glaser, 1981, for a useful discussion of the history and present status of research on intelligence).

The question that has produced the most dissent, because it is so tied to social policy, is whether differences in intelligence are inherited or are acquired as a result of differences in experience. Posed in this way, the question has no single answer, and it often evokes social and political rather than scientific responses. The understanding of intelligence becomes much more tractable when one raises more pointed questions about what constitutes intelligence and how schools and other educational institutions can best respond to individual differences. These are questions to which current cognitive research on the nature of reasoning, problem solving, and learning can successfully respond.

In so doing, there are two fundamental ways of thinking about intelligence. One is to treat intelligence as something that children (or adult learners) bring with them to an educational experience. In this view, intelligence and aptitudes set the range and limits of the learning that can be expected. This view of intelligence can be held regardless of whether one believes that intelligence is set by heredity or formed by experience. Whatever the origins of individual differences, by the time people present themselves for a particular lesson or course of study, particular aptitudes may determine what kinds of learning activities will be most successful, and established capabilities for learning will set boundaries on what can be expected in a given period of time. A large amount of recent research has centered on trying to identify the cognitive processes that are involved in various kinds of intelligent performances. This knowledge, it is hoped, will provide the basis for more effectively adapting instruction and teaching to the intellectual capacities and propensities that people bring to school with them.

The second view of intelligence and aptitude is that they are processes of thinking and reasoning that can be formed by instruction. This view need not imply a total rejection of a hereditary basis for individual differences. It only requires a belief that environmental factors, including instruction, can make some significant difference in subsequent abilities to learn and reason. Although the hope of improving intelligence and learning skills through deliberate cultivation of certain ways of thinking is an old one—witness a long history of programs for improving memory, problem solving, and other learning abilities—and one that has often been disappointed, recent research on the nature of skilled learning and performance in many domains is building a more scientific basis for these efforts. Although a magic potion for curing failures in human learning and intelligence is hardly in the offing, current lines of investigation are refocusing the issue in profitable ways, and there is room for reasonable optimism about eventual developments that will extend the limits of human learning capacities.

Intelligence Brought to School: Aptitude-Treatment Interactions

If intelligence and learning ability are viewed as capacities already formed in people before they enroll in an educational program, what education can best do is adapt to intelligence—that is, provide forms of instruction that are optimally matched to the aptitudes the individual already has. This is a very old and honorable ambition of educators, although viewpoints on effective and appropriate ways of adapting to individual differences have shifted over time in response to both political and social pressures on the educational system and to available psychological theory about the nature of individual differences.

The first deliberate effort to adapt educational offerings to individual differences was made by separating (i.e., tracking) children into groups according to their different ability levels. The general idea supporting such practices was that people differed in the speed at which they could learn and perhaps also in the highest levels of abstraction to which they could aspire. By grouping faster learners with faster and slower with slower, both groups could proceed at a pace suited to their natural abilities. This, it was proposed, would produce optimal—but not necessarily equal—outcomes for each group. This theory of grouping and tracking was totally consonant with theories of intelligence and aptitude that were dominant from the end of the 19th century through at least the 1920s. Intelligence was viewed as a largely fixed trait, hardly modifiable by experience, and as a unitary trait: *general* intelligence was what determined speed and ease of learning in all domains. Binet's intelligence test and its various offspring, some still in use today, are based on this view of intelligence, as are many of the landmark research studies on intelligence and school learning of the early part of this century (see Carroll, 1982, for this history).

Beginning in the 1930s a more differentiated view of intelligence and mental abilities became predominant among psychologists, who had, through factor analysis and related techniques, identified a variety of *differential aptitudes* in which people might vary. The new viewpoint was that specific aptitudes, rather than general intelligence, were what suited people for specific forms of learning and job performance. This view of intelligence fit well with a new social and political mood that became dominant after World War II. People began to question the suitability of an educational system that more or less permanently classified children as either fast or slow learners and thus limited the potential aspirations of those characterized as slower. Further, increasing sensitivity to ethnic and cultural variations in the American population began to produce the view that recognizing different aptitudes and approaches to learning, rather than emphasizing deficits in general intelligence, would be a more suitable way to optimize educational outcomes. Glaser (1977) called this a shift from a selective theory of education to an *adaptive* one.

The shift to an adaptive theory of education and a more differentiated concept of aptitude and intelligence has produced a search for qualitatively different instructional treatments that would be optimally matched to learners with different characteristics. The result has been research on *aptitude-treatment interactions* (ATIs). This research seeks situations in which a given instructional treatment produces different outcomes in people of different aptitudes. Optimally, one would hope for interactions that allow one to choose a treatment for each individual that will produce the highest level of performance possible in a domain, thus eliminating overall differences in performance. In fact, such ideal interactions are almost never found.

The most typical finding in ATI research is one in which a single aptitude measure—some form of a general intelligence measure—interacts with two broad classes of instructional approaches. Highly structured treatments (e.g., careful sequencing of instructional materials, required responding at specified points, teacher control, and instructions to process in a particular way) reduce the correlation between general intelligence and achievement, whereas unstructured treatments (e.g., much student control of sequence and pace, "discovery-learning" conditions, and open-ended problem setting) maintain a correlation that favors high general intelligence students. That is, low intelligence students do better under structured conditions, which are interpreted as reducing the burden of information processing for the learner (Snow, 1976). Many theories (e.g., Cronbach, 1970) suggest that high general intelligence students should do less well under these circumstances. Only a few studies, however, show such a suppression. This may be due to the fact that the tests used to assess learning often do not permit high intelligence students to demonstrate the additional knowledge or skill that they have in fact acquired in the less-structured teaching conditions.

It should not be surprising, on reflection, that the ATI enterprise as traditionally conducted has not resulted in the kind of strong basis for adapting instruction to aptitudes that had been sought. The near-total dependence in ATI research, until very recently, on standardized tests as measures of intelligence and aptitude has meant that the research attempted to match aptitudes whose characteristics were ill-understood to instructional treatments defined only in very global terms (structured versus unstructured, for example). To break this logjam, and to discover whether there are in fact ways of adapting instruction to specific rather than general capacities for learning, it is necessary to understand better what mental processes are actually involved in the various traits called aptitudes, and what kinds of processes are actually called upon in the various instructional treatments. In other words, cognitive analyses of both aptitudes and instructional treatments are required.

Cognitive Analyses of Aptitudes

Responding to this need, there has been considerable effort in recent years to reanalyze the constructs of intelligence and aptitude in terms of cognitive processes and constructs (Friedman, Das, & O'Connor, 1980; Resnick, 1976; Snow, Federico, & Montague, 1980; Sternberg & Detterman, 1979). Most of this new work began with traditional aptitude tests (for which there is a considerable validation history, based largely in factor-analytic research) and sought to redescribe these aptitudes in terms of current cognitive constructs and parameters. Pellegrino and Glaser (1979) have made a useful distinction between a *cognitive correlates* approach and a *cognitive components* approach to the study of intelligence. The correlates approach uses an aptitude test as a criterion measure and seeks more elementary cognitive processes that are highly correlated with the test criterion. The cognitive components approach uses the test items as tasks to be analyzed in a search for the component processes of test performance itself.

Cognitive correlates of aptitude. Much research is being done to identify basic cognitive processes that distinguish between high and low scorers on a particular aptitude test. The primitive processing parameters for study are drawn from the mainstream of basic research on cognitive processes, especially memory processes. This line of research was initiated by Hunt (1978), who suggested that verbal performance requires both the specific verbal knowledge that is called upon by the task and the exercise of certain mechanistic processes by which information is manipulated. According to Hunt's theory, individuals with less efficient mechanistic processes have to work harder at learning tasks involving verbal information. Over time this handicap produces relatively large individual differences in verbal skill and knowledge.

The theoretical argument is buttressed by data from studies that have investigated the relations between performance on laboratory information-processing tasks and scores on global measures of aptitude, such as IQ tests and college admissions tests. Although early efforts (e.g., Hunt, Frost, & Lunneborg, 1973) were attempts to find associations with quantitative as well as verbal ability, the main findings have shown correlations with tests of verbal aptitude or general intelligence measures that are heavily verbal in character.

The most robust finding in this literature reveals differences in the amount of time that various people need to access name codes in long-term memory. *Code access* time is inferred from the difference between the time it takes a person to decide whether two stimuli that look different have the same name and the time it takes the person to decide that two other stimuli are physically identical. For example, a subject might be shown a lowercase *a* and an uppercase *A* (different physical form, but same name). On a subsequent trial, the subject might be shown two uppercase *A*s (same physical form). The subject will take longer to decide that the pair of stimuli with different physical forms nevertheless has the same name than to decide that the other pair of stimuli has the same form. The longer time is needed to access the name code in memory. The extent of the difference in the time required for the two decisions correlates with verbal aptitude. Across a number of studies, the time difference tends to increase as one moves from highly verbal university students to young adults not in a university, to normal elementary school children, and finally to mildly retarded school children (cf., Bisanz, Danner, & Resnick, 1979; Hunt, 1978). Several other tasks, all requiring speed in particular kinds of microprocesses, have also been shown to discriminate high and low scorers on verbal aptitude tests.

All told, there seems to be enough evidence of individual and age differences in primitive parameters of mental processing to make plausible Hunt's notion that small differences in mechanistic processes could cumulate over time to produce considerable differences in verbal skill and knowledge. It is important to note, however, that a large portion of the findings clearly associating these parameters with individual differences comes from Hunt's own laboratory. Wider replication is needed before strong conclusions about specific associations are drawn. A recent summary and useful critique of this research appears in Cooper and Regan (1982).

Cognitive components of aptitude. Carroll (1976) and Simon (1976) first suggested the analysis of test items as cognitive tasks, and several research programs subsequently focused on uncovering the processes that are required in actually performing the items in intelligence and aptitude tests. Perhaps the most ambitious program in terms of the range of tasks studied is Sternberg's work on what he calls a "componential analysis" of intelligence (1977a, 1977b, 1980). Sternberg's analyses begin with a specification of the components that are hypothesized to be involved in the performance of a test item. Several models are then defined that differ in the components called on, the sequence of the components, the number of times each component needs to be executed, and the manner of execution (e.g., exhaustive or self-terminating searches). These models permit predictions of reaction time and error patterns under varying conditions of stimulus structure and task presentation.

Empirical tests of models generated for analogies, for example, have identified a "best fit" model and provided estimates of which processes absorbed most of the processing time. For verbal analogies, encoding of the stimulus terms accounted for about half of the solution time, while 30 percent of the time was spent on attribute comparison operations. For geometric analogies, attribute comparisons took longer, both as a percentage of total time (57 percent) and in absolute terms. Sternberg has extended the analysis of analogies to children, making it possible to chart developmental changes in the various components. The most important developmental observation has been that children have a greater tendency to rely on associations between the words in the analogy than to analyze all of the relations.

Other research on analogies performance is largely in agreement with Sternberg's findings on the importance of encoding. Some of the studies have analyzed the encoding process itself further, with particular attention paid to which aspects of the stimuli are encoded. For example, Mulholland, Pellegrino, and Glaser (1980) showed that in geometric analogies, individuals analyze stimuli in a systematic serial manner, so that latency of responding is a function of both the number of elements that must be encoded and the number of transformations that must be performed on each element. They found a sharp increase in both reaction time and errors when multiple transformations on multiple stimuli had to be processed, suggesting that working memory limitations are important in analogy processing. For verbal analogies, studies by Pellegrino and Glaser (1980) and Sternberg (1977a, 1977b) all show that individuals with high aptitude test scores specify more precisely the set of semantic features that relate the word pairs in an analogy, and that the extra time they spend on this process allows them to spend less time on subsequent decision and response processes.

Other test-like tasks that have been subjected to similar analysis include series completion, syllogistic reasoning and transitive inference, spatial abilities tasks such as mental rotation and visual comparison, block designs, and tasks from the Ravens Progressive Matrices test. Not all of this work has been explicitly oriented toward detecting individual differences. Instead, much has been inspired by the Piaget-generated debates over how and when various logical abilities develop in children, and over whether language or spatial representations are central (see Resnick, 1981a for a review).

It seems likely that as efforts to understand performance on such tasks proceed, individual differences will have to be considered if the data are to be sensibly interpreted. An interesting case in point is Cooper's (1980) research on visual comparison, in which subjects separate naturally into two quite different subgroups, one using a holistic and one an analytic comparison strategy. The two strategies produced very different patterns of latencies, and the groups responded in predictably different ways to variations of task instructions and of stimuli. Cooper and Regan (1982) have suggested that differences in preferred strategy for various tasks, verbal as well as visual, may account for aptitudes even more strongly than across-the-board differences in speed of basic processes. Their discussion suggests ways in which correlational and componential approaches to the analysis of aptitude may have to be joined before really adequate theories of the nature of individual differences in test performance can be developed.

Intelligence Shaped by School: Teaching Learning Skills

If one views intelligence and aptitude as a set of capacities that are formed partly by instruction, one is led to pose two questions. First, what skills of learning are sufficiently pervasive and general (that is, not limited to specific subject matters or specific situations of application) that they warrant concerted attention as the goals of educational programs? Second, how are these skills acquired, and correlatively, how might they be most directly taught? The search for general skills of learning has been a long one, and it has been pursued from many points of view. Before proceeding to a consideration of particular skills of learning and their acquisition, it is worth pausing to ask whether it is likely that such generalizable abilities exist at all.

Skepticism about the existence of general abilities. There are two bodies of evidence, one old and established, one quite recent, that must lead to skepticism toward the claim that cognitive abilities are really very general. The first set of evidence is the repeated failure, over decades of trying, to produce convincing demonstrations of widespread transfer of learning from one domain to another. The second is evidence of the central role of specific knowledge in intelligence performance and in learning.

There has been a recurrent view that certain school subjects would "discipline the mind" and should therefore be taught not so much for their inherent value as for their value in facilitating other learning. Latin was defended for many years in these terms; mathematics and formal logic are often so defended today. Most recently, learning to program computers has been offered as a way to develop general problem-solving and reasoning abilities, appropriate even when no computers are available or applicable to the situation at hand (Papert, 1980), and a variety of courses and programs claiming to teach reasoning and problem-solving abilities have been developed and promoted (see Segal, Chipman, & Glaser, in press; Nickerson, Salter, Shepard, & Herrnstein, 1984). This view of transfer from a particularly powerful or nodal knowledge has never been supported empirically. In the 1920s, Thorndike (1922) studied transfer among school subject matters and found that it was always more efficient to study the subject of interest directly (English vocabulary, for example) than to study some other subject (Latin, for example) that "prepared" one's mind. Subsequent reviews of research on transfer of school subject matter have reconfirmed Thorndike's finding, and there is as yet no empirical evidence of transfer to other activities from specific kinds of problem-solving courses or from learning to program computers.

The second source of evidence that weakens claims for generalized abilities is the research yielding repeated demonstrations that specific knowledge plays a central role in reasoning, thinking, and learning of all kinds. Several examples of the role of specific knowledge have been developed in the course of this essay. For example, specific knowledge about the topic of a text affects the processes of language comprehension, and specific, acquired schemata underlie problem-solving performances as varied as those in primary school arithmetic and college-level physics and political science. Glaser (1984) further described evidence of the role of domain-specific knowledge in a variety of tasks that have traditionally been viewed as indicators of aptitude or intelligence.

Belief in the reality of general skills. Despite the evidence that opposes transfer and that favors the importance of domain-specific knowledge, there are some equally compelling factors that have sustained psychologists' belief in the reality of general competencies in learning. First, there is a positive correlation between almost any two cognitive performances that have ever been measured, except when tests have been specifically designed not to correlate with IQ (as, for example, certain creativity tests). This *positive manifold* is the basis for the factor analytic tradition in intelligence research: Factor analysis uses patterns of covariance to infer what various tests may have in common, and thus what the basic dimensions of human aptitude are. Tests that are positively correlated—that is, that share variance—also presumably share underlying processes. The fact that most tests correlate positively with each other, and that a general factor can always be found if the statistical methods used do not insist on completely uncorrelated factors, suggests that all tests have some processes in common. These common processes are, presumably, general abilities.

Second, when cognitive scientists do information-processing analyses of complex skills, they find that the same kinds of basic problem-solving processes are used in task after task. Several examples of this have come up in the course of this essay. For example, although the original General Problem Solver (GPS), built to solve symbolic logic problems, was not in fact very general in the range of problems it could solve, the kinds of processes used by GPS appear over and over again in simulations of human performances on complex tasks. For example, means–ends analysis, generate-and-test routines, subgoal formation, and other kinds of planning are used in tasks as varied as inventing buggy arithmetic routines, planning compositions, constructing geometry proofs, and troubleshooting electronic devices. The reason that a single artificial intelligence program cannot solve a wide variety of problems is apparently not that the fundamental processes it applies are widely different across domains, but rather that the program must apply these processes to very specific, organized bodies of knowledge. Each simulation must build in the relevant knowledge, and so it becomes specific to its knowledge base (see Dehn & Schank, 1982).

Third, a variety of basic processes such as perceiving stimuli, encoding, classifying, generating responses, and executing responses are quite obviously involved in a number of different cognitive performances. These are the building block processes of intelligence and aptitude of the kind studied by Hunt and other students of the cognitive correlates of intelligence. Some years ago, Simon (1976), considering what information processing analyses of various tasks might suggest about the nature of intelligence, suggested that very low-level components (such as the building blocks) and very high-level ones (such as means–ends analysis and the like) are shared across many tasks and are therefore general abilities. The specific knowledge varies from task to task, however, producing the domain-specificity of cognitive abilities.

Finally, in some of the most recent and provocative work on the nature of intelligence, an apparently common body of "executive" or self-regulatory processes have been identified. Processes such as keeping track of one's own understanding or knowledge, initiating review or rehearsal activities when needed, deliberately organizing one's attention and other resources in order to learn something, or planning a set of actions so as to meet goals within the limits of certain constraints are all activities that have been shown to be characteristic of effective learners, good readers of texts, good writers, and strong problem solvers. These processes are relatively absent in younger or less intelligent individuals. These higher order or metacognitive skills, as they are often called, have become the object of an important recent line of research.

Self-Monitoring and Metacognition

Metacognition is surely one of the "boom" fields of recent cognitive psychology. The term *metacognition* is a relatively new one, whose field of reference has so exploded in just a few years that thoughtful scholars (cf., A. L. Brown, Bransford, Ferrara, & Campione, 1983) are beginning to suggest that it be abandoned as confusing, and that more specific terms such as *self-monitoring* and *self-regulation* should be substituted. The broad domain of metacognition includes (a) knowledge about cognition in general, (b) knowledge about one's own knowledge or cognitive strategies, and (c) application of these two kinds of knowledge to the planning and execution of appropriate mental activities in learning and problem-solving situations.

Several investigators have documented the fact that knowledge about cognition increases with age, and that older children are better able than younger ones to describe what one *ought* to do to remember something—for example, how to remember to take one's skates to school the next day. There is also a small body of evidence showing that younger children and the "developmentally young" (i.e., the retarded) are less able than older children to assess when they have understood a message, when they are ready for a test, and the like. Convergent with this set of findings is a line of research showing that much of the deficit of retarded people in simple learning tasks, such as memorization, comes from their failure to apply well-known strategies such as rehearsal or information of mnemonics.

A number of studies have shown impressive gains in immediate performance on such tasks by simply instructing individuals to rehearse or to engage in verbal elaboration. In these studies, however, there was almost complete lack of transfer even to only slightly modified tasks. This led to a search for superordinate (Belmont, Butterfield, & Ferretti, 1982) or metacognitive skills (A. L. Brown, 1978), such as assessing one's own readiness for a test, apportioning study time, or deciding when to use rehearsal, imagery, or self-interrogation strategies that might promote general improvement. Some modest successes have been reported, but not enough for cognitive scientists to be convinced yet that even mild retardation can be overcome by training in superordinate skills of the kind studied thus far.

Most of the initial research on metacognitive training focused on memorization tasks that require very specialized kinds of strategies and that may have only a limited function outside of the laboratory and certain very specialized kinds of school learning (e.g., vocabulary lists). Recent research on memory, showing the power of chunked and organized knowledge in extending memory power (Chi, 1978), calls into question the extent to which strategies for artificial memorizing are likely to be an optimal approach to take even in simple school learning. A very recent shift toward the study of processes of self-control and self-regulation in more complex kinds of learning and performance, ranging from reading comprehension to writing compositions to learning new subject-matter domains, offers a more promising perspective on the development of learning abilities and the improvement of a variety of learning competencies.

Effects of reciprocal teaching. To illustrate this new perspective, I describe a recent training study which embodies many of the ideas under consideration in the field. The experiments were conducted by Palincsar and Brown (1984) with middle school children who had extremely weak reading comprehension skills. The children were divided into small groups, and with an adult, each group engaged in a process called "reciprocal teaching." The children took turns posing questions about and summarizing short texts that they read. The other members of the group commented on the quality of the questions or summaries and tried to help formulate better questions or summaries. Reciprocal teaching sessions were conducted daily for several weeks. During the intervention, there were daily assessments in which children individually read passages and answered questions about them. Assessments continued for several generalization days after the intervention ended, and there also were 3 days of assessment after an 8-week break. In addition, there were some generalization and transfer tests. In the generalization tests, students read social studies and science texts in their regular classrooms and answered comprehension questions about them. The children were not aware that these tests had anything to do with the experimental teaching in which they had participated.

Table 1 contains some protocol segments from reciprocal teaching sessions with one of the weaker readers in the study. In these segments, there is a very great shift apparent in the child's ability to pose questions about the texts. At first the child cannot formulate questions at all and does not even produce full sentences. Later the child is able to pose coherent questions and by Day 15 is able to formulate a single question that addresses the main point of the passage. The protocol clearly shows the role of the adult in this process. At the beginning the teacher actually formulates the questions and the child does little more than repeat them. Later the adult provides portions of the questions, often the initial words of a sentence that will produce an appropriate question. By the end the child has taken over the entire process. Notice

Table 1
Protocol Excerpts Showing the Acquisition of Question-Asking by a Seventh-Grade Student (C) With Reciprocal Teaching

Day 1:

TEXT: The water moccasin, somewhat longer than the copperhead, is found in the southeastern states. It lives in swampy regions. It belongs, as do also the copperhead and the rattlesnakes, to a group of poisonous snakes called pit vipers. They have pits between their eyes and their nostrils which, because they are sensitive to heat, help the snakes tell when they are near a warm-blooded animal. Another name for the water moccasin is "cottonmouth." This name comes from the white lining of the snake's mouth.

C: What is found in the southeastern snakes, also the copperhead, rattlesnakes, vipers—they have. I'm not doing this right.

T: All right. Do you want to know about the pit vipers?

C: Yeah.

T: What would be a good question about the pit vipers that starts with the word "why?"

C: (No response)

T: How about, "Why are the snakes called pit vipers?"

C: Why do they want to know that they are called pit vipers?

T: Try it again.

C: Why do they, pit vipers in a pit?

T: How about, "Why do they call the snakes pit vipers?"

C: Why do they call the snakes pit vipers?

T: There you go! Good for you.

Table 1, continued

Day 7:

TEXT: Perhaps you are wondering where the lava and other volcanic products come from. Deep within our earth there are pockets of molten rock called magma. Forced upward in part by gas pressure, this molten rock continually tries to reach the surface. Eventually—by means of cracks in the crustal rocks or some similar zone of weakness—the magma may break out of the ground. It then flows from the vent as lava, or spews skyward as dense clouds of lava particles.

C: How does the pressure from below push the mass of hot rock against the opening? Is that it?

T: Not quite. Start your question with, "What happens when?"

C: What happens when the pressure from below pushes the mass of hot rock against the opening?

T: Good for you! Good job.

Day 15:

TEXT: Scientists also come to the South Pole to study the strange lights that glow overhead during the Antarctic night. (It's a cold and lonely world for the few hardy people who "winter over" the polar night.) These "southern lights" are caused by the Earth acting like a magnet on electrical particles in the air. They are clues that may help us understand the Earth's core and the upper edges of its blanket of air.

C: Why do scientists come to the south pole to study?

T: Excellent question! That is what this paragraph is all about.

Note: T = teacher, C = student (Charles). Adapted from Palincsar and Brown (1984) by permission.

also that the standards for what the adult accepts as a good question from the child keep changing; stiffer requirements are applied toward the end than in the first days of the reciprocal teaching.

According to various measures this process greatly affected reading comprehension. Figure 9 shows increases in the percentage of assessment questions answered correctly by several students during the various phases of the first experiment. From a preintervention baseline measurement of very few questions answered correctly, most of the children moved up to about an 80 percent correct response rate, and they remained there after an 8-week break. Several control groups showed no increase in correct assessment responding during the same period. Figure 10 shows the effects of the training on the generalization tasks in regular classrooms. Again, the reciprocal teaching experience was shown to have a powerful effect on comprehension in a very different physical setting and under quite different measurement conditions. The experiment was replicated under more ordinary school conditions, as part of the regular instruction offered by the teacher in reading. Very similar results were obtained.

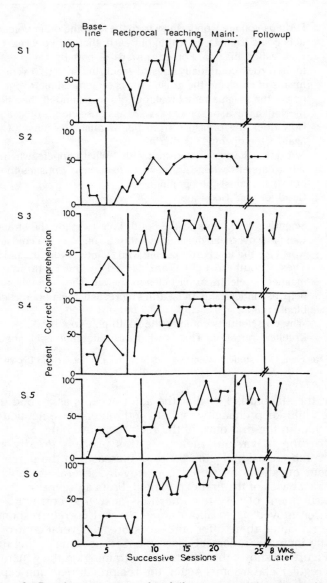

Figure 9. Results correct on the daily assessment passages for the six subjects in the Reciprocal Teaching Group of Study 1. Reprinted from Palincsar and Brown (1984) by permission.

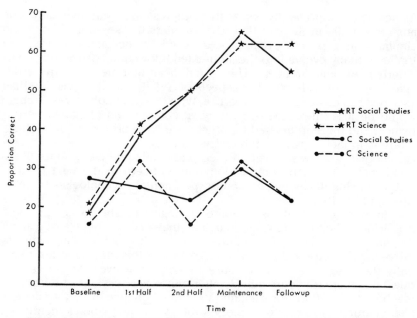

Figure 10. Percent correct on the classroom generalization probes of Study 1 for the Reciprocal Teaching (RT) and untreated control (C) groups in both science and social studies classes. Reprinted from Palincsar and Brown (1984) by permission.

The Palincsar and Brown study is not only a dramatic success story in educational intervention. It also illustrates many of the issues being studied in today's research on self-monitoring and cognitive strategy learning. First, the skills in question asking and summarizing that the children in the study practiced are probably not directly called upon in skilled reading. The automatic nature of many reading comprehension processes, the speed at which reading proceeds, and its sequential nature make it implausible that in the normal course of skilled reading, people actually pose questions or create summaries for themselves. There is, then, only an indirect relation between the strategies taught and what was probably involved in the children's subsequent relatively skilled reading performance. This indirect relation between strategies taught and skilled performance is also characteristic of findings in other metacognitive training research.

This raises the question of how instruction that focuses on overt, self-conscious strategies that are not components of skilled performance might improve processes that progress quite automatically. The answer may lie in the fact that when readers use self-questioning and similar strategies, they evoke processes of inference and interpretation that eventually evolve into the automated information processing characteristic of skilled readers. This would mean that metacognitive strategies are better understood as aspects of cognitive skill acquisition than as aspects of cognitive skill expertise. With this assumption, researchers would be less interested in identifying components of skilled performance, and more interested in directly studying processes of learning. There is in fact a growing interest within cognitive science in the processes of cognitive acquisition (see Anderson, 1981) and some likelihood that this will become a dominant concern in the next decade, further linking developmental and experimental psychologists (cf. A. L. Brown et al., 1983).

Another possibility is that the strategies taught do not promote acquiring skilled processes so much as they activate or release capacities already available. The relative speed with which reading skill improved with reciprocal teaching suggests that this may be at least partially the case. As shown in Figure 10, correct answers to assessment questions increased very quickly after only a few sessions of reciprocal teaching for most of the students. Very rapid change in performance is also characteristic of the memory strategy training studies mentioned earlier. To the extent that strategy training releases rather than builds processing capability, one would expect this kind of instruction to be effective only if the relevant capabilities were already present.

There is some evidence that certain forms of metacognitive training can actually suppress performance, at least temporarily, if the knowledge or skills necessary to use new information is not already present. Scardamalia and Paris (in press) taught children to recognize and identify certain rhetorical devices that are known to affect the self-monitoring performance of skilled writers. This training increased the students' use of these rhetorical devices in their written compositions. However, no improvement, and even some depression, in overall organization and coherence of the compositions resulted. Scardamalia and Paris attributed this to a fundamental strategy that children use for composing, one they call "knowledge telling." The strategy involves little planning and the child writes down in sequence everything he or she thinks of relating to the topic. Because there was no overall planning, the children could not use these rhetorical devices to form the framework for a well-organized argument as adult writers would do.

A third important point is that reciprocal teaching is a special form of social interaction that may in fact be central to the acquisition of generalized cognitive skill. Traditional views of the way in which social interaction affects learning focus on the adult as provider of new information, as a modeler of correct performance, and as a selective reinforcer of children's tries at producing the performance. The reciprocal teaching of the Palincsar and Brown study was inspired by a different view of social processes in learning that is attracting increased attention among cognitive psychologists interested in the development of general cognitive competence. The Soviet psychologist Vygotsky (1978; see also Wertsch, 1978) has argued that cognition begins in social situations in which a child shares responsibility for producing a complete performance with an adult. The child does what he or she can, the adult the rest. In this way, practice on components occurs in the context of the full performance. In naturally occurring interactions of this kind, the adult will gradually increase expectations of how much of the full performance the child can be responsible for.

It should be clear that the Palincsar and Brown experiments should properly be regarded as more provocative than definitive. Their success in teaching a socially valuable skill, after many failures over the years, is stimulating. However, cognitive scientists do not really know what component in the reciprocal teaching method actually produced the success. So many elements of instruction were combined that it is impossible to determine from this study alone which parts of the instruction were essential. Further, it is not clear exactly what was taught. It is obvious that the children learned to ask questions and to summarize. However, the true target skill was neither of these, but rather skillful reading comprehension, and it is not completely clear why practice in asking questions and summarizing should produce that skill.

None of this is said in the spirit of criticizing the Palincsar and Brown experiments. Rather, it is said in order to emphasize that research on self-monitoring and metacognitive skills is at this time a highly promising but still largely unexplored domain. It is attracting considerable attention because there is some broad theory that suggests that it ought to work, and because a few studies such as the one cited have produced some dramatic successes. However, considerable caution in interpretation and in expectations for the future is necessary or psychologists risk another round of enthusiastic faddism.

Conclusion: Learning in the Future

The examples of cognitive research on learning and thinking developed in the course of this essay have been intended to convey the sense of excitement and of open possibilities that now pervade many branches of cognitive psychology. A major feature of current cognitive research is its focus on complex forms of intellectual competence. This has the effect of making large segments of fundamental research more immediately relevant to questions of instruction than has usually been the case for psychological research on learning. As a result, a new cognitive instructional psychology is growing up as a special branch of cognitive psychology.

The emergence of instruction as an arena of concern for cognitive psychology is helping to focus the field's attention on questions of cognitive change. Instructional psychology seeks to formulate principles that can guide interventions designed to help people to learn. People learn, however, even when they are not taught, and so instruction must be construed as interventions in a learner's ongoing processes of knowledge acquisition. To develop principles of intervention, therefore, it is essential that we know what these acquisition processes are like. For this reason instructional psychology requires strong theories of the processes involved in cognitive change.

For a considerable period of time cognitive psychologists had given up the long-standing interest of experimental psychologists in questions of how changes in performance and competence come about. During this period, cognitive psychology focused instead on building detailed descriptions of given states of cognitive competence. Expert and novice states were often compared, but little was done to explain how people might pass from one state to the other. This inattention to processes of change is ending. In fact, the topic of learning is high on today's cognitive science agenda and will probably draw more and more attention in the next few years.

Most cognitive research on learning up to now has been concerned with accounting for changes in performance skills—that is, for developing speed and accuracy in doing things like solving algebra equations or programming computers. Some elegant and highly plausible theories of how early states of competence are transformed in the course of practice now exist. However, there has been little attention thus far to the question of how conceptual knowledge is acquired. Cognitive scientists can show how schemata influence learning from texts, for example, but their models of how the schemata themselves are learned are poorly developed. This lacuna in knowledge is widely recognized among cognitive scientists and some are now beginning to turn their attention to questions associated with the acquisition processes of conceptual learning. Psychologists can probably expect a new generation of cognitive learning theories to emerge in the next few years that will substantially modify the theoretical landscape. As this happens instructional questions are likely to become even more visible and central in cognitive psychology.

References

Anderson, J. R. (Ed.). (1981). *Cognitive skills and their acquisition.* Hillsdale, NJ: Erlbaum.

Anderson, R. C., Reynolds, R. E., Schallert, E. T., & Goetz, E. T. (1977). Frameworks for comprehending discourse. *American Educational Research Journal, 14,* 367–381.

Baroody, A. J., & Gannon, K. E. (1984). The development of the commutativity principle and economical addition strategies. *Cognition and Instruction, 1*(3), 321–339.

Bartlett, F. C. (1932). *Remembering: A study in experimental and social psychology.* New York: Cambridge University Press.

Belmont, J. M., Butterfield, E. C., & Ferretti, R. P. (1982). To secure transfer of training to instruct self-management skills. In D. K. Detterman & R. J. Sternberg (Eds.), *How and how much can intelligence be increased?* (pp. 147–155). Norwood, NJ: Ablex.

Bisanz, J., Danner, F., & Resnick, L. B. (1979). Changes with age in measures of processing efficiency. *Child Development, 50,* pp. 132–141.

Bransford, J. D., & Johnson, M. K. (1972). Contextual prerequisites for understanding: Some investigations of comprehension and recall. *Journal of Verbal Learning and Verbal Behavior, 11,* 717–726.

Briars, D. J., & Larkin, J. H. (1984). An integrated model of skill in solving elementary word problems. *Cognition and Instruction, 1*(3), 245–296.

Brown, A. L. (1978). Knowing when, where, and how to remember: A problem of metacognition. In R. Glaser (Ed.), *Advances in instructional psychology* (Vol. 1, pp. 77–165). Hillsdale, NJ: Erlbaum.

Brown, A. L., Bransford, J. D., Ferrara, R. A., & Campione, J. C. (1983). Learning, remembering, and understanding. In J. H. Flavell and E. M. Markman (Eds.), *Handbook of child psychology: Vol. 3. Cognitive development* (4th ed., pp. 420–494). New York: Wiley.

Brown, J. S., & Burton, R. R. (1978). Diagnostic models for procedural bugs in basic mathematical skills. *Cognitive Science, 2*(2), 155–192.

Brown, J. S., & VanLehn, K. (1982). Towards a generative theory of "bugs." In T. P. Carpenter, J. M. Moser, & T. A. Romberg (Eds.), *Addition and subtraction: A cognitive perspective* (pp. 117–135). Hillsdale, NJ: Erlbaum.

Burton, R. R. (1982). Diagnosing bugs in a simple procedural skill. In D. Sleeman & J. S. Brown (Eds.), *Intelligent tutoring systems* (pp. 157–183). New York: Academic Press.

Buswell, G. T. (1920). An experimental study of eye–voice span in reading. *Supplementary Educational Monographs,* No. 17. Chicago: University of Chicago Press.

Carpenter, T. P., Hiebert, J., & Moser, J. M. (1981). The effect of problem structure on first graders' initial solution processes for simple addition and subtraction problems. *Journal for Research in Mathematics Education, 12*(1), 27–39.

Carpenter, T. P., & Moser, J. M. (1982). The development of addition and subtraction problem-solving skills. In T. P. Carpenter, J. M. Moser, & T. A. Romberg (Eds.), *Addition and subtraction: A cognitive perspective* (pp. 9–24). Hillsdale, NJ: Erlbaum.

Carroll, J. B. (1976). Psychometric tests as cognitive tasks: A new "structure of intellect." In L. B. Resnick (Ed.), *The nature of intelligence* (pp. 27–56). Hillsdale, NJ: Erlbaum.

Carroll, J. B. (1982). The measurement of intelligence. In R. J. Sternberg (Ed.), *Handbook of human intelligence* (pp. 29–120). Cambridge, MA: Harvard University Press.

Carry, L. R., Lewis, C., & Bernard, J. E. (1980). *Psychology of equation solving—an information-processing study.* Austin: University of Texas.

Cattell, J. M. (1886). The time it takes to see and name objects. *Mind, 11,* 63–65.

Chi, M. T. H. (1978). Knowledge structures and memory development. In R. Siegler (Ed.), *Children's thinking: What develops?* (pp. 73–96). Hillsdale, NJ: Erlbaum.

Chi, M. T. H., Feltovich, P. J., & Glaser, R. (1981). Categorization and representation of physics problems by experts and novices. *Cognitive Science, 5*(2), 121–152.

Chiesi, H. L., Spilich, G. J., & Voss, J. F. (1979). Acquisition of domain-related information in relation to high and low domain knowledge. *Journal of Verbal Learning and Verbal Behavior, 18,* 257–274.

Cooper, L. A. (1980). Spatial information processing: Strategies for research. In R. E. Snow, P. A. Federico, & W. E. Montague (Eds.), *Aptitude, learning, and instruction* (Vol. 1, pp. 149–176). Hillsdale, NJ: Erlbaum.

Cooper, L. A., & Regan, D. T. (1982). Attention, perception, and intelligence. In R. J. Sternberg (Ed.), *Handbook of human intelligence* (pp. 123–169). Cambridge, MA: Harvard University Press.

Cronbach, L. J. (1970). *Essentials of psychological testing* (3rd ed.). New York: Harper & Row.

Curtis, M. E., & Glaser, R. (1981). Changing conceptions of intelligence. *Review of Research in Education, 9,* 111–148.

Davis, R. B. (1983). Complex mathematical cognition. In H. P. Ginsburg (Ed.), *The development of mathematical thinking* (pp. 253–290). New York: Academic Press.

Dehn, N., & Schank, R. (1982). Artificial and human intelligence. In R. J. Sternberg (Ed.), *Handbook of human intelligence* (pp. 352–391). Cambridge, MA: Harvard University Press.

Ernst, G. W., & Newell, A. (1969). *GPS: A case study in generality and problem solving.* New York: Academic Press.

Ericsson, K. A., & Simon, H. A. (1984). *Protocol analysis: Verbal reports as data.* Cambridge, MA: MIT Press.

Flammer, A., & Kintsch, W. (Eds.). (1982). *Discourse processing: (Vol. 8) Advances in psychology.* Amsterdam: North-Holland.

Fleisher, L. S., & Jenkins, J. R. (1978). Effects of contextualized and decontextualized practice conditions on word recognition. *Learning Disabilities Quarterly, 1*(3), 39–47.

Frederiksen, C. H. (1979). Discourse comprehension and early reading. In L. B. Resnick & P. A. Weaver (Eds.), *Theory and practice of early reading* (Vol. 1, pp. 155–186). Hillsdale, NJ: Erlbaum.

Frederiksen, J. R., Warren, B. M., & Rosebery, A. S. (in press). A componential approach to training reading skills. *Cognition and Instruction.*

Friedman, M., Das, J., & O'Connor, N. (Eds.). (1980). *Intelligence and learning.* New York: Plenum Press.

Fuson, K. C. (1982). An analysis of the counting-on solution procedure in addition. In T. P. Carpenter, J. M. Moser, & T. A. Romberg (Eds.), *Addition and subtraction: A cognitive perspective* (pp. 67–81). Hillsdale, NJ: Erlbaum.

Gelman, R., & Gallistel, C. R. (1978). *The child's understanding of number.* Cambridge, MA: Harvard University Press.

Ginsburg, H. P. (1977). *Children's arithmetic: The learning process.* New York: Van Nostrand Reinhold.

Ginsburg, H. P. (Ed.). (1983). *The development of mathematical thinking.* New York: Academic Press.

Glaser, R. (1977). *Adaptive education: Individual diversity and learning.* New York: Holt, Rinehart & Winston.

Glaser, R. (1984). Education and thinking: The role of knowledge. *American Psychologist, 39*(1), 93–104.

Greeno, J. G. (1983, August). *Investigations of a cognitive skill.* Paper presented at the Annual meeting of the American Psychological Association, Anaheim, CA.

Greeno, J. G., Riley, M. S., & Gelman, R. (1984). Conceptual competence and children's counting. *Cognitive Psychology, 16*(1), 94–143.

Groen, G. J., & Parkman, J. M. (1972). A chronometric analysis of simple addition. *Psychological Review, 79*(4), 329–343.

Groen, G. J., & Poll, M. (1973). Subtraction and the solution of open sentence problems. *Journal of Experimental Child Psychology, 16,* 292–302.

Groen, G. J., & Resnick, L. B. (1977). Can preschool children invent addition algorithms? *Journal of Educational Psychology, 69*(6), 645–652.

Halliday, D., & Resnick, R. (1974). *Fundamentals of physics.* New York: Wiley.

Houlihan, D. M., & Ginsburg, H. P. (1981). The addition methods of first- and second-grade children. *Journal for Research in Mathematics Education, 12*(2), 95–106.

Huey, E. G. (1968). *The psychology and pedagogy of reading.* Cambridge, MA: MIT Press. (Original work published 1908)

Hunt, E. (1978). Mechanics of verbal ability. *Psychological Review, 85,* 109–130.

Hunt, E., Frost, N., & Lunneborg, C. (1973). Individual differences in cognition: A new approach to intelligence. In G. H. Bower (Ed.), *The psychology of learning and motivation* (Vol. 7, pp. 87–122). New York: Academic Press.

Kieras, D. (1977). Problems of reference in text comprehension. In M. A. Just & P. A. Carpenter (Eds.), *Cognitive processes in comprehension* (pp. 249–270). Hillsdale, NJ: Erlbaum.

Kintsch, W. (1979). On modeling comprehension. *Educational Psychologist, 14,* 3–14.

Kintsch, W., & vanDijk, T. A. (1978). Toward a model of text comprehension and production. *Psychological Review, 85,* 363–394.

Lesgold, A. M., & Resnick, L. B. (1983). How reading difficulties develop: Perspectives from a longitudinal study. In J. P. Das, R. Mulcahy, & A. E. Wall (Eds.), *Theory and research in learning disability* (pp. 155–188). New York: Plenum Press.

Magone, M. E. (1977). *Goal analysis and feature detection as processes in the solution of an insight problem.* Unpublished master's thesis, University of Pittsburgh, Pittsburgh, PA.

Mandler, J. M. (1978). A code in the node: The use of a story schema in retrieval. *Discourse Processes, 1,* 14–35.

Mandler, J. M., & Johnson, N. S. (1977). Remembrance of things parsed: Story structure and recall. *Cognitive Psychology, 9,* 111–151.

Matz, M. (1982). Towards a process model for high school algebra errors. In D. Sleeman & J. S. Brown (Eds.), *Intelligent tutoring systems* (pp. 25–50). New York: Academic Press.

Meyer, B. J. F. (1975). *The organization of prose and its effect on recall.* Amsterdam: Elsevier.

Meyer, B. J. F. (1984). Text dimensions and cognitive processing. In H. Mandl, N. L. Stein, & T. Trabasso (Eds.), *Learning and comprehension of text* (pp. 3–51). Hillsdale, NJ: Erlbaum.

Miller, G. A. (1956). The magical number seven, plus or minus two: Some limits on our capacity for processing information. *Psychological Review, 63,* 81–97.

Mulholland, T. M., Pellegrino, J. W., & Glaser, R. (1980). Components of geometric analogy solution. *Cognitive Psychology, 12,* 252–284.

Neches, R. (1981). *Models of heuristic procedure modification.* Unpublished doctoral dissertation, Carnegie-Mellon University, Pittsburgh, PA.

Nesher, P. (1982). Levels of description in the analysis of addition and subtraction word problems. In T. P. Carpenter, J. M. Moser, & T. A. Romberg (Eds.), *Addition and subtraction: A cognitive perspective* (pp. 25–38). Hillsdale, NJ: Erlbaum.

Nesher, P., & Teubal, E. (1975). Verbal cues as an interfering factor in verbal problem solving. *Educational Studies in Mathematics, 6,* 41–51.

Newell, A., & Simon, H. A. (1972). *Human problem solving.* Englewood Cliffs, NJ: Prentice-Hall.

Nickerson, R. S., Salter, W., Shepard, S., & Herrnstein, J. (1984). *The teaching of learning strategies.* Cambridge, MA: Bolt, Beranek, and Newman.

Palincsar, A. S., & Brown, A. L. (1984). Reciprocal teaching of comprehension-fostering and comprehension-monitoring activities. *Cognition and Instruction, 1*(2), 117–175.

Papert, S. A. (1980). *Mindstorms.* New York: Basic Books.

Pellegrino, J. W., & Glaser, R. (1979). Cognitive correlates and components in the analysis of individual differences. *Intelligence, 3,* 187–214.

Pellegrino, J. W., & Glaser, R. (1980). Components of inductive reasoning. In R. E. Snow, P. A. Federico, & W. E. Montague (Eds.), *Aptitude, learning and instruction* (Vol. 1, pp. 177–218). Hillsdale, NJ: Erlbaum.

Perfetti, C. A. (Ed.). (in press). *Reading Ability.* New York: Oxford University Press.

Piaget, J. (1965). *The child's conception of number.* New York: Norton. (Original work published 1941)

Resnick, L. B. (Ed.). (1976). *The nature of intelligence.* Hillsdale, NJ: Erlbaum.

Resnick, L. B. (1981a). Instructional psychology. In M. R. Rosenzweig & L. W. Porter (Eds.), *Annual review of psychology* (Vol. 32, pp. 659–704).

Resnick, L. B. (1981b). Social assumptions as a conflict for science: Some reflections on psychology and education. *Educational Psychologist, 16*(1), 1–10. [University of Pittsburgh, Learning Research and Development Center, LRDC Reprint Series 1981/18.]

Resnick, L. B. (1982). Syntax and semantics in learning to subtract. In T. P. Carpenter, J. M. Moser, & T. A. Romberg (Eds.), *Addition and subtraction: A cognitive perspective* (pp. 136–155). Hillsdale, NJ: Erlbaum.

Resnick, L. B. (1983). A developmental theory of number understanding. In H. P. Ginsburg (Ed.), *The development of mathematical thinking* (pp. 109–151). New York: Academic Press.

Resnick, L. B., & Neches, R. (1984). Factors affecting individual differences in learning ability. In R. J. Sternberg (Ed.), *Advances in the psychology of human intelligence* (Vol. 2, pp. 275–323) Hillsdale, NJ: Erlbaum.

Resnick, L. B., & Omanson, S. F. (in press). Learning to understand arithmetic. In R. Glaser (Ed.), *Advances in instructional psychology* (Vol. 3). Hillsdale, NJ: Erlbaum.

Riley, M. S., Greeno, J. G., & Heller, J. I. (1983). The development of children's problem-solving ability in arithmetic. In H. P. Ginsburg (Ed.), *The development of mathematical thinking* (pp. 153–196). New York: Academic Press.

Rumelhart, D. E., & McClelland, J. L. (1981). Interactive processing through spreading activation. In A. M. Lesgold & C. A. Perfetti (Eds.), *Interactive processes in reading* (pp. 37–60). Hillsdale, NJ: Erlbaum.

Scardamalia, M., & Paris, P. (in press). The function of explicit discourse knowledge in the development of text representations. *Cognition and Instruction.*

Schank, R., & Abelson, R. (1977). *Scripts, plans, goals, and understanding: An inquiry into human knowledge structures.* Hillsdale, NJ: Erlbaum.

Segal, J. W., Chipman, S. F., & Glaser, R. (Eds.). (1985). *Thinking and learning skills: Relating instruction to research,* (Vol. 1). Hillsdale, NJ. Erlbaum.

Simon, H. A. (1976). Identifying basic abilities underlying intelligent performance of complex tasks. In L. B. Resnick (Ed.), *The nature of intelligence* (pp. 65–98). Hillsdale, NJ: Erlbaum.

Sleeman, D. (1982). Assessing aspects of competence in basic algebra. In D. Sleeman & J. S. Brown (Eds.), *Intelligent tutoring systems* (pp. 185–199). New York: Academic Press.

Snow, R. E. (1976). Research on aptitudes: A progress report. In L. S. Shulman (Ed.), *Review of research in education* (Vol. 4, pp. 50–105). Itasca, IL: Peacock.

Snow, R. E., Federico, P. A., & Montague, W. E. (Eds.). (1980). *Aptitude, learning, and instruction* (Vols. 1–2). Hillsdale, NJ: Erlbaum.

Spilich, G. J., Vesonder, G. T., Chiesi, H. L., & Voss, J. F. (1979). Text-processing of domain-related information for individuals with high and low domain knowledge. *Journal of Verbal Learning and Verbal Behavior, 18,* 275–290.

Steffe, L., Thompson, P., & Richards, J. (1982). Children's counting in arithmetical problem solving. In T. P. Carpenter, J. M. Moser, & T. A. Romberg (Eds.), *Addition and subtraction: A cognitive perspective* (pp. 83–97). Hillsdale, NJ: Erlbaum.

Stein, N. L., & Glenn, C. G. (1979). An analysis of story comprehension in elementary school children. In R. O. Freedle (Ed.), *New directions in discourse processing* (Vol. 2, pp. 53–120). Norwood, NJ: Ablex.

Stein, N. L., & Trabasso, T. (1983). What's in a story: An approach to comprehension and instruction. In R. Glaser (Ed.), *Advances in instructional psychology* (Vol. 2, pp. 213–267). Hillsdale, NJ: Erlbaum.

Sternberg, R. J. (1977a). Component processes in analogical reasoning. *Psychological Review, 84*(4), 353–378.

Sternberg, R. J. (1977b). *Intelligence, information processing, and analogical reasoning: The componential analysis of human abilities.* Hillsdale, NJ: Erlbaum.

Sternberg, R. J. (1980). Sketch of a componential subtheory of human intelligence. *Behavior and Brain Sciences, 3,* 573–584.

Sternberg, R. J., & Detterman, D. K. (Eds.). (1979). *Human intelligence: Perspectives on its theory and measurement.* Norwood, NJ: Ablex.

Svenson, O., & Broquist, S. (1975). Strategies for solving simple addition problems: A comparison of normal and subnormal children. *Scandinavian Journal of Psychology, 16,* 143–151.

Svenson, O., & Hedenborg, M. L. (1979). Strategies used by children when solving simple subtractions. *Acta Psychologica, 43,* 1–13.

Svenson, O., Hedenborg, M. L., & Lingman, L. (1976). On children's heuristics for solving simple additions. *Scandinavian Journal of Educational Research, 20,* 161–173.

Thibadeau, R., Just, M. A., & Carpenter, P. A. (in press). A model of the time course and content of reading. *Cognitive Science.*

Thorndike, E. L. (1922). *The psychology of arithmetic.* New York: Macmillan.

Thorndyke, P. W. (1977). Cognitive structures in comprehension and memory of narrative discourse. *Cognitive Psychology, 9*(1), 77–110.

Trabasso, T., Secco, T., & van den Broek, P. (1984). Causal cohesion and story coherence. In H. Mandl, N. L. Stein, & T. Trabasso (Eds.), *Learning and comprehension of text* (pp. 83–111). Hillsdale, NJ: Erlbaum.

Venezky, R. L., & Massaro, D. W. (1979). The role of orthographic regularity in word recognition. In L. B. Resnick & P. A. Weaver (Eds.), *Theory and practice of early reading,* (Vol. 1, pp. 85–107). Hillsdale, NJ: Erlbaum.

Vergnaud, G. (1982). A classification of cognitive tasks and operations of thought involved in addition and subtraction problems. In T. P. Carpenter. J. M. Moser, & T. A. Romberg (Eds.), *Addition and subtraction: A cognitive perspective* (pp. 39–59). Hillsdale, NJ: Erlbaum.

Voss, J. F. (1984). On learning and learning from text. In H. Mandl, N. L. Stein, & T. Trabasso (Eds.), *Learning and comprehension of text* (pp. 193–212). Hillsdale, NJ: Erlbaum.

Vygotsky, L. S. (1978). *Mind in society: The development of higher psychological process.* M. Cole, V. John-Steiner, S. Scribner, & E. Souberman (Eds. and Trans.). Cambridge, MA: Harvard University Press.

Wertsch, J. V. (1978). Adult-child interaction and the roots of metacognition. *Quarterly Newsletter of the Institute for Comparative Human Development, 1,* 15–18.

Woods, S. S., Resnick, L. B., & Groen, G. J. (1975). An experimental test of five process models for subtraction. *Journal of Educational Psychology, 67*(1), 17–21.

EVOLUTION OF LEARNING MECHANISMS

John Garcia is a professor of psychology and psychiatry at the University of California, Los Angeles. He was a farm-worker, a mechanic, and a soldier before entering the University of California, Berkeley at age 29. Employed by the U.S. Navy to research the effects of ionizing radiation, he published his first paper at age 39 and earned his PhD at age 48.

Controversy arose when Garcia and his associates discovered that animals were extremely radiosensitive, acting as if X-rays were odorous and poisonous. Their animals did not always obey the theoretical laws of associative learning. They remembered the cues that naturally went with reinforcing consequences and ignored the others. Noise went with shock, flavor went with poison, and odor went with either one depending on what the animal had in mind. Garcia contends that, although he is quite conventional, his animals often misbehave because their quirky brains are tuned to the urgencies of nature rather than to the regulations issued by ivy-covered learning labs.

Garcia was elected to the National Academy of Sciences. He received the Warren Medal from the Society of Experimental Psychologists and the Distinguished Scientific Contribution Awards from the American and the California Psychological Associations.

EVOLUTION OF LEARNING MECHANISMS

Seven Historic Principles of Learning

History is selectively recalled at each point in time according to the purpose of the day. Our purpose is to introduce seven scientific principles of learning that have endured over the last five centuries of psychological thought and study. Seven is the favored integer when professors are enumerating universal laws, basic ethics, or personal homilies. Miller (1956) discussed this human proclivity in a delightful paper entitled "The Magical Number Seven, Plus or Minus Two: Some Limits on Our Capacity for Processing Information." People tend to distinguish seven shades of gray and feel seven degrees of wonder. That integer nicely describes their span of apprehension and comfortably fills their capacity for short-term memory. Call seven the "psychobiological number" because this memory capacity must be the endpoint of a long evolutionary process of adaptation to this earth. Seven may not be the perfect capacity, because evolution does not strive for perfection; evolution is a blind process resulting from differential reproductive success due to biological variations among organisms.

John Garcia presented a Master Lecture at the 1984 APA Convention. The lecture was based on this paper, which he wrote in collaboration with his son, Rodrigo Garcia y Robertson, who earned a PhD in the history of science and technology at UCLA. Rodrigo is the father of Anneke Garcia y Beach, the infant girl described on page 11 and depicted in Figure 14. All the figures were drawn by John Garcia.

First, let us recommend an excellent source for those who enjoy reading the historic literature in psychology. Sahakian (1981) skillfully compiled and edited the writings of many philosophers and psychologists, creating a single coherent volume entitled *History of Psychology*. The excerpts in that book give the reader an insight into many important figures, beginning with ancient Greek and Latin philosophers, coursing through medieval scholars and Renaissance dissidents, and culminating with the evolutionists, the experimentalists, and the behaviorists. The book provides an exciting preview and a useful guide to the history of psychological thought.

The beginnings of modern learning theories can be traced to the writers of the European Renaissance who rejected the medieval notion of a soul oriented toward the deduction of heavenly wisdom and proposed instead an inductive, associationistic mind focused on earthly observations. In doing so, they set up the basic principles of learning that exist to this day. These writers were not giants nor are modern authors dwarfs, but following the reasoning of Juan Luis Vives, we become taller visionaries by adding their stature to our own, providing we do not throw away our advantage by prostrating ourselves before these famed authorities. Vives advised his students and colleagues to cease their disputations on antiquities and to study nature (Watson, 1915).

Because of our Spanish surname, readers might question our objectivity in citing Juan Luis Vives, a Catholic philosopher and educator born in Valencia, Spain. However, it was a Welsh scholar, Foster Watson (1915), who called Vives "The Father of Modern Psychology." Furthermore, Sahakian (1981) recorded Vives' birth in 1492 as a "landmark in Psychology," identifying his work, *De Anima et Vita,* as the precursor of "modern psychology." Zilborg (1941) described Vives as the humanitarian advocate of the first psychiatric revolution against demonology. Zilborg cited Vives' empirical advice for treatment of the insane as follows: "Remedies suited to the individual patients should be used. Some need medical care and attention to their mode of life; others need gentle and friendly treatment, so that like wild animals they may gradually grow gentle; still others need instructions" (1941, p. 188). This statement, which so resembles the "watching, wondering and taming procedures" for treating autistic children Tinbergen (1974) suggested in his Nobel Laureate address, was written about three centuries before Philippe Pinel began the final psychiatric revolution in France by providing medical treatment for demented human beings and removing their chains.

Vives is well known in Europe and Latin America, but he is an obscure figure in American psychology because of political and religious persecution. He was a member of the English court and a lecturer at Oxford, but because he was Spanish and Catholic he fell from favor during the divorce of Catherine of Aragon and Henry VIII and the schism between the Tudors and the Catholic popes. His humanistic writings were largely expurgated from English letters during the subsequent rivalry between Elizabeth I of England and Phillip II of Spain. Ironically, his father was persecuted in Spain for being a Jew, and Vives, who escaped from England to Flanders, never returned to his beloved Valencia (Watson, 1915, 1922).

Vives deserves a prominent place in the history of science for several reasons. First, he taught empiricism at Oxford two generations before Frances Bacon; moreover, Vives self-consciously applied empiricism to human psychological problems in a way that Bacon did not. Empiricism was a radical transition from the prevailing medieval viewpoint. For example, Saint Augustine, discussing the soullike nature of mind, excluded from consideration all outside knowledge received through the senses of the body and began with the dictum that all minds know and are certain of themselves (see Sahakian, 1981, p. 16). In contrast, Vives wrote, "The senses are our first teachers in whose home our mind is enclosed" (in Watson, 1915, p. 344). Vives was not concerned with the essence of the soul, only with the practical manifestations of soul in mind and action. Furthermore, knowledge was of no value to Vives until it was applied to social problems (Watson, 1915, p. 344). Thus, Vives provides the basis for the first principle of learning: I. *Empirical analysis begins with the observations of nature and proceeds to explanation by inductive logic, then returns to nature for verification.*

Second, Vives analyzed the behavior of animals and people, as well as his own introspective memories and feelings. In his age, equating soulless animals with godlike humans was a courageous stand for a Church scholar. Nevertheless, Vives noted that if an animal is called and then treated kindly, subsequently it will run toward the caller readily. But if the animal is called and beaten, it will be frightened by the memory of the beating when it is called again. The same is true of people: When something joyful occurs in a certain place, pleasant memories of that place are formed, but if a sad event happens the memories of that place are sad. Vives recalled his own memories as a child eating cherries in Valencia while ill with a fever. "For many years afterwards," he said, "whenever I tasted fruit, I not only recalled the fever but also seemed to experience it again" (Watson, 1915, p. 334). This attention to a broad spectrum of evidence extending from the behavior of other living forms to self-reports implies the second principle of learning: II. *There is a continuity of mind and behavior among living organisms so that information obtained in observing one organism can be generalized to other organisms.*

Third, Vives formulated associationism two centuries before John Locke. According to this theory of mental chemistry that underlies all modern psychology, the mind is a recording system that stores and integrates mental elements. These discrete sensations, motives, and reactions emanating from the body are formed into compounds called ideas by the action of three basic laws of association, as follows: III. *Mental elements are associated (1) by their contiguity in time and space, (2) by their similarity to each other, and (3) by their cause and effect relational sequences.*

For Vives, as for most modern theorists, contiguity was the most important associative law. When two things have been perceived together, the appearance of one recalls the other to mind, he said. On recalling a place, a person recalls the people encountered there and the fears, emotions, and motives felt there. The various elements are welded together in the conscious stream of memory and thought (Watson, 1915).

Association by similarity hardly needs elaboration; it is represented in modern psychology by discrimination and generalization learning. Association by cause and effect can be viewed in two ways. It can be viewed physicalistically, as it was by David Hume (1739/1969), who argued that it could not be distinguished from association by contiguity. But Hume rejected feelings from his analysis; psychologically, cause and effect comes from feelings of causality. The association expressed by Vives, when he said each time he tasted cherries he seemed to feel the fever again, is an example of association by cause and effect, now known as the Law of Effect.

Vives suffered obscurity in modern textbooks, but Locke suffered a worse fate, distortion and defamation. He is often depicted as the originator of the ridiculous behavioristic idea known as the *tabula rasa,* which refers to the mind of a newborn babe as a blank slate that passively records external inputs. In truth, Locke was a brilliant physician with an astonishingly modern view of sensory integration and reflexive action. In our judgment, he is the outstanding physiological psychologist of his age or any other age. It is a humbling experience to read his *An Essay Concerning Human Understanding* (1690/1981), written three centuries ago; we have made so little progress since then (see Sahakian, 1981, pp. 32–34). Locke delineated two sources of knowledge, from which this principle is derived. IV. *The sensations induced by external objects and events are transmitted by the nerves to the sensorium, then the innate connections and operations of the body give rise to the reflections of the mind.*

Sensation and reflection foreshadowed stimulus and response as well as releasing signal and species-specific reaction. Locke knew that the mind and the body were inseparable. Over a century before, Johannes Muller (1838/1848) proclaimed the "doctrine of specific energies of nerves." Locke defined the doctrine and provided examples. He said, in effect, the following: V. *Sensations do not exist in external events and objects. Sensations are the effects produced in our receptors, nerves, and brains by external events. The external world is constructed for each organism by the organism itself.*

In discussing manna, a dried exudate of plants used as a medicinal purge, Locke (1690/1981) explained that the sensations of whiteness, sweetness, and illness did not exist in manna, but were the effects produced by manna on eye, palate, and gut, respectively. In an analysis employing the notion of kinetic energy as heat, he explained how a cool left hand and a warm right hand plunged into the same basin of tepid water sense warmth and coolness respectively at the same time. Obviously, the water cannot be both cool and warm. The opposing sensations of heat and cold must be due to changes in the motion of the tiny particles in the nerves, increasing in the left hand and decreasing in the right hand, caused by the intermediate motion of tiny particles in the water.

This example has broad implications for the comparative study of those organisms that have receptors and nerves different from our own. Locke (1690/1981) warned that in this vast universe there are many mansions occupied by different organisms, of whose mental faculties we have as little knowledge "as a worm shut up in one drawer of a cabinet, hath of the senses or the understanding of a Man" (p. 120). Therefore, generalization from one organism to another must be preceded by a comparative analysis of their sensory systems and their brains.

Locke scrubbed the theoretical mind clean of the accumulation of two millennia of Platonic rationalizations, but he enriched it with biological structure and function. He was a political rebel, disputing the heavenly knowledge dispensed by the religious hierarchy. He favored the civil rights of individuals over the divine rights of kings. Asked what distinguishes the mind of the king from that of the commoner, Locke replied, "Experience." How could a commoner acquire the knowledge to rule? Locke replied, "By observing." This thesis is presented in a most entertaining form by George Bernard Shaw in *Pygmalion* and in the musical comedy version of this play, *My Fair Lady,* in which a linguist turns a flower girl into a "princess" by educating her in aristocratic speech and manner, the behavioral manifestations of a royal mind.

The reply to Locke's theory of mind came in 1781 from Immanuel Kant (1781/1896), who conceded everything to empiricism except a few a priori intuitions that, he argued, must exist in the mind prior to any experience (see Sahakian, 1981, pp. 69–72). Kant is credited with two propositions that set the context for recording all phenomena in mind and memory and that provide the basis for the sixth and seventh principles of learning. VI. *An a priori appreciation of space is a necessary representation in mind that precedes perception of external objects.*

With this proposition Kant argued that although it is possible to imagine space without objects, it is impossible to imagine objects without space. Therefore, space is not determined by objects, but rather a sense of space is a necessary contextual condition for the perception of objects (see Sahakian, 1981, p. 69). Most organisms studied seem to be able to remember spatial arrangements of objects as if they acquire a cognitive map of their territory. Kant made a similar argument for a sense of time: VII. *An a priori appreciation of time is a necessary representation of mind that precedes perception of external events.*

Kant said that although it is possible to imagine time without events, it is impossible to imagine events without time. Therefore, time is not determined by a sequence of events, but rather a sense of time is a necessary contextual condition for the perception of events (see Sahakian, 1981, p. 71). It is also true that most animals seem to have cyclical functions that operate like biological clocks. Whether space exists prior to exploration, and whether biological clocks run free of external events, is open to question. However, it seems certain that a mature mind cannot function adequately without senses of space and time with which to categorize objects and events, however those senses may come into being.

The Seven Principles and The Biopsyche

Undergraduate studies refer to the dual major of biology and psychology as "biopsych;" thus the modern concept of mind could aptly be called the "biopsyche." Despite the protestations of the behaviorists, we doubt if anyone is really interested in behavior per se. Everyone is interested in behavioral indicators of those central states of motivation and memory that give rise to the characteristic habitual patterns of an individual or of a species. The central nervous system, principally the brain, is the structure of the biopsyche in humans. The functional biopsyche is the brain in action. Brain structure and function represent a single inseparable product of evolution.

Evolution is a divergent process driven by variation of structure and function. Theoretically, all forms of life emerged from a single form because of biological variation. The varying individuals fanned out upon this earth to find ecological niches best suited to their idiosyncracies of structure and function in a process called *adaptive radiation.*

The ecological niche is an important, yet circular, concept because the niche cannot be described without recourse to the organism filling it. No biologist would ever have conceived of an ecological niche composed of a low winter territory in India and a high summer territory in Tibet joined by a long narrow flight path arching above the world's highest mountains, yet this is the niche created by the bar-head goose. Conversely, the special structures and functions of any organism cannot be understood without recourse to the ecological niche in which the organism evolved. To traverse the distant regions of its niche, the bar-head goose has acquired the brain capacity to navigate over "the hump" of the world and the cardiopulmonary capacity to fly at 30,000 feet, honking at every beat of its wings. When flying in the pressurized cabin of a jet plane, we often wonder how a warm-bodied creature, such as the bar-head goose, can survive in what is a cold, hostile environment to us. But the organism and its niche are two aspects of the same phenomenon, and the bar-head goose must be comfortable out there.

The Acquisition of Structure and Knowledge

Principle I refers to the general process of accumulating scientific knowledge through empiricial observation and arriving at tentative explanations through inductive logic. This dynamic method is also present in nature. As Lorenz (1965) pointed out, the acquisition of specialized anatomical structure through evolution and the acquisition of individual knowledge through experience are similar empirical, inductive processes: First, by individual death and survival, a species acquires the specialized structure enabling it to survive in its niche. Therefore, adaptive structure represents eons of ecological information accumulated through natural selection and encoded into the genome for transmission to succeeding generations. Second, by failure and success, each individual acquires information about the vagaries of its particular niche and encodes it into memory for use when similar situations arise again.

Behavior is manifested at the juncture between the organism and its niche, and learning is an adjustive process that eases the misfits at that juncture. All organisms inherently possess the basic behavioral patterns that enable them to survive in their niches, but learning provides the fine tuning necessary for successful adaptation. Even fetal organisms learn. For example, if a rat fetus is presented with lemon flavor while it is in the uterus, it will show a higher preference for lemon-flavored nipples on its mother after it is born. If a flavor presented to the fetus is followed by a mild toxicosis in utero, the newborn rat will display a reduced preference for a nipple marked with that flavor (Kolata, 1984; Pedersen, Williams, & Blass, 1982; Smotherman, 1982; Stickrod, Kimble, & Smotherman, 1982).

Newborn human infants demonstrate inherent wisdom concerning food and flavor. Tickle a baby's cheek with a cotton swab, and the baby will turn its head and engulf the swab in its mouth though it has never eaten before. If the swab is bitter, the baby will grimace and thrust out its tongue as if it knows that bitter is the natural signal for poison. If the swab is sweet, the baby will suck with a benign expression as if it knows that sweet signifies nutritious calories (see Garcia & Hankins, 1975; Garcia, Rusiniak, Kiefer, & Bermudez-Rattoni, 1982). This inherent human preference can be modified in utero, as the rat data indicate.

This conjecture is almost certainly true because infants of both species have the required homologous brain structures, and rat infants are less developed than human infants at birth.

In the first few days of life, the human infant demonstrates a preference for its mother's voice over another woman's voice and for its mother's heartbeat over its father's voice. The infant also prefers to listen to a poem it heard in the womb, as its mother read it, than to another poem with a different meter when both poems are read by its mother. These preferences have been determined by allowing babies to select what they want to hear by sucking in different patterns on non-nutritive rubber nipples (DeCasper & Fifer, 1980; Kolata, 1984). Certainly the newest member of our family was far from helpless at birth. She immediately created her niche, eliciting a maternal embrace and attaching herself to her mother's breast. At seven months, she has developed vocalizations and expressive movements to enthrall her parents and grandparents and smiles to reward them for assisting her to achieve her ends. For example, establishing eye contact with her grandfather, she made authoritative sounds from the back of her throat before picking the forbidden eyeglasses out of his shirt pocket. Then, forestalling him with another stern "declaration," she began chewing on the ear bows. So meaningful were her intonations and so exquisite was her timing that, without uttering a single word, she effectively argued her rights to expropriate his glasses.

Nature and Nurture

In discussions of children's development, the nature–nurture argument inevitably arises, usually phrased in the following form: Which is more important, heredity or environment? Attempts to answer the question employ simple statistical formulations, such as $V_H^2 + V_E^2 = 1$, which means that the variance in a trait can be divided into a hereditary component (V_H^2) and an environmental component (V_E^2). Ponder this equation for a moment. If V_E^2 decreases, then V_H^2 must increase, and vice versa. Furthermore, either component can be reduced to zero. Such a statistical function makes no biological sense.

Of course, the people who use such formulations say that these are merely simplifying assumptions dealing with the relative variance in measured traits of groups. These people also say that the reasonableness of the assumptions varies with the particular application and that the resulting proportions obtained from groups cannot be meaningfully applied to any individual. Nevertheless, the pronouncements issued following these statistical studies usually sound like value judgments with definite implications for social policy. Indubitably, there are genetic differences between groups of people, but because scientists cannot predict the future with much precision, they cannot tell which genetic variants, if any, will prove more adaptive in the long run.

The hereditary and environmental influences are so completely intermingled that it is impossible to determine to what degree either influence is responsible for any structure or trait displayed by an organism. As we have already pointed out, the genome itself can be considered the results of an accumulation of interactions between heredity and environment. Furthermore, from the zygote stage through every step of development, the living organism is the result of a series of interactions, as the genetic code is expressed on an environmental substrate by biochemical reactions, much as an image is developed on a photographic plate. Change the light striking the emulsion and the picture changes; change the emulsion receiving the light and the picture changes. Which is more important pictorially, light or emulsion?

Arguments on nature versus nurture remind us of how Pudd'nhead Wilson got his name (Twain, 1893, p. 16). Listening to a dog yelping, snarling, howling, and making a disagreeable nuisance of itself, Wilson said,

> "I wish I owned half of that dog."
> "Why?" somebody asked.
> "Because I would kill my half."

The group that heard Wilson's comments retired to discuss him in privacy. Obviously, it did not matter biologically if Wilson meant to kill his end of the dog as opposed to the other person's end or if he meant to kill his half-interest in the general dog. However, in the latter case, it would be more difficult to determine legally whose half he had killed. Finally, the puzzled group deemed him a fool and thereafter called him "Pudd'nhead."

Pervasive Ecological Influences

Large organisms resemble each other, in part because they all share a common ancestor, and in part because they have been shaped by the same general environmental forces, such as oxygen, temperature, and gravity. By "large organisms," we mean minnows, shrews, and hummingbirds, as well as sharks, elephants, and ostriches. Most insects are also large. Minute organisms occupying mansions where surface tension and fluid viscosity are greater impediments to movement than gravity are excluded from this discussion, although the remote ancestor of all large organisms must have been a tiny cell living in such a world. Minute organisms are excluded because, as Locke said, we have little knowledge about the universe in which they cope.

Five of the seven principles of learning can also be considered pervasive external influences on all large organisms. Two of the principles, IV (senses and reflexes) and V (neural transduction), deal with the internal structures common to all large organisms. We have already made the case for the pervasive influence of Principle I (empiricism) when we discussed the inductive logic of natural selection and of individual experience. We also made the case for Principle II (continuity of life) when we discussed fetal learning in the rat and human. It is intuitively obvious that Principle VI (space) and Principle VII (time) are relevant to all organisms.

Let us now consider the pervasive influences of Principle III (associationism). If two objects are close together in space, or if two noises are heard in quick succession, it is probably safer to assume they are connected than to assume they are separated. Thus, association by contiguity has a degree of ecological validity for all large organisms. If two objects look or feel the same, it is probably safer to treat them the same than to treat them differently. Therefore, association by similarity is an adaptive process acquired by all large organisms through natural selection. If a stimulus such as taste is followed by a sensation such as illness, it is adaptive to consider the stimuli as cause and effect. The same can be said for a noise followed immediately by a painful insult to the skin; it is adaptive to run or hide when that noise is heard again.

Associative learning and acquired habits played a critical role in Darwinian theory from its inception, as is illustrated in Figure 1. Charles Darwin's (1871/1936) volume on the origin of species contains numerous examples of the coevolution of plants and animals. The common example is blossoms and honey bees. Bees go from flower to flower, collecting nectar and delivering fertile pollen as they do so. This process becomes marvelously complex as plants evolve special visual signals to beckon certain bees and special mechanisms such as a lock on the "nectar cabinet" that can be tripped effectively by heavy bumblebees. Thus bumblebees are encouraged to specialize in specific blossoms, making them efficient pollinators of particular plant species. Since Darwin's time scientists have learned that bees are tiny learning machines capable of associating arbitrary signals with food under artificial experimental conditions. For general references on the coevolution of animals and plants, see Alcock (1979) and Gilbert and Raven (1980).

Lamarck, Darwin, and the Giraffe's Neck

Learning may be a causal factor in evolution. That is, the capacity to associate sequences and patterns of events in time and space, and to retain this information, may have given rise to the differentiation of modern animals from common primal ancestors. This is an old idea

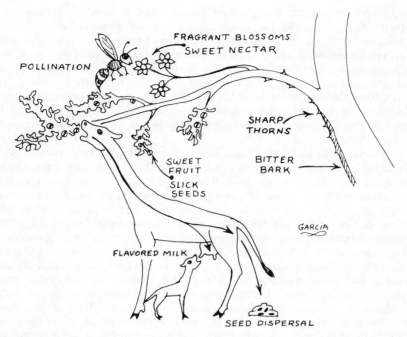

Figure 1. Darwin's associationism: The fruit tree as an S-S conditioning program. The tree has sharp thorns and bitter bark to protect its vital structures from browsers. With fragrant blossoms, it signals bees that sweet nectar is available, and the bee carries its pollen to a similar blossom in another tree of the same species. Fruit is a combination of nutritious pulp and slick indigestible seeds. The animal digests the pulp and drops the seed in far-off places. The tree benefits because animals learn. Mammals acquire preferences for certain foods, food flavors the milk, thus the offspring acquires a preference for the same food as the mother. In the case of the giraffe, an acquired preference for the leaves of tall trees may have set the stage for natural selection of long necks.

considered a heresy in modern biology, and it is attributed to Jean Baptiste de Lamarck, who published a theory of evolution in 1801 (1801/1970). Lamarck believed that differentiation of animal forms arose out of the use or disuse of organs during adaptation to the environment. Through habitual exercise, some organs were developed and some were neglected; these acquired characteristics were passed on to the next generation. He described the giraffe's neck as an example of the effects of habitual use on specific structure.

Fifty years later, Darwin (1871/1936) used the same example of Lamarckian evolution in *The Origin of Species:* For some unknown reason, the primal ancestor of the modern giraffe began browsing on the leaves of tall trees. In hard times when leaves were scarce, the individuals stretching their necks the longest survived and passed this acquired characteristic to their progeny. "By this process," wrote Darwin, "... combined no doubt in a most important manner with the inherited effects of the increased use of parts, it seems to me almost certain that an ordinary hoofed quadruped might be converted into a giraffe" (p. 161). Now Darwin is credited for establishing Darwinian evolution and Lamarck is discredited for proposing Lamarckian evolution, which proves that science as well as mythology needs its heroes and its heretics clearly delineated.

Darwin was not wrong in cribbing from Lamarck; he simply lacked detailed knowledge of the way in which characteristics were transmitted from one generation to another, though he made some shrewd guesses foreshadowing two types of inheritance mechanisms, genes and habits. Ironically, at the very time he was engrossed in this problem of transmission, Gregor Johann Mendel (1865/1959) was establishing the principles of genetic transmission, working with flowering sweet peas in a monastery garden in Monrovia. Ultimately, this new science indicated that the habits of animals have no direct effect on their genes. In the case of the giraffe, the genetic changes that resulted in long necks were random, like the toss of dice, and the lucky giraffes who got the long necks survived and passed their genes on to their offspring. Environmental pressure, operating blindly and mechanistically through gene selection, encoded information about a way of life into the anatomical structure of the giraffe.

However, genetic mechanisms are not the only mode of transmission from parents to offspring. Learning is another mode, as Lamarck and Darwin foresaw. Consider again the ancient quadruped munching on the leaves of tall trees. During consumption, sensors on the tongue sent taste information, and sensors lower down in the gut sent nutritional information to the brain. Midbrain mechanisms increased the palatability of leaves from tall trees so that the animal acquired the habit of eating such leaves. The diet of the mother flavored her milk so the acquired preference was transmitted to her young, and thus the stage was set for the competition wherein the length of the neck was a crucial factor (see Figure 1).

As we have explained, natural selection and associative learning operate together. Bitter is the natural signal for poison, and any animal insensitive to bitter is at risk. This risk is reduced if the animal nibbles at new foods and is able to associate bitter flavor with mild toxicosis. Sweet is the natural signal for highly caloric nutrients, and an animal insensitive to sweet is also at a disadvantage, but it also can compensate for this deficiency by associative learning mechanisms. A wide variety of animals, including neonate rats and humans, have the inherent predispositions toward food selection and the associative food-effect mechanisms directed to the same end.

Three Modern Conditioning Theories

As the 19th century turned into the 20th century, Darwin, Pavlov, and Thorndike put forth modern conditioning theories. All three theories were based on the seven principles of learning in general, and on associationism in particular. They were modern theories, which is to say the word *stimuli* replaced *sensations* and the word *responses* replaced *reflections*. Also, habits replaced ideas as psychological compounds, theorizing and hypothesis testing replaced introspection, and experimentation and data collection resolved arguments.

Darwin, Pavlov, and Thorndike did not compete with each other by offering alternative explanations for the same set of facts. Each theory dealt with a different data base and was compatible with the other two. All three theories focused on feeding behavior and invoked biological adaptation and associations in their explanations. The theories can be viewed as explaining three phases of the feeding process. Thorndike explained how the organism copes with the problem of obtaining food. This instrumental phase begins when food is placed beyond a barrier of time and space and ends when the food is accessible to the animal. Pavlov explained how food is utilized. This consummatory phase begins when food-related stimuli elicit anticipatory oral responses and ends when food is ingested. Darwin was interested in the ultimate effects of the food chain. The ultimate adaptive phase begins with prey coloration and predator reactions and ends with natural selection.

Darwin and the Gaudy Caterpillar

Darwin's hypothetical-deductive learning model antedated the classical conditioning and instrumental conditioning theories by nearly a half century (Garcia & Hankins, 1975). Darwin was interested in the adaptive value of camouflage. Cryptic form and coloration is a popular defense against predators in the natural world, as it is against the enemy in human warfare. Yet some caterpillars flaunt their brilliant colors on the tips of bare twigs and catch the eye of every passing bird. These facts placed a severe burden on Darwin's theory of adaptation through natural selection. He presented his dilemma to his coevolutionist A. R. Wallace and then recorded Wallace's hypothesis:

> From such considerations Mr. Wallace thought it probable that conspicuously-coloured caterpillars were protected by having a nauseous taste; but as their skin is extremely tender, and as their intestines readily protrude from a wound, a slight peck from the beak of a bird would be as fatal to them as if they had been devoured. Hence, as Mr. Wallace remarks, "distastefulness alone

would be insufficient to protect a caterpillar unless some outward sign indicated to its would-be destroyer that its prey was a disgusting morsel." Under these circumstances it would be highly advantageous to a caterpillar to be instantaneously and certainly recognized as unpalatable by all birds and other animals. Thus the most gaudy colours would be serviceable, and might have been gained by variation and the survival of the most easily-recognized individuals. (Darwin, 1896, p. 668)

Wallace presented his hypothesis to the Entomological Society of London in 1866. Twenty years later, E. B. Poulton (1887) reviewed the evidence substantiating a theory of conditioned taste aversions in a remarkable 83-page paper entitled "The Experimental Proof of the Protective Value of Color and Markings in Insects in Reference to Their Vertebrate Enemies." He described how a food becomes aversive when it is followed by toxicosis in a chain of behavioral reactions. A few unpleasant experiences are sufficient to establish a prejudice against an insect and against any eatable species that resemble the noxious one.

Darwin (1896) summarized his own conclusion as follows:

> When the birds rejected a caterpillar, they plainly shewed, by shaking their heads, and cleansing their beaks, that they were disgusted by the taste. Three conspicuous kinds of caterpillars and moths were also given to some lizards and frogs, by Mr. A. Butler, and were rejected, though other kinds were eagerly eaten. Thus, the probability of Mr. Wallace's view is confirmed, namely, that certain caterpillars have been made conspicuous for their own good, so as to be easily recognized by their enemies, on nearly the same principle that poisons are sold in coloured bottles by druggists for the good of man. (p. 669)

This tradition of studying associative generalizations and discriminations in natural settings is still vigorous, as exemplified by the research of Brower (1969). Brower demonstrated that certain caterpillars feeding on toxic plants metamorphose into toxic monarch butterflies. He showed that bluejays that eat toxic monarch butterflies become sick and vomit; thereafter they avoid monarch butterflies and also viceroy butterflies, which are similar to monarchs in color and pattern (see Figure 2).

This Darwinian conditioning model and its related line of research is rarely presented as a model in texts and tomes of psychology, although it is well represented in biology volumes. However, it is a well-documented learning theory. Furthermore, it antedates the comparable conditioning theories of Pavlov (1903/1955) and Thorndike (1911) by several decades. Perhaps Darwin's theory was overlooked because the

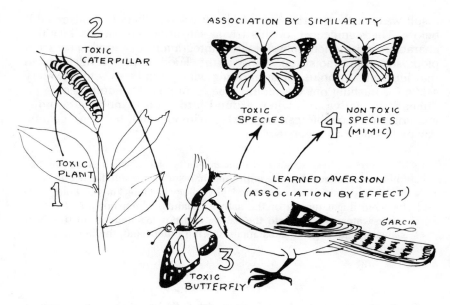

Figure 2. Brower's toxic ecology: A taste aversion is acquired in a natural setting and the effect spreads to visual cues. Through natural selection, the milkweed plant evolves a toxic defense against herbivores. The caterpillar consumes the leaves and sequesters the toxin in its exoskeleton for its own protection. The toxic caterpillar metamorphoses into a toxic monarch butterfly. The bluejay eats a toxic monarch and vomits, thus acquiring an aversive reaction to the taste and the visual patterns of the monarch. The bluejay also avoids the viceroy butterfly, which is similar to the monarch. Learning is embedded in ecology (based on Brower, 1969).

animal under investigation did not learn the association in question. The caterpillar merely carried the warning signals and the punishing noxious effects. The caterpillar's enemies, amphibians, reptiles, birds, and mammals, did the learning. Nevertheless, Poulton (1887) clearly delineated the mechanism of associative learning in his comprehensive paper.

Pavlov and the Drooling Dog

Pavlov focused on the neural mechanisms within the brain of a learning organism (Principles IV and V). In his classic experiment with dogs, the sound of a bell was immediately followed by the presentation of food. After repeated trials the dogs salivated whenever the bell rang. This result was hardly surprising, for as Pavlov said, others had observed it before. The significance of this trivial salivating act was its adaptive character and its neurophysiological integration. Dry food causes copious salivation; moist food causes little. Food induces a thick mucin that lubricates a bolus for swallowing; vinegar induces a thin, watery saliva for flushing out the mouth (see Figure 3). A smooth pebble induces little saliva, but when ground into sand it induces copious amounts, for a pebble can be ejected without fluid, but sand cannot. Pavlov (1903/1955) theorized:

> Here we have exact and constant facts—facts which seem to imply intelligence. But the entire mechanism of this intelligence is absolutely plain. On the one hand, physiology has long known about the centrifugal nerves of the salivary glands, which now chiefly cause water to enter into the saliva, and now accumulate in the saliva special organic substances. On the other hand, the internal

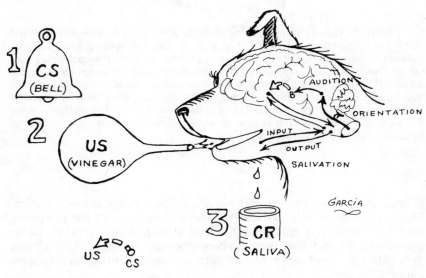

Figure 3. Pavlov's temporary connection. Pavlov selected a vinegar-like fluid to produce a reliable salivary reflex because he understood the neurology of that system. He selected an auditory stimulus (bell) because that stimulus caused the dog to pay attention (orient), but the bell did not cause the dog to salivate before training. After bell-vinegar training, the dog salivated at the sound of the bell. Pavlov argued that a new temporary connection had been established between the auditory system and the salivary system. That temporary brain process induced by learning was the critical issue in Pavlov's problem.

lining of the oral cavity consists of separate areas which act as receptors of different special stimuli—mechanical, chemical, thermal . . . [where] the specific centripetal nerves have their origin. (p. 386)

Pavlov was, after all, a Darwinian physiologist who wanted to study intellectual behavior in an objective way; brain mechanisms were absolutely plain, that is, clear of the obscurities of idealistic mentalism. Conditioning was a method of establishing a new temporary association in the biopsyche of the dog. Before conditioning, the dog salivated at food, but did not salivate at the bell; therefore, the brain center that received food stimuli controlled the salivary motor center and the auditory center did not. After conditioning, the dog salivated at the bell as if a new cortical pathway from the auditory center to the salivary center had been established by temporal contiguity (see Figure 3).

Thorndike and the Restless Cat

Like Pavlov, Thorndike was a Darwinian functionalist concerned with neurophysiological mechanisms, at least in the beginning. Consider his classic study: A cat was locked in a box containing a mechanical latch controlling the door. Food was outside. By accident, the cat tripped the latch, obtaining freedom and food. With repeated trials, the cat used the same response to free itself with increasing promptness. The cat's increasing skill was not surprising; it must have been observed eons earlier by neolithic pet owners, much as they also witnessed the anticipatory salivation of their dogs. But Thorndike had a theory based on the cause and effect sequences described in Principle III. He called it the Law of Effect. Of the various responses made in the closed box, the one closely followed by satisfaction to the animal becomes the response most firmly connected to the response elicited in the box situation. Describing satisfaction, Thorndike (1911) wrote,

The satisfiers for any animal in a given condition cannot be determined with precision and surety save by observation. Food when hungry, society when lonesome, sleep when fatigued, relief from pain, are samples of the common occurrence that what favors the life of a species satisfies its individual members. . . . The annoyers for any animal follow the rough rules that alterations of the animal's "natural" or "normal" structure—as by cuts, bruises, blows, and the like—and deprivations of or interference with its "natural" or "normal" activities—as by capture, starvation, solitude, or indigestion—are intolerable. (p. 245)

Thus, Thorndike paid his debt to Darwin, but he was troubled by exceptions to the survival rule. Humans learn many bad habits—drug abuse, alcoholism, and overeating to name a few—that do not promote survival. Thorndike (1911) explained:

> Upon examination it appears that the pernicious states of affairs which an animal welcomes are not pernicious *at the time, to the neurones.* We learn many bad habits, such as morphinism, because there is incomplete adaptation of all of the interests of the body-state to the temporary interests of its ruling class, the neurones . . . satisfaction and discomfort, welcoming and avoiding, thus seem to be related to the maintenance and hindrance of the life processes of the neurones rather than of the animal as a whole, and to the temporary rather than permanent maintenance and hindrance. (p. 245).

Like Pavlov, young Thorndike knew it is the mechanisms of the brain that control adaptation and intelligence. Neither survival of the species nor survival of the individual could explain self-destructive acts. His Law of Effect operated on the "selfish neurone" to the detriment of the whole organism at times.

These notions have an oddly modern ring. More recent research has shown that animals shock themselves repeatedly in the brain when electrodes are implanted in the septal region, as if specific neurones are being satisfied. Individual neurones respond to specifically complex precepts or numbers and pontifical neurones respond to categories and abstractions. Endogenous opiatelike endorphins and their antagonists are secreted by the central nervous system as well. Such agents may yet explain the deranged self-destruction that puzzled Thorndike.

Critique of Pure Behaviorism

In the beginning of the 20th century, the scientific study of learning sprang from a Darwinian view of natural selection and adaptive structure. Then about 30 years later, a schism occurred. A competitive theory was proclaimed. The psychology of learning was separated from biology and became "pure behaviorism." Pavlov's and Thorndike's systems were stripped of both their adaptive implications and their neurophysiological mechanisms. Charismatic theoreticians, such as Watson (1925), Spence (1947), and Skinner (1966), offered psychologists marvelously simple programs for controlling an animal's behavior without studying its natural ecological niche or its central nervous system.

The way that the behaviorists accepted the methods of Pavlov and Thorndike and stripped their systems of adaptive biology is reminiscent of the way in which the empirical philosophers created the mind by stripping the soul of its medieval metaphysical rationalizations. But in this case, the study of learning was denied the genuine benefits of unification with the other empirical life sciences. Nevertheless, psychologists decided to go it alone. It was a mistake, a great mistake, but mistakes are part of the learning process, so this one must be critically reviewed.

Eviscerating the Organism

This stripping process culminated in behavioral engineering. In a series of position papers and a book entitled *Behavior of Organisms,* Skinner (1938) offered a simple system for controlling behavior based on economic theory. As profit operated in a free market to produce the required goods and services, so reinforcement would act on a free organism to produce the required behavioral patterns. In this view, the organism had a repertoire of responses that it freely emitted, each at a given rate. In order to control the animal, Skinner applied a reinforcer immediately after the organism did what Skinner wanted it to do. The reinforcer increased the rate of the chosen response. If the organism did not do exactly what Skinner wanted, he reinforced the responses that were most similar to the target response. As the organism repeated the similar responses with some variation, Skinner (1959) reinforced those variants that were even more similar to the target response. Gradually, the organism's behavior was *shaped* in the direction of the target behavior, like clay in the hands of a sculptor, according to Skinner. The reinforcer was both a guide to what the experimenter wanted and a payoff for "correct" responding.

In order to clear the way for his new behaviorism, Skinner replaced the structured organism with an empty black box. He dismissed Pavlov's notions of an eliciting stimulus and its centripetal neurones and an evoked response with its centrifugal neurones. The reflex was emptied of any connotation of the active push of the stimulus and studied as an event appearing spontaneously with a given frequency. Skinner also preferred to speak of a response as an *operant,* stressing its operational effect on the environment rather than its intrinsic topography. For example, the important datum for a rat in Skinner's box was the excursion of the lever; it did not matter whether the rat depressed the lever with its left paw, its right paw, its chin, or its rump. All methods yielded the same environmental effect, the automatic advancement of the food delivery mechanism and the response counter. In fact, some professors covered the peekholes in their Skinner boxes so that their students' concentration on the response counters would not be disrupted by observations of the rats or the pigeons in action.

Emptying the Reinforcer

Thorndike's (1911) neural reinforcement was dismissed as well; Skinner's reinforcement worked on the whole organism without regard to internal hook-ups. The survival value of reinforcement and the satisfaction of the subject were of no concern. The reinforcer was simply defined by the following test: Any stimulus applied immediately after an emitted response that increased the frequency of that response was a reinforcer. Of course, no one applied this rule because it was too cumbersome. For example, some bats prefer the nectar of flowers and some prefer the blood of cattle. It is much simpler to find this out by observing bats in their natural habitats or examining their specialized oral structures than by empirically offering an unknown bat an endless series of foodstuffs. In practice, operant conditioners merely selected a pigeon or a rat, starved it 80 percent of its free-feeding weight, and offered it the standard laboratory fare.

The empirical rule for defining the reinforcer makes more sense in attempting to modify the behavior of inmates in a psychiatric ward. The therapist must carefully record the various responses of oddly behaving patients, noting the responses' frequencies. In doing so, the therapist learns a good deal about the patients (Juan Luis Vives would have approved). Then the therapist can arrange a contingency between a low-frequency response, for example, washing up and making the bed, and a high-frequency normal response, for example, shopping in the commissary, in order to modify a patient's behavior toward normalcy. But many patients are in the psychiatric wards because their idiosyncratic reinforcers are abnormal and cannot be applied ethically or legally. Other patients apparently respond to intrinsic reinforcement that cannot be metered out by the therapist. Skinner, in effect, buried too many psychological problems in the empirical reinforcement rule. His method was limited because it failed to address the nature of reinforcement and because it provided no hypotheses to explain modifying reinforcers.

Premack's (1965) probabilistic description of reinforcement completed the reduction of operant conditioning into a methodology empty of biological purpose. According to Thorndike's way of thinking, if a thirsty rat were placed in an activity wheel connected to a water spout, running responses would be reinforced by water, which would promote the rat's survival. A thirsty rat running to water seems natural, but Premack said that this sequence is arbitrary. He said water was neither a required substance nor a reinforcing stimulus. Running and drinking were simply two operants, each with an empirical probability of occurring depending on the situation arranged by the experimenter. If the experimenter deprived the rat of water, drinking would be more probable than running, and so the rat would run to drink. But, if the experimenter deprived the rat of exercise, the rat would drink in order to run. Premack demonstrated this phenomenon with drinking spouts connected to running wheels. Thirsty rats ran in the wheels in order to drink. Restless rats licked the water spout to unlock the running wheel. In a similar experiment, children who wanted candy played pinball games in order to eat, while children who preferred pinball games ate candy in order to play.

Thus, Premack eliminated the distinction between operants and reinforcers. Operant responses became the only behavioral elements, probabilities of occurrence were their essential properties, and contingency relationships established their associations. The system was as empty of biological properties as classical celestial mechanics (mass, velocity, gravity, time, and distance) was empty of geological properties. Pure behaviorism had reached its culmination.

Eliminating Biological Variation

Skinner also rejected biological variation as a necessary ingredient for learning theory. He rejected variation of responses displayed by a single organism saying, "I suggest that the dynamic properties of operant behavior may be studied in a single reflex" (1959, p. 2). He also rejected the importance of biological variation between species in the following oft-quoted passage (1959). Describing the similar response patterns of different animals in a Skinner box on a fixed-interval schedule, he said,

> Pigeon, rat, monkey, which is which? It doesn't matter. Of course these species have behavioral repertoires which are as different as their anatomies. But once you have allowed for differences in the ways in which they make contact with the environment, and in the ways which they act upon the environment, what remains of their behavior shows astonishingly similar properties. (p. 2)

Apparently, it did not occur to Skinner that any method that cannot distinguish among pigeons, rats, and monkeys has serious limitations or that species differences in behavioral repertoires and environmental contacts are the central concern of psychology.

Skinner selected pecking by the pigeon as the single reflex he would use to study the basic laws of operant behavior. It is necessary to describe his behavioral paradigm in some detail. A pigeon was starved until it was at 80% of its normal weight. It was placed in a Skinner box, which had a small translucent disk called the key. Whenever the key was illuminated, any depression of the key would activate a mechanical feeder, making grain available for a few moments on an experimental schedule. Note that Skinner's pigeon had to work for the food payoff, whereas Pavlov's dog was presented with bell and vinegar no matter how it behaved. This was a crucial difference between the two systems, or so it seemed. The Skinner box proved to be so convenient that all sorts of animals were placed in operant boxes—rats, cats, monkeys, and even dogs served as subjects.

Operant conditioning thrived for a while almost unchallenged. Complex "purposive" behavior directed at temporally and spatially distant goals was simulated by a chaining procedure in which operant elements were linked into long sequences. For example, a rat could be shaped into picking up a marble by immediate reinforcement. Subsequent training phases could shape the rat into carrying the marble to the foot of a stairs, then up a ladder, and so forth. Finally, the entire behavioral compound of picking up marbles, carrying them upstairs, and dropping them down a chute to operate a food delivery mechanism could be engineered. Innocent observers of the ultimate behavior sequence, unaware of the long history of shaping and chaining, might proclaim the rat's behavior to be purposive and intelligent, as they might also see purpose and intelligence in the mechanistic evolutionary process of random variation and natural selection. From a strictly Skinnerian point of view, intelligence and purpose are only a socially defined collection of operants in a chained sequence. Simply define those operants that you consider intelligent and reinforce them. This theory was put to practice in teaching machines and programmed courses of instruction.

The Return of Instinct

No sooner had the crowning touches been placed on the elegant and empty edifice of operant conditioning than Skinner's students and followers began to undermine its foundations. Keller and Marian Breland left the operant laboratory, well trained in shaping and chaining responses, to establish a business training animals for amusement parks and television commercials. In the main, they were successful, but they had some difficulties that posed serious problems for operant theory. For example, they conditioned a pig to put a large wooden coin, or token, into a slot in a bank. The token tripped a mechanism delivering food. In the beginning, the pig would quickly pick up a token and drop it in the bank, run back, pick up another token, bank it, and repeat the process until the food mechanism delivered reinforcement. After a few weeks, though, problems developed. The pig eagerly ran to pick up the token, but on the way to the bank it dropped the token, rooted it along the floor, and played with it before reluctantly depositing it in the bank. The operantly conditioned "middle-class" behavior was progressively replaced by piglike behavior that delayed, or eliminated, reinforcement, in direct contradiction with operant principles. Making the pig hungrier did not eliminate the "pig-headed" behavior. The same problem occurred with pig after pig. Each time, the Brelands found it simpler to train a new pig than to rehabilitate the old one.

In a similar way, operantly conditioned behavior in amusement displays was disrupted by natural behavior in species after species. Cats left the manipulanda to stalk the food slot. Raccoons refused to deposit their tokens in banks, rubbing and washing them instead. Chickens refused to operate the bat and pecked at the baseball. In the end, the Brelands turned away from arbitrary operants and reinforced natural acts instead: Scratching chickens were trained to "dance," and dabbling ducks were trained to "play the piano" with their bills, but their roles could not be easily reversed. Breland and Breland (1961) described their experiences in an article entitled "The Misbehavior of Organisms," obviously aimed at their mentor. Operantly engineered behavior, they said, drifted back toward the unconditioned behavioral repertoire of the species.

The Cat Behind the Glass Door

The return of instinct, now called *species-specific behavior,* to psychological explanations of learning is exemplified by two similar experiments separated by a third of a century. In the original version, Guthrie and Horton (1946) confined a cat in a puzzle-box behind a glass door. The glass door could be opened by jostling a vertical rod approximately 12 inches tall and 12 inches from the door. Cats placed in the box one after the other rubbed up against the rod and released themselves in a stereotypic manner.

Guthrie's explanation of the cats' behavior was an ingenious example of pure behaviorism: On the first trial, each cat eventually rubbed against the rod and was immediately released, so the cat made no further "box responses" to interfere with the memory of rubbing the rod. Upon return to the box, the cat retrieved the memory of the last "box response" and thus repeated the rubbing behavior. The box stimuli and the rubbing response were thus welded together by contiguity in time and space; the cat, lacking insight into the lever mechanism, repeated itself in a blind, superstitious manner. Guthrie offered this general explanation: The last coping response is always learned because reinforcement takes the organism out of the problem situation; food ends hunger responses, water ends thirst responses, and sex ends courting responses. Guthrie's hypothesis was not completely different from Premack's or Skinner's explanations.

Moore and Stuttard (1979) repeated the study with a slight variation. The rod was disconnected from the door so that the cats could not release themselves. Nevertheless, the cats rubbed the rod just as Guthrie and Horton's cats did many cat generations before. However, when Moore and Stuttard absented themselves from the cats' view, the cats stopped rubbing. When the experimenters returned, the cats rubbed on the rod again. The cats were greeting Moore and Stuttard as the prior cats had greeted Guthrie and Horton. Rubbing was neither learned nor reinforced in either experiment.

Moore and Stuttard pointed out that many members of *Felidae*, including lions, tigers, jaguars, ocelots, and domestic cats, display flank rubbing and head rubbing during greeting rituals and courtship. Typically, one cat moves sinuously past another, brushing the object of its affection with its back arched and tail held high. Alternatively, when the other cat is not within reach, the cat will rub itself sensuously against inanimate objects, such as vertical rods. Domestic cats will greet humans the same way, as if the humans were conspecifics. The behavior is one of those stereotypic patterns that can be used to phylogenetically classify organisms.

When a conditioning program runs counter to species-specific behavior, the animal may fail to perform even though it may learn the required association. For example, Brett (L. Brett, personal communication, 1976) attempted to increase the growling responses of a polar bear with food reinforcement. Polar bears growl menacingly to drive away competitors and rivals in the wild. When the bear began to associate Brett and food, it became understandably reluctant to growl and threaten its source of food. But it seemed to recognize that vocalizations were required. The confused animal made some strange sounds in its effort to cope. Failure to growl on cue was not an indication of failure to associate; to growl appropriately, the bear would have to be trained to control its emotions like a method actor.

The Pigeon's Dilemma in Skinner's Box

Ultimately, Skinner paid the price for dismissing Pavlovian mechanisms in an ironic way. As Moore (1973) effectively argued, the pigeon's key-peck was not a freely emitted operant, nor was it shaped by Skinner. The peck was a Pavlovian response evoked by the lighted key. Observations of pigeons with slow-motion film techniques indicated that, like Pavlov's dogs salivating at a conditioned stimulus, the pigeons were directing consummatory responses toward the lighted key. When the lighted key was paired with food, the pigeons pecked at the key as if it were grain. When the lighted key was paired with water, the pigeons acted as if they were trying to drink the key.

Brown and Jenkins (1968) altered the Skinner box in a simple yet theoretically significant way. They lit the key and then made the food available at a fixed time later, no matter what the pigeon did. The bird did not have to work the key but could simply eat the food. Actually this was a Pavlovian arrangement; the key light was the conditioned stimulus (CS) that elicited orientation, and food was the unconditioned stimulus (US) that elicited pecking, the unconditioned response (UR). As Pavlov would have predicted, the pigeon first pecked at the food, but after repeated light-food pairings it began to peck at the lighted key, just as Pavlov's dog came to salivate at the bell paired with food. Pecking the key was a conditioned response (CR).

Staddon and Simmelhag (1971) gave their pigeons free grain every 12 seconds regardless of the pigeons' behavior. Nevertheless, the pigeons oriented towards the feeder and pecked at the nearby wall even though no such response was required. After a time the pigeons demonstrated temporal discrimination, pecking at the end of each 12-second interval, when grain was imminent. The general phenomenon, called *autoshaping* as opposed to *experimenter shaping,* was verified in other species.

Williams and Williams (1969) took autoshaping one step further; they withheld reinforcement whenever their pigeons pecked the lighted key. That is, grain was not presented if a pigeon pecked at the key, but grain was presented if the pigeon refrained from pecking the lighted key. Many pigeons continued to peck at the key for hundreds of trials. Pigeons are not stupid; their pecking response is as involuntary as a dog's salivary response, or a human's for that matter. Consider yourself to be the subject of such an omission-training autoshaping experiment: You are ravenously hungry, I show you a plate of your favorite food, and all you have to do in order to eat is to refrain from salivating!

The pigeon is a marvelously adaptive creature capable of making fine discriminations. It can cope with time and distance, displaying a sophisticated learning capacity for navigation as it forages for food and returns to its loft. But once it begins to eat, plasticity is limited. As illustrated in Figure 4, a seed offers the pigeon in its natural niche (1) the occasion to peck, (2) the target to peck, and (3) the reinforcement for pecking. The Skinner box breaks up that natural event into three arbitrary components. The light signals the occasion, the key provides the target, and the food cup provides the reinforcement for pecking. When these three factors are clustered in close spatiotemporal proximity, as they were in the original Skinner box, the pigeon adapts effectively. But if the three factors are widely separated, the pigeon is relatively helpless. It simply cannot watch for a signal in one place, peck at a different place, and receive its food in yet another place. The seed in its natural niche has been pulled apart far beyond the pigeon's capacity to adapt.

The degree of learning involved in instrumental responses at the beginning of a behavioral sequence and the consummatory reactions ending the sequence in the pigeon was discussed by Craig (1917) long before the advent of operant conditioning as follows:

> An appetite is accompanied by a certain *readiness to act.* When most fully predetermined, this has the form of a chain reflex. But in the case of most supposedly innate chain reflexes, the reactions

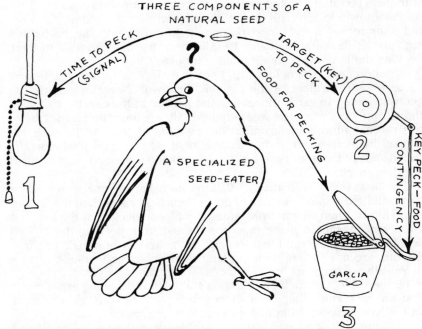

THREE COMPONENTS OF A
NATURAL SEED

Figure 4. The pigeon's dilemma in Skinner's automated box. In the natural world, the seed provides the signal to peck, the target to peck, and the reward for pecking. As long as these three components are clustered together in one place, the pigeon is effective. However, the pigeon finds it extremely difficult to look at one signal and to peck at another target in order to get food at a third place. If the signal is presented on the target, the pigeon will readily peck at the signal-target, but it has difficulty in learning not to peck at the signal-target in order to obtain food. If the signal-target and food delivery are paired, with the keypeck-food contingency disconnected, the bird will peck at the signal-target nevertheless. When food is imminent, the hungrey pigeon pecks just as the hungry dog salivates (based on Moore, 1973).

> of the beginning or the middle part of the series are not innate, or
> not completely innate, but must be learned by trial. The end action
> of the series, the consummatory action, is always innate. (p. 92)

The Selective Pressure of the Food Chain

Darwin noted that everything that is born is bound to eat—and to be eaten. Plants are eaten by herbivores, herbivores are eaten by carnivores, and carnivores are eaten by scavengers. The wastes from feeding and dying return to feed the plants. The food chain is like a vast fabric that includes bacteria, biting insects, internal parasites, and dung beetles as well as the larger animals. To forestall extinction, each animal must delay the final alternative until it has eaten and reproduced; thus, the food chain exerts a powerful selective pressure on the evolution of corporal structure, instinctive behavior, and learning mechanisms.

Even plants resist being eaten, employing germicides, pesticides, and appetite suppressors. Many herbivorous insects utilize plant poisons for their own defense, as illustrated in Figure 2. Humans also utilize plant toxins for their own purposes. Quinine and other alkaloids are extracted from the bitter cinchona bark of trees and introduced into human blood to help people resist the ravages of malarial parasites. The substance digitalis, extracted from the genus of herbs (*Digitalis*) including foxglove, contains important glycosides and serves human cardiovascular patients as a heart stimulant. The glycosides serve the herbs by turning off the appetites of herbivores. Caffeine is extracted from coffee beans and used to suppress appetite and promote diuresis in those wishing to retain a slim, fashionable figure. Caffeine is also used to excite the central nervous system, acting as an antidepressant. In nature, it may make an animal too excited to eat. Because the most common complaint of those who stop smoking is that they gain weight, one can infer that nicotine in tobacco also probably works to excite nervous activity and suppress appetite. In addition, humans use nicotine as an insecticide, and nicotine also serves this function in plants. Natural herbs are used all over the world for medicinal purposes, but it must be remembered that herbal chemicals evolved to promote the survival of the herbs; they are not nature's gift to humans.

All this chemical warfare in the plant kingdom and in the first links of the food chain presents the intermediate feeders with food selection problems. Meanwhile, larger predators always on the hunt for meat pose a second safety problem for the feeders caught in the middle. All species occupy this vulnerable intermediate position in the food chain, or occupied it at some point in their phylogeny. In a similar way, all individuals occupy the same middle position, or occupied it at some point in their ontogeny. Thus, all animals have evolved two defense systems, one to protect their gut from poison and the other to defend their skin from predators (Garcia, Forthman Quick, & White, 1984; Garcia, Lasiter, Bermudez-Rattoni, & Deems, in press).

Body and Brain

The dichotomous structure of the feeder in the middle is illustrated in Figure 5. A salamander is represented, but all vertebrates possess the same general body plan. The gut for processing food, essentially a long tube lined with sensors and fitted with sphincters at both ends, occupies a ventral position in the body. Digestion is a comparatively sluggish process attended by glandular secretions and actions of smooth muscles. The taste receptors at the oral end of the tube provide the CS by chemical analysis of the food. The visceral receptors of the midgut report on the effects of the food, thus providing the US. If the food is bitter it is usually rejected at the mouth. If a toxin enters the system, it may be ejected by vomiting or speeded on its way out by diarrhea. Gut defense is only one subsystem within the larger homeostatic system protecting the internal environment.

Similarly, skin defense is one subsystem within the greater system designed to cope with the external environment. Skin defense is essentially a motor system designed for escape, replete with early-warning

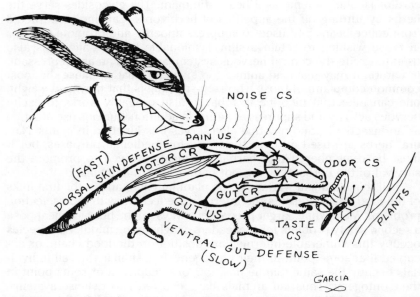

Figure 5. Herrick's salamander: To eat or to be eaten? This drawing depicts natural selection pressure inherent in the food chain and its effect upon the body and brain of the salamander and other vertebrates. The brain is divided into two systems. Distal noises and proximal insults protect the skin against predatory attack. The output from these mechanisms converge to dorsal brain mechanisms engaging striated muscular reactions of avoidance and escape. Food taste and visceral feedback from consumption converge to mechanisms in the ventral regions of the brain where taste preferences are established commensurate with food effects. The output from this system flows to the smooth muscles of the gastrointestinal tract. Olfaction (and vision) can be used in either the dorsal or ventral systems (based on Herrick, 1948).

alarms and proximal damage sensors located in the dorsal position. Since the attack of the predator is sudden and swift, skin defense is characterized by fast motor reactions of striated muscles. Although vision and olfaction provide excellent distal cues, they tend to be directional and possess blind spots. In most vertebrates, audition is the principal warning system, picking up signals from all around the organism and remaining on guard during rest and sleep. It is no accident that modern burglar alarms emit noisy vibrations and that public buildings have visual signs to point to escape routes.

The mouth plays a pivotal role in both external and internal systems. After the vertebrate feeder arises from its rest, its first reaction is to examine its immediate surroundings for danger. If all is well, the animal forages for food in the external world. Food thus acts as a Thorndikian reinforcement for the instrumental phase of the feeding sequence. Feeding cues act as CSs and food in the mouth acts as a Pavlovian US in the consummatory phase. In the third, homeostatic or Darwinian phase, food in the mouth acts as a CS and the effects of food on the gut act as the US. The homeostatic US can operate in both directions; toxin is a negative US and nutrition is a positive US.

The dorsal-ventral duality so obvious in the vertebrate body is also reflected in the organization of the brain. Herrick (1956) described it most eloquently:

> Precise localization of function stops at this place where the peripheral nerve fibers make contact with the central nerve cells in a dense feltwork of interlaced fibers, termed neuropil. One of these pools—the visceral sensory neuropil associated with the fasciculus solitarius—receives all fibers of gustatory and general visceral sensibility and discharges into the visceral motor mechanisms. The other pool—the somatic sensory neuropil—receives fibers of all types of cutaneous and deep sensibility that are concerned with adjustment to the external environment, i.e., the exteroceptive and proprioceptive systems of Sherrington's analysis. This neuropil discharges into somatic motor apparatus that controls the movements of the skeletal system.
>
> This segregation of all sensory nerve fibers, except those of vision and olfaction, into only two receptive centers is the only well-defined localization of sensory functions present in the medulla oblongata. It corresponds with the fundamental difference in behavior between internal visceral activities and somatic sensorimotor activities that have an external reference. The visceral movements are for the most part of total pattern type. This is as true in men as in salamanders. Accordingly, there is little more specialization or separate localization of function in the fasciculus solitarius neuropil of men than of salamanders. (pp. 245–246)

Prey and Predator

Some odd behavior results when incompatible conditioning has taken place in the external and internal systems of a wild predator. Figure 6 provides an example of a confused wolf. Several days before, the wolf was given a "mutton burger" containing capsules of lithium chloride. The wolf bolted down everything. The wolf did not smell or taste the lithium chloride, which was enclosed in tasteless capsules that were swallowed whole. The mutton burger smelled and tasted like a sheep, but did not look like a live sheep. About a half hour later, the wolf became sick and vomited, then recovered rapidly (Gustavson, Kelly, Sweeney, & Garcia, 1976).

Several days later a sheep was let into the wolf's compound. The hungry wolf charged eagerly, ears up and tail carried high like a cavalier's plume. It went for the throat, burying its muzzle in the wool of its prey, then abruptly broke off the attack. Circling its potential victim, the wolf attempted a hamstring attack, but again it recoiled as soon as it made contact. Then, continuously orienting to the sheep, the wolf

Figure 6. The wolf's dilemma after toxicosis. Previously, the wolf was given some mutton laced with lithium chloride. About a half an hour later, it retched and vomited. When confronted by its customary prey, the wolf was attracted by the visual aspects of a possible meal, but repelled by the odor and taste of the sheep. As a result of this conflict, the behavioral attack pattern of this canid species was replaced by another species-specific pattern, that is, an invitation to play (based on Gustavson, Kelly, Sweeney, & Garcia, 1976).

circled again and again, obviously reluctant to close in on its prey. As the hour-long test wore on, the distance between the predator and its prey increased, and the behavior of both animals changed dramatically. The sheep began to make short charges, lowering its woolly head as if it bore horns. The wolf dodged and made submissive species-specific gestures. It bowed the way canine puppies bow, head and thorax on the group, rump in the air, inviting the sheep to play (see Figure 6). It never attacked again. When a rabbit was introduced into the pen, the wolf immediately killed and ate it. After feeding, the wolf no longer paid attention to the sheep, acting as if its former prey no longer existed.

As a result of the mutton–lithium treatment, the wolf had acquired an aversion for the odor and taste of the sheep, but no aversion for the sight of the sheep, presumably because the poisoned mutton did not look like the living sheep. The wolf was in conflict, visually attracted to the sheep but repelled by its odor and taste. The wolf resolved the conflict by treating its former prey as a dominant conspecific. Social play behavior displaced attack behavior. When the wolf's hunger was satisfied by rabbit flesh, the curious social contract between prey and predator was dissolved; the wolf ignored the sheep and the sheep ignored the wolf. Another wolf tested at the same time responded in the same way (Gustavson et al., 1976).

Figure 7 provides an example of the curious behavior of avian predators poisoned after eating the flesh of their natural prey (Brett, Hankins, & Garcia, 1976). In contrast to the wolf, the hawk normally searches for prey with its keen vision from high in the air, then swoops to kill with taloned feet, never tasting the prey in the instrumental phase. In captivity, the broad-winged hawks used in this experiment were normally fed white mice as a necessary part of their diet. On conditioning trials, the first hawk was given a black mouse and later injected with a lithium chloride solution. Because the hawk was accustomed to eating mice it had no discriminatory taste cue for the injected poison, but it had an excellent visual cue. Several days later, when the hawk was tested with black and white mice, it ate them both with no sign of discrimination. When two more black-poison conditioning trials were imposed, the hawk refused both black and white mice. The hawk had a taste aversion for mouse flesh but no visual aversion for black mice.

A second hawk was conditioned the same way except that the black mouse was dipped into a mildly bitter solution. The hawk ate the bitter black mouse without undue hesitation. Several days later, an identical black mouse was placed on the floor of the large cage with the hawk on its perch 4 feet above. The hawk looked down and smacked its beak but refused to strike. Efforts to tease the hawk into action by moving the dead mouse were of no avail; the hawk merely looked and smacked its beak. Apparently the black mouse was evoking conditioned illness in the hawk, because beak smacking is a symptom of nausea. When the

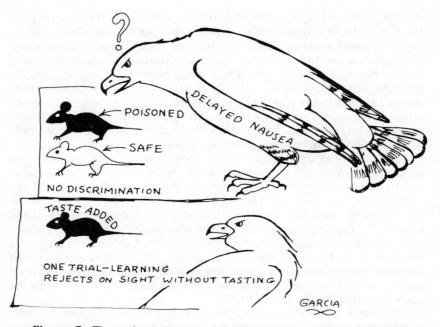

POISONED

SAFE

NO DISCRIMINATION

DELAYED NAUSEA

TASTE ADDED

ONE TRIAL-LEARNING
REJECTS ON SIGHT WITHOUT TASTING

GARCIA

Figure 7. The red-tailed hawks and the tainted mice. What an animal cannot learn is often more informative than what it can learn. Hawks fed on a diet of white mice, and occasionally given a black mouse followed by an emetic injection, cannot learn to discriminate black from white, presumably because both mice taste the same. When a distinctive taste is added to the black mouse, the hawk learns to avoid black mice on sight after a single black mouse–emesis episode. The taste cue has potentiated the color cue (based on Brett, Hankins, & Garcia, 1976).

experimenter, Brett, picked up the black mouse and placed it on the perch, the hawk retreated in obvious disgust. This hawk had a visual aversion as well as a taste aversion.

A third hawk was conditioned the same way, except that a bitter white mouse was paired with the lithium injection. Thus, this hawk, not included in Figure 7, had a taste cue but not a color cue. In this test, the hawk seized a second bitter white mouse in its talons, but on tasting it, the bird refused to eat. The third hawk had a taste aversion for bitter but no visual aversion for the mouse. Three other hawks tested under the same three conditions showed essentially the same behavior patterns (Brett et al., 1976).

The hawk experiments yielded a new empirical finding with broad theoretical implications. The first hawk demonstrated that black coat color, used alone, was a weak CS for a toxic US. The third hawk proved that bitter flavor, used alone, was a strong CS under the same conditions. According to classical learning theory, when a strong CS and a weak CS are combined into a compound CS, the strong component should block conditioning to the weak component. This makes sense; if a strong cue is available, why bother with weak cues. Much evidence has been accumulated for this principle, called *overshadowing* or *blocking* (Kamin, 1969). However, in the hawk experiment, the strong bitter cue potentiated conditioning to the weak color cue. Significantly, all the evidence for blocking comes from conditioning in the external sphere, whereas the hawk experiment dealt with internal, homeostatic conditioning. (For a general review of studies with wolves, coyotes, and hawks, see Garcia & Brett, 1977.)

The Memory for Poison

The dual organization of the vertebrate brain is best illustrated by a series of behavioral experiments with rats (Garcia & Koelling, 1967). Essentially the method was very simple: Rats were presented with a variety of cues and given a toxic treatment inducing a mild bout of nausea. Then the rats were tested with each cue separately to see which cues the rats treated as poison. It was discovered that if a rat is given a drink with a novel saccharin taste and becomes nauseous an hour later, it acquires an aversion for saccharin. If it is given a drink of plain water in a novel compartment, again followed by nausea, it is not likely to acquire a strong aversion for the novel compartment.

People display the same sort of selective learning and memory because, as Herrick described, they possess similar neural systems for control of feeding. If people become ill after a novel meal, they blame the food, not, for example, the new wallpaper on the dining room wall. This reaction seems cognitive and rational, but it is not. As any ship's steward knows, when the seas become stormy, the bilious voyager first blames the food, not the sea. After a bout of seasickness, the passenger may have fond memories of the ship and long for the sea again, but will retain a strong aversion for the sardine lunch eaten just before the storm, knowing full well that the storm and not the sardines caused the nausea. The ship's rat eating the sardine scraps in the hold will display the same pattern of aversions, but perhaps not the same cognitions. Radiation and chemical treatment for cancer often produce nausea in patients, and the resultant patterns of aversions resemble those displayed by laboratory animals, as we have discussed in an extensive review of the problem (Garcia y Robertson & Garcia, in press).

Many people think that the flavor of food is due mostly to smell rather than taste. A heavy cold clogging the nose with mucous will destroy a good meal, it is often said, proving that olfaction is more important than gustation in the appreciation of food flavor. Recent experiments with rats revealed that odor and taste play completely different roles in feeding behavior but that taste is the prime arbiter of what is fit to eat. As such, taste designates specific olfactory and visual stimuli to act as food cues for the delayed effects of a meal (Garcia & Rusiniak, 1980).

Figures 8 and 9 illustrate the results obtained in a recent study demonstrating the utilization of odor and taste cues in gut and skin defense. Thirsty rats were habitually given their daily ration of water in an experimental apparatus where every lick at a water spout was recorded. The spout protruded through a "nose cone," where an odor was presented as scheduled. Taste was presented in the water according to the experimental schedule. Care was taken to prevent the rats from tasting the odorant or smelling the tastant. On the conditioning days, the drinking spout was marked with the novel taste, odor cues, or both. One half hour later, the gut-defense rats were intubated with a mild dose of lithium chloride, producing obvious malaise. The rats recovered in a few hours. Several days later, the odor and taste cues were administered in separate tests (Rusiniak, Palmerino, Rice, Forthman, & Garcia, 1982).

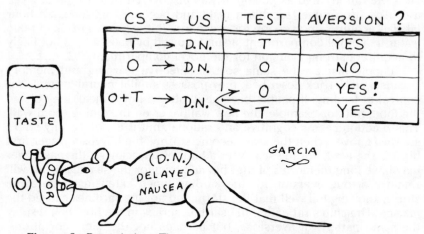

Figure 8. Potentiation: The memory of the poisoned rat. This drawing presents a "scoreboard" with the results obtained in rats given a drink marked with taste and/or odor cues followed 30 minutes later by an emetic treatment. If odor is used alone, the rat does not acquire an odor aversion. If taste is used alone, the rat acquires a taste aversion. If odor and taste cues are used in combination, then the rat acquires an aversion for odor as well as for taste. Taste has potentiated odor. Compare these results with those obtained in Figure 9 where rats received immediate foot shock. Note also the explanation offered in Figure 10 (based on Rusiniak, Palmerino, Rice, Forthman, & Garcia, 1982).

The scoreboard in Figure 8 summarizes the gut-defense groups, their treatments, and the results of the tests. When taste alone was used as the CS, the rats acquired a taste aversion. When odor alone was used as the CS, the rats did not acquire an odor aversion. However, when odor and taste were combined and used as a compound CS, the odor component proved to be extremely aversive when tested alone. The taste component was also aversive, but not more so than when taste alone served as the CS. As in the case of the broad-winged hawks depicted in Figure 7, the stronger taste cue potentiated the weaker odor cue, in direct contradiction to the classic theory of overshadowing or blocking.

The Memory for Pain

The half of the experiment demonstrating the utilization of odor and taste cues in skin defense is illustrated in Figure 9. The experimental

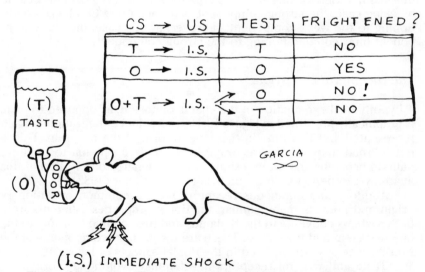

Figure 9. Blocking: The memory of the frightened rat. This drawing presents a "scoreboard" with the results obtained in rats given a drink marked with taste and/or odor cues followed a few seconds later by mild shock to the feet. If taste is used alone, the rat acquires no fear of the taste. If odor is used alone, the rat acquires a fear of the odor. If odor and taste are used in combination, the rat does not acquire a fear of the taste or of the odor. Taste has blocked odor. Compare these results with those obtained in Figure 8 with rats receiving delayed emetic treatment. Note also the explanation offered in Figure 10 (based on Rusiniak et al., 1982).

setup was exactly the same, except for the reinforcement conditions. The skin-defense rats received an immediate foot shock when they drank instead of the delayed-illness treatment. Food shocks and poisons both suppress drinking responses in the Skinnerian sense, but the two punishments are completely different in every other regard. A foot shock is a sharp external insult coming from the floor, whereas nausea is a dull internal malaise stemming from the gut. Shock produces fear of a place on the floor; nausea does not. To strip events of their bio-psychological manifestations was Skinner's error. It was also Hume's error when he argued that causality could not be differentiated from contiguity.

The scoreboard in Figure 9 gives the results of the skin-defense experiments, which stand in opposition to the poison experiments shown in Figure 8. When taste alone was followed by immediate shock, the rats did not develop an aversion to taste. When odor alone was followed by shock, the rats developed a fear of odor and suppressed their drinking. When combined odor and taste were followed by shock, the taste component blocked conditioning to the odor component. But this was not the blocking effect described by Kamin (1969). In the classic blocking case, the strong component of a compound CS blocks conditioning to the weak component. However, in this case, the weak component blocked conditioning to the strong component.

The Bicameral Biopsyche

A hypothetical explanation of the effects of poison, as opposed to pain, is graphically presented in Figure 10. Herrick's dual organization is again represented, but this time in the general form of the rat brain. This is not a "road map" of the rat brain; it is simply a schema to organize data on behavior and brain lesions. A more detailed description of this anatomy can be found in Braun, Lasiter, and Kiefer (1982).

Auditory and cutaneous receptors have a common evolutionary origin and possess many similar functional properties. Afferents from both systems converge to the thalamus and then course rostrally to the limbic system and the cortex. These are the primary components of the skin-defense system depicted in the dorsal aspects of Figure 10.

Taste and visceral receptors have similar evolutionary origins in the lining of the primitive gut. Afferents from these two systems converge to the nucleus of the solitary tract in the brain stem, and then the two afferent systems course together through the parabrachial area to the gustatory thalamic relay, the limbic system, and the gustatory neocortex. The two afferent systems form the principal components of the gut-defense system depicted in the ventral aspects of Figure 10.

The skin-defense and gut-defense systems as depicted in Figure 10 are separated by reciprocal inhibition, but also integrated by a sensory gate. The reciprocal inhibition underlies the common observation that

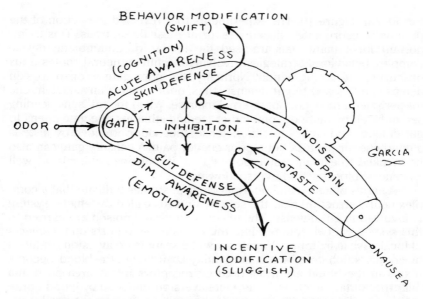

Figure 10. The defensive biopsyche. This drawing depicts an elaboration of the schema presented in Figure 5. It is an explanation of the results shown on the scoreboards of Figures 8 and 9. Noise and immediate shock enter the dorsal brain areas to modify behavioral patterns of skin-defense. Taste and delayed nausea enter the ventral brain areas to modify incentive value of food commensurate with food effects in defense of the gut. Fast reactions, acute awareness, and cognition are characteristic of skin-defense. Sluggish reactions, dim awareness, and emotion characterize gut-defense. Odor enters either system: When taste is absent, odor enters the dorsal mechanism. When taste is present, odor enters the gut-defense. Test the implications of the gate with the results shown in Figures 8 and 9. Construct a similar explanation for the behavior of the hawk in Figure 7.

vertebrate organisms tend to allocate energy as needed to one or the other of the two systems. After a heavy meal, digestion is promoted by activity of visceral smooth muscles and glands; striated muscles are relaxed, high-amplitude slow waves sweep over the cortex, and the organism prepares for sleep. In contrast, if an alarm sounds, excitement reigns in the skin-defense system, whereas appetite vanishes and gastric stasis ensues in the visceral system.

Herrick (1956), in his description of the segregation of function in the amphibian brain, noted that olfaction and vision did not participate in the two great neural pools in the medulla oblongata. Significantly, it was in these two systems that potentiation was discovered, as illustrated in Figures 7 and 8. Potentiation has been extensively studied in the olfactory system of the rat, and accordingly is depicted as a gate for odor in Figure 10. The experiments that revealed the action of the putative sensory gate utilized one, or at most three, trials. This is important, for if many trials are used, the animal will undoubtedly devise complex behavioral strategies involving circuitous neural routes, thus obscuring the gating action. Normally, the odor gate is open to skin defense and closed to gut defense; thus, odor alone is an excellent cue for peripheral pain, but not internal malaise. When the rat is in a feeding set, induced by taste or some other feeding stimulus, the gate opens to gut defense and closes to skin defense; thus, odor attended by taste is a good cue for malaise but a poor cue for pain. A sensory gate can also be invoked to explain visual potentiation in poisoned animals, as well as general blocking and overshadowing.

A series of lesion and pharmacological studies indicate that a complex neural structure near the solitary nucleus called the emetic system is involved in gut defense. The effects of ingested poison are carried to this system via two routes. First, the vagus nerve reports on the effects of local gastric irritation. Vagotomy will disrupt taste aversions induced by copper sulphate, which is not readily absorbed in the blood. Second, toxins in the blood are monitored by receptors in the area postrema near the solitary nucleus. Thus, taste aversions induced by blood-borne toxins are disrupted by lesions of the area postrema, but not by vagotomy. The odor gating mechanism is apparently located in the limbic system and the lateral aspect of the forebrain cortex. Pharmacological agents supplied to the amygdala or the hippocampus have selective effects on potentiated odor aversions, but not on taste aversions or odor-shock avoidance responses. Punctate lesions in the upper part of the gustatory neocortex in the lateral forebrain disrupt taste aversions but, oddly enough, spare taste potentiation of odor. Punctate lesions a few millimeters lower disrupt conditioning to both odor and taste components. So, empirical exploration of the rat brain supports the model in Figure 10 (Garcia, Rusiniak et al., 1982; Garcia, Lasiter et al., in press).

Behavior modification in the time and space of the external world is characterized by associations spanning relatively brief interstimulus intervals. For optimal learning, noise must be followed promptly by peripheral pain in classical conditioning, and the rat's reaction times are also brief. Likewise, responses must be followed promptly by reinforcers in instrumental conditioning. In the external world, the vertebrate organism is acutely aware of its stimulus surroundings. (The organism orients to signals and responds precisely to reinforcers.) Subsequently, the organism will display a memory for the locus of the reinforcer and for the temporal relationship between the signal and the reinforcer. Response to a CS can be described as cognitive, because an organism utilizes neutral stimuli to cope with a painful reinforcer in an objective way.

Incentive modification, exemplified by gut defense, operates in a completely different manner. For one thing, a toxin can take its effect long after a meal, when the organism is asleep, and the palatability of a meal is automatically adjusted commensurate with the meal's utility within the internal economy. If a meal delivers nutritive calories required by homeostasis, that meal will be more palatable the next time it is encountered. If a meal produces toxicosis during sleep, that meal will be disgusting at the next encounter, even though the organism cannot remember the illness. Since sleep often follows a meal, the unconscious adjustment of palatability without awareness of the US is a matter of necessity. (A more extensive discussion of the evidence for incentive modification can be found in Garcia, Hankins, & Rusiniak, 1974 and in Garcia, Lasiter et al., in press.)

Sensory Hedonics

Affective, or hedonic, changes are cardinal features of homeostatic conditioning. After eating a tainted meal and becoming ill, a person does not coolly decide to avoid that meal in the future because it may cause nausea again. The flavor of the meal now upsets the stomach and inhibits the appetite. In similar situations, coyotes retch and hawks smack their beaks in disgust. What was once delicious food is now disgusting. The CR is an emotional response directed at the CS, not a coping strategy directed at a fear-inducing US (Garcia et al., 1984). This same hedonic change is characteristic of other homeostatic systems, such as temperature regulation. When the core temperature of a vertebrate organism is cool, a warm stimulus on the skin feels pleasant; when the core is warm, the same warm stimulus is unpleasant. Thus, the Law of Effect directs the organism to a region of optimal temperature. Cabanac (1979) discussed homeostatic regulation in a lucid article with broad psychobiological implications appropriately entitled "Sensory Pleasure." Richter's (1942–1943) Harvey lecture on self-regulatory functions is a classic in this field.

The best example of this automatic adjustment taking place in the primitive nether regions of the brain is the prolonged delay of poison gradients, illustrated in Figure 11 (Palmerino, Rusiniak, & Garcia, 1980). Odor alone can be associated with poison if the toxin takes effect within 20 minutes. In contrast, taste alone is an effective CS even when the poison is delayed for several hours. When odor and taste are combined into a compound CS, odor is potentiated by taste so that the odor component yields a long delay gradient when tested alone in extinction. Therefore, long-delay learning is not an exclusive function of taste; the long-delay function will be displayed by any sensory system shunted into the homeostatic gut-defense system.

The delay gradients in Figure 11 were established using rats raised in barren laboratory cages. A recent experiment (Rusiniak, Garcia, Palmerino, & Cabral, 1983) demonstrated that the slopes are changed dra-

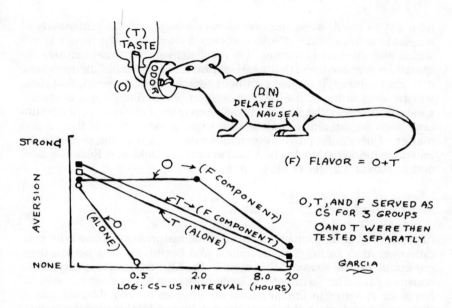

Figure 11. Potentiation of odor by taste. Depicted here is the span of association for the flavor and the effect of a tainted meal. Emetic injections were given various delays after rats had consumed flavored fluid. When odor was used alone, aversions were absent when the delay of injection was a half hour or longer. When taste was used alone, significant aversions were obtained at two hours and longer. When flavor was followed by varied delays of the emetic US and the odor and taste components were tested alone, the taste gradient was unchanged but the odor gradient was extended. Again taste potentiated odor cues for delayed illness (based on Palmerino, Rusiniak, & Garcia, 1980).

matically if rats are given extended experience with a single taste and odor in their cages. Later, when the rats are challenged with a different odor and taste paired with poison, the experienced rats utilize odor cues much more effectively than the naive rats, easily spanning a 30-minute delay before the poison when odor alone is the CS. The odor component of a compound odor-taste CS also serves as a much more potent CS for experienced rats. In contrast, the taste gradients are relatively unchanged by the enriched experience with odor and taste. Recall that odor cues are used to search for food in the instrumental phase of the feeding sequence and taste cues are used in the consummatory phase. Thus, these data support Craig's contention (1917) that the earlier (odor) components of a behavioral sequence tend to be plastic, whereas the consummatory (taste) components tend to be more fixed.

The Science of Learning in the Context of Evolution

The geological record reveals mainly the hard structural parts of our ancestors; their soft physiological parts are less well recorded. Behavioral patterns are virtually never recorded, and therefore behavior is of little concern to the paleontologist; a habit is not worth a coprolith. This is unfortunate because behavioral patterns in one animal can serve the same ends that anatomical structure and physiological functions serve in another. For example, horses and rodents feed on sandy grass and gritty vegetation, wearing their teeth away, but their teeth compensate by continuous growth and repair. Primates do not have such dental specializations, so baboons must clean gritty vegetation by hand. Some Japanese macaques learned to toss sandy rice into the sea to separate the lighter food from the heavier grit. This strategy soon spread by imitation to other members of the troop (see Gould, 1982, p. 299).

People tend to think that behavioral solutions to survival problems are superior to physiological ones. Consequently monkeys, who are closely related to humans, seem more intelligent than horses and rodents, more distant relatives. This is a self-serving conceit, as it is a simple matter to find instances in which humans use physiological adaptations whereas distant relatives use behavioral strategies. For example, humans burn up a lot of calories as fuel to maintain a constant body temperature. Behavior strategies, such as seeking shelter, using fire, and lying in the sun, also serve that purpose. But reptiles are the real experts in behavioral use of solar energy and thus require about one tenth the food calories that mammals require. Lizards shuttle back and forth between shade and sun to maintain a constant body temperature. As the temperature rises, marine iguanas position themselves parallel to the sun's rays, standing with their bodies lifted off the heated rocks of the Galapagos Islands. When the iguanas dive into the cold Pacific to feed on seaweed they rapidly dissipate their body heat and lose their mobility, so they come out to flatten themselves on hot rocks, raising their body temperature for the next dive. Attenborough (1979) discussed reptilian temperature control in his book *Life on Earth,* which summarizes the entire evolutionary history of life in about 300 remarkable pages of entertaining and thoughtful discussion illustrated with beautiful photographs. A more extended discussion of the topics in this section can be found in the ethological textbooks written by Gould (1982), Barnett (1981), and Alcock (1979). There are a number of other excellent volumes, usually with ethology, evolution, or animal behavior somewhere in the title.

The Imprinting Option: Innate and Acquired?

The subtle interplay between instinct and learning is best illustrated by what is simplistically called *imprinting.* Consider Lorenz and the gray-lag gosling illustrated in Figure 12. Speaking metaphorically, there are two evolutionary options for introducing a newly hatched gosling to its mother. Nature could have provided the gosling with a hereditary locket containing the portrait of its mother. The gosling would then simply match the mother's features with the mental portrait to discriminate its protective mother from the predatory fox. Alternatively, nature could have provided the gosling with a learning camera and the following instructions: As you come out of the egg, take a picture of whatever you see moving about; that is your mother. Run to her and follow her; she will protect you from the fox. Now, if for some reason the mother is absent and the fox is present, the gosling with the hereditary locket

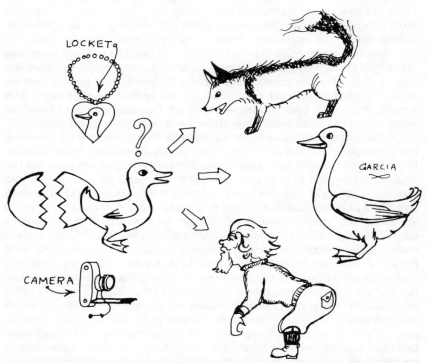

Figure 12. The imprinting option. Nature can ensure that the gosling will recognize its mother by giving it a picture of its mother in a hereditary locket. The gosling could then easily discriminate between its mother and the fox, but this information is not of much help since the newborn gosling has no defense against foxes. The mother must be nearby when the gosling hatches if it is to survive. In the latter case, an imprinting mechanism like a camera operates just as well, as Konrad Lorenz demonstrated. A learning mechanism performs the same function as an innate mechanism.

will run away and the gosling with the learning camera will run toward the fox, but that will make no difference. Neither gosling would survive because the predatory fox is incredibly swift and sly.

By squatting on his heels before hatching goslings and calling like a mother goose, Lorenz induced the goslings to follow him as he duck-walked through weeds to a pond. Lorenz's original observations are now criticized because it is difficult to tell which features of his body or behavior enticed the goslings to follow him. But he demonstrated that whatever the signs were, the goslings became attached to him as the parent. When the goslings developed into mature geese, they were also attached to him as a sex object (see Gould, 1982, pp. 61–65, 267–277). This is reminiscent of Freud's early theory of hysteria: During psychosexual development, a young girl who is traumatically molested has her sexual energy drained in an aberrant way. Later, her sexuality is expressed in a hysterical manner related to the initial trauma. In a like manner, Lorenz may have "traumatized" the gray-lag goslings. The important point is that the gosling is born into a structured evolutionary classroom with the predisposition to learn a great deal about its mother in a brief critical period. The learning mechanisms serve as well as hereditary knowledge because in either case, the mother must be nearby if the gosling is to survive the critical period of hatching.

Imprinting always appears in a structured context. For example, the white crown-sparrow is also born into an evolutionary classroom. From its nest it can always hear its father singing the species song in defense of the nesting territory. Later, peering over the nest, it can also watch its father sing. The nestling memorizes its father's song in silence, and the following year, it practices and perfects the song.

Imprinting occurs at any age because organisms learn what they must, when they must, in order to ensure infant survival during the critical period. The mother herring gull nesting in an open area with flocks of other mother gulls becomes imprinted on the individual features of her own chicks. She will accept any chick as her own for two days after hatching; after that she is likely to kill and eat a strange chick put into her nesting area by an experimenter. The Kittiwake gull nests in the narrow crags and crevasses of rocky cliffs and does not need to memorize the features of her own offspring because no strange chicks are apt to come wandering in. She will accept any chick the experimenter puts in her nest (see Gould, 1982, pp. 267–268). Each species of gull has its own program of imprinting congruent with its environmental niche.

Inherent responses are sometimes directed to very specific features. For example, a red spot on a moving beak is the feature needed to reliably evoke the pecking response of a herring gull chick. The mother waves her beak, the chick pecks at the spot, and the mother delivers the food. The chick will peck at a sharpened pencil with some painted bands on its tip as readily as it will peck at a model of its mother's beak (see Gould, 1982, pp. 54–61).

Imprinting is not limited to birds; it occurs probably more often than scientists know in mammals as well. For example, goats become attached to the smell of their kids when cleaning off the afterbirth tissues (Klopher, Adams, & Klopher, 1964). The same thing may happen in sheep, for sheepherders often induce a lactating mother whose lamb has died to accept an orphan by wrapping the skin of her dead offspring around the strange lamb.

Shepher (1983) presented the case for an apparent human imprinting phenomenon in a slim volume documenting his hypothesis with extensive sociological evidence. In the kibbutzim of Israel, unrelated children in the same age range are raised together in nurseries and kindergartens. They form sibling attachments, but not erotic attachments. As children, they explore each others' sexual apparatus, playing "doctor," but as they approach puberty, they shy away from such intimate contact and act like brothers and sisters. They never court or marry one of their own age group. Shepher examined thousands of longitudinal case histories without finding a single sexual attachment between unrelated adults raised together between the ages of one to six years.

Shepher said that the kibbutz nurseries "fooled mother nature" into believing unrelated children are siblings. The primitive nuclear family was the evolutionary classroom where children learned that their siblings were not suitable mates. Those variants that did not learn this lesson presumably died out because inbred children did not survive as well as outbred children. Shepher's thesis may be controversial, but his evidence is most impressive. Furthermore, the same phenomenon has been observed in other primates. When apes are reared together from birth in a zoo, they also form sibling relationships, and it is extremely difficult to induce them to mate, according to Warren Thomas, director of the Los Angeles Zoo (personal communication, 1983).

Convergent Evolutionary Forces

As we pointed out at the beginning of this chapter, evolution is usually considered a divergent process. Individual members of a species radiate outward, finding different niches suited to their individual traits. However, there are convergent forces also. Different species often evolve superficially similar structures in adapting to similar niches. For example, flowers hang at the end of long slender stems in high places, offering deep pools with nectar at the bottom to passing animals. In order to harvest the nectar, animals need siphons and the ability to hover in the air flying forward and backward. At least three completely different animals can do this: the nectar-sipping bat, a mammal; the hawk moth, an insect; and the hummingbird, of course, a bird. According to evolutionary theory, all three animals diverged from a common ancestor long ago. But more recently in evolutionary time, their differential anatomical mechanisms converged to adapt to the same behavioral niche.

The belief in convergent evolution may encourage people to believe that pure behavior can be fruitfully studied without attention to anatomical structure. However, that would mean studying "empty" niches, and as we said in the case of the bar-head goose, a niche cannot be defined independently of the organism that creates it.

Figure 13 illustrates the universal "signposts" used by all long-distance navigators, no matter what species they belong to. Although different species may converge upon the same signs, each species usually does so in a unique way. For example, the geomagnetic field around the earth provides a reliable directional cue used by humans, birds, and bees. Humans use a compass with a magnetized needle that points northward. (The needle also points downward near the North Pole because the lines of magnetic force converge down toward the pole.) Humans use the lateral component of magnetic force, but the European robin uses the vertical component (Wiltschko & Wiltschko, 1972). In actual practice, humans, birds, and bees use geographic features in conjunction with magnetic north to reach their destinations.

Stars also provide reliable cues for the long-distance traveler. The circumpolar constellations are especially valuable. In the northern hemisphere that means the Big Dipper. The two stars forming the front surface of the dipper opposite the handle point to the North Star, which swings in a small arc directly and constantly above the North Pole. Black slaves escaping from the South followed this "drinking gourd" to freedom in Canada. They learned about the constellations through human linguistic communication. The indigo bunting (a songbird) also learns about the circumpolar stars and constellations, but in an entirely different way. Each individual studies the sky while growing up during the summer and, in the fall, is prepared to travel south. When raised in an artificial planetarium, indigo buntings will learn an arbitrary sky circling an arbitrary pole (Emlen, 1975).

The migration of the monarch butterfly presents a most intriguing mystery. One population spends the winter in Mexico, north of the capital city. In the spring, the first generation flies northward, completing only a small part of the migratory cycle before reproducing. The second generation flies further north and reproduces. At the end of the summer, some of the final generations find themselves in Canada. They do not reproduce, conserving energy for the long trek back to their ancestral home in Mexico, which they have never seen (Brower, 1977, in press). Imagine being orphaned in Canada, equipped with hereditary maps, innate navigational gear, and genetic instructions to find a grand-

Figure 13. Convergent evolution: Various navigators use the same sign posts. Some of the most reliable sign posts for long distance travelers are the sun, the stars, the moon, geomagnetism, prevailing winds. Recent research demonstrates that birds and bees utilize geomagnetic forces to navigate, while humans use the compass for the same purpose. Circumpolar stars and constellations are also used by birds in spring migrations and were used by humans seeking refuge in the north. Polynesian navigators used the stars and surface patterns of waves and swells to navigate thousands of miles across the Pacific. Monarch butterflies migrate from Mexico to Canada and back over several summer generations, finding their goal in some as yet unknown way. These various species, with their different evolutionary histories, have evolved independent mechanisms to converge upon the same reliable signs for traveling great distances.

parental home in the mountains north of Mexico City. The genetic instructions must be matched against a terrain the individual butterfly has never traversed. The course must be maintained over thousands of miles by a body too light to make headway against a stiff breeze. This mystery may never be solved because human populations moving into the butterflies' territory are altering the butterflies' niche beyond their capacity to adapt.

The Polynesians were able to migrate over vast reaches of the ocean, without features salient to the untrained human eye. Navigational skills were learned over repeated voyages and taught to countless generations. The Polynesians discovered that the ocean's surface is not featureless even when the sun and stars are screened out by an overcast sky. Winds and current provide a grid of swells and waves to steer by. Flotsam on the surface indicates the leeward side of islands, and birds in the air provide similar cues. If a coral island is beyond the horizon, the green of the jungle and the blue of the lagoon are reflected on the bottom of the overcast sky. Putting together these bits of lore, the Polynesians learned to steer true courses for thousands of miles without the aid of instruments. The same cues are available to avian navigators and are no doubt used by them in different ways.

When Did Learning Begin?

The evolutionary origin of learning may never be known, but musing over the question is fun. According to a hypothesis of divergence, learning capacity emerged from a single ancient ancestor common to all learning organisms. According to a hypothesis of convergence, many different organisms independently evolved learning mechanisms in response to similar pressures. The second alternative seems more likely, but perhaps the first is true for some learning mechanisms, like gut defense. Anatomically, the gut is an ancient structure common to invertebrates and vertebrates and appearing early in the fossil record. Gut defense, a learning function of the integrated gut, must have coevolved with toxic defense of plants.

The intractable problem of determining the evolutionary origin of learning is illustrated in Figure 14. The honeybee, depicted on the left branch, is a master of the external environment (see Lindauer, 1961; von Frisch, 1967). It can locate nectar far from its hive, and on its return, it will communicate the locus of its find to its hivemates in a symbolic dance. On a flat, sunlit surface, the central axis of the dance points in the direction of the nectar, and the cadence gives the distance, indicating the energy expenditure required to reach the goal. When dancing on a vertical surface in a dark hive, the dancer uses gravity as a reference point for the sun. The vertical angle formed by the gravity vector and the axis of the dance is equal to the horizontal angle formed by a vector to the sun and the direct flight path to the nectar. The dancer gives its hivemates a theoretical heading based on its own flight, correcting for the sun's movement and the wind's drift. Research on the bee's anatomy indicates that the bee senses these vectors in ways we do not, thus supporting the hypothesis of convergence.

The garden slug depicted on the right branch in Figure 14 has been proven to be an expert in learning in the internal sphere (Gelperin, Wieland, & Barry, 1984; Sahley, Rudy, & Gelperin, 1984). The garden slug can learn a taste aversion in one trial, and it can learn a second-order conditioned aversion in just a few trials when tested with vege-

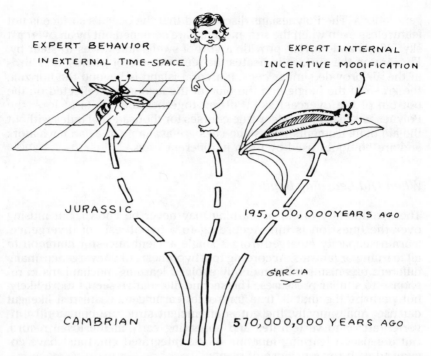

Figure 14. Divergent evolution, illustrated by the honey bee, the human, and the garden slug. Research has demonstrated the remarkable ability of the honey bee to learn locations of food sources and to communicate this information to her hive mates. More recent research has demonstrated the capacity of the garden slug to learn taste-toxin aversions in a single trial. Humans have both capacities. When the same function, learning in this case, is evident in widely divergent species, it is assumed that the function is of ancient evolutionary origin. Alternatively, convergent evolution pressure in more recent times may have forced three different organisms to develop similar learning capacities.

table stimuli from its own niche in the garden. After a single trial in which potato is paired with a plant poison in single-order conditioning, the slug will avoid potato. Then, if carrot is followed by potato in second-order conditioning, the slug will avoid carrot also. Examination of the neural mechanisms of the snail's gut defense reveals specialized mechanisms unlike any human mechanisms. When the sensory oral receptors and the motor components driving the snail's rasping tongue are excised along with their connections to the integrative relay stations in the central nervous system, the resultant neural apparatus will learn in isolation. This evidence points to convergence.

The ancestral line in the center of Figure 14 culminates in Anneke, the latest addition to our family, whom we consider to be the ultimate product of evolution. Like all vertebrates, she has the capacity for external skin defense and internal gut defense. Herrick's research indicated that modern amphibians possess both systems, and the assumption is that both systems were in place when an ancient ancestral amphibian crawled out of the sea about 350 million years ago.

Fish also possess the homologues for amphibious duality, so the homologues of the bicameral biopsyche must be sought in even more distant relatives, hypothetically pointing to an origin in a more remote ancestor. Most evolutionary biologists agree that the human ancestral lineage runs as follows: primates, insectivores, reptiles, amphibians, lobe-finned fish, early jawed fish, and jawless fish. The line of ancestors ends with the myxinoid jawless fish, appearing in the Ordovician period about 500 million years ago. No satisfactory probable ancestor of the myxinoids has been recognized.

Jensen (1960, 1963) suggested that hoplonemertines are good candidates as the missing link between the myxinoids and the more remote human ancestors. These small ribbon worms possess presumptive homologues for a large number of myxinoid and vertebrate organs: the notochord; the glandular hypophysis; the muscular somites; the skeletal cartilage and horny teeth; the nasopharyngeal duct, mouth, and gill slits; the digestive tract with liver and anus; the circulatory system with a dorsal vessel and red and white blood cells; the paired eyes with inverted retinas and a pineal eye; the labyrinths; the neuromast organs; the olfactory organs; the neural tube, alar, and basal plates of the brain and spinal cord; the sensory, mixed, and motor nerves; and the neural hypophysis.

This little worm is not a relative to be proud of, but it may prove to be a difficult one to deny. It is predatory, like most human relatives and ancestors. Its hunting weapon, a tubular proboscis, is a curious blend of external and internal components functioning like a harpoon and line. Taking aim at its prey with its paired eyes, the worm fires its proboscis, everting the tube and exposing a horny, barbed stylus that impales the victim. Then the worm retracts the proboscis, dragging its prey into its orifice. According to Jensen, this eversible proboscis contains the homologue for the notochord of the lower chordates. Certainly, this creature must have the capacity to improve its hunting and aiming with repeated trials and to acquire preferences for nutritious prey and aversions for noxious prey. If that is true, this predatory worm must be admitted into the human family.

It is rather obvious that the hoplonemertine pattern of foraging is dictated by the structure of the worm's proboscis. For all animals, including the human animal, learning is always an adjustment of a natural behavioral pattern inherent in anatomical structure. Polar concepts such as learning and instinct cause confusion because they cannot exist without each other. Edward Tolman used to tell his students to study only that which was fun. He knew that assignments are often irksome, but that self-directed learning is joyous. Thus, a semantic paradox is revealed: Learning is an instinct. Verily, learning is the primary instinct, because it converts a potentially hostile environment into a comfortable home where secondary instinctual processes, such as drinking, eating, and mating, can take place in safety. Fulfilling these instincts promoting the survival of the species pleases the individual, as Thorndike theorized, or as Tolman said, "Learning is fun."

References

Alcock, J. (1979). *Animal behavior: An evolutionary approach.* Sunderlind, MA: Sinauer Associates.

Attenborough, D. (1979). *Life on earth.* Boston: Little, Brown.

Barnett, S. A. (1981). *Modern ethology: Science of animal behavior.* New York: Oxford University Press.

Braun, J. J., Lasiter, P. S., & Kiefer, S. W. (1982). The gustatory neocortex of the rat. *Physiological Psychology, 10,* 13–45.

Breland, K., & Breland, M. (1961). The misbehavior of organisms. *American Psychologist, 16,* 681.

Brett, L. P., Hankins, W. G., & Garcia, J. (1976). Prey-lithium aversions III: Buteo hawks. *Behavioral Biology, 17,* 87–98.

Brower, L. P. (1969). Ecological chemistry. *Scientific American, 220,* 22–30.

Brower, L. P. (1977). Monarch migration. *Natural History, 86*(June–July), 40–53.

Brower, L. P. (in press). New perspectives on the migration biology of the monarch butterfly, *Danaus plexippus L.* In M. A. Rankin (Ed.), *Migration: Mechanisms and adaptive significance* (*Contributions to Marine Science 27* Supplement). Port Aransas, TX: University of Texas at Austin Marine Science Institute.

Brown, P. L., & Jenkins, H. M. (1968). Autoshaping of the pigeon's key-peck. *Journal of the Experimental Analysis of Behavior, 2,* 1–8.

Cabanac, M. Sensory pleasure. (1979). *The Quarterly Review of Biology, 54,* 1–29.

Craig, W. (1917). Appetites and aversions as constituents of instincts. *Biological Bulletin of the Marine Biological Laboratory, No. 33.* Woods Hole, MA.

Darwin, C. (1896). *Mental powers of man and woman: The descent of man and selection in relation to sex.* New York: Appleton.

Darwin, C. (1936). *The origin of species by means of natural selection: Or, the preservation of favoured races in the struggle for life and the descent of man and selection in relation to sex.* New York: Modern Library. (Original work published 1871)

DeCasper, A. J., & Fifer, W. P. (1980). Of human bonding: Newborns prefer their mothers' voices. *Science, 208,* 1174–1176.

Emlen, S. T. (1975). The stellar-orientation system of a migratory bird. *Scientific American, 223,* 102–111.

Garcia, J., & Brett, L. P. (1977). Conditioned responses to food odor and taste in rats and wild predators. In M. Kare & O. Maller (Eds.), *The chemical senses and nutrition* (pp. 277–389). New York: Academic Press.

Garcia, J., Forthman Quick, D. L., & White, B. (1984). Conditioned disgust and fear from mollusk to monkey. In D. L. Alkon & J. Farley (Eds.), *Primary neural substrates of learning and behavioral change* (pp. 47–61). New York: Cambridge University Press.

Garcia, J., & Hankins, W. G. (1975). The evolution of bitter and the acquisition of toxiphobia. In D. Denton & J. Coghlan (Eds.), *Olfaction and taste, V* (pp. 39–41). New York: Academic Press.

Garcia, J., Hankins, W. G., & Rusiniak, K. W. (1974). Behavioral regulation of the milieu interne in man and rat. *Science, 184,* 824–831.

Garcia, J., & Knoelling, R. A. (1967). A comparison of aversions induced by x-rays, drugs, and toxins. *Radiation Research, Supplement 7,* 439–450.

Garcia, J., Lasiter, P. S., Bermudez-Rattoni, F., & Deems, D. (in press). A general theory of aversion learning. *Annals of the New York Academy of Sciences.*

Garcia, J., & Rusiniak, K. W. (1980). What the nose learns from the mouth. In D. Muller-Schwarze & R. M. Silverstein (Eds.), *Chemical signals* (pp. 141–156). New York: Plenum Press.

Garcia, J., Rusiniak, K. W., Kiefer, S. W., & Bermudez-Rattoni, F. (1982). The neural integration of feeding and drinking habits. In C. D. Woody (Ed.), *Conditioning: Representation of involved neural functions* (pp. 567–579). New York: Plenum Press.

Garcia y Robertson, R., & Garcia, J. (in press). Xrays and learned taste aversions: Historical and psychological ramifications. In T. G. Burish, S. M. Levy, & B. E. Meyerowitz (Eds.), *Cancer, nutrition and eating behavior: A biobehavioral perspective* (pp. 11–41). Hillsdale, NJ: Erlbaum.

Gelperin, A., Wieland, S. J., & Barry, S. R. A strategy for cellular analysis of associative learning in a terrestrial mollusk. In D. L. Alkon & J. Farley (Eds.), *Primary neural substrates of learning and behavioral change* (pp. 229–242). New York: Cambridge University Press.

Gilbert, L. E., & Raven, P. H. (Eds.). (1980). *Coevolution of animals and plants.* Austin, TX: University of Austin Press.

Gould, J. L. (1982). *Ethology: The mechanisms and evolution of behavior.* New York: Norton.

Gustavson, C. R., Kelly, D. J., Sweeney, M., & Garcia. J. (1976). Prey-lithium aversion: I. Coyotes and wolves. *Behavioral Biology, 17,* 16–72.

Guthrie, E. R., & Horton, G. P. (1946). *Cats in a puzzle box.* New York: Rinehart.

Herrick, C. J. (1956). *The evolution of human nature.* Austin: University of Texas Press.

Hume, D. (1969). A treatise on human nature. In R. P. Wolff (Ed.), *The essential David Hume* (p. 35). New York: New American Library. (Original work published 1739)

Jensen, D. D. (1960). Hoplonemertines, myxinoids and deuterostome origins. *Nature, 188,* 649–650.

Jensen, D. D. (1963). Hoplonemertines, myxinoids and vertebrate origins. In E. C. Dougherty, Z. N. Brown, E. D. Hanson, & W. D. Hartman (Eds.), *The lower Metazoa; Comparative biology and phylogeny* (pp. 113–126). Berkeley: University of California Press.

Kamin, L. J. (1969). Predictability, surprise, attention, and conditioning. In B. A. Campbell & R. M. Church (Eds.), *Punishment and aversive behavior* (pp. 279–296). New York: Appleton-Century-Crofts.

Kant, I. (1896). *Critique of pure reason.* (F. M. Muller, Trans.). New York: Macmillan. (Original work published 1781)

Klopher, P. H., Adams, D. K., & Klopher, M. S. (1964). Maternal imprinting in goats. *Proceedings of the National Academy of Science, 52,* 911–914.

Kolata, G. (1984). Studying learning in the womb. *Science, 225,* 302–303.

Lamarck, J. (1970). Philosophie zoologique. In C. Gillispie (Ed.), *Dictionary of scientific biography* (Vol. 7, pp. 590–592). New York: Scribner's. (Original work published 1801)

Lindauer, M. (1961). *Communication among social bees.* Cambridge, MA: Harvard University Press.

Locke, J. (1981). *An essay concerning human understanding.* (P. H. Nidditch, Ed.). Oxford, England: Clarendon Press. (Original work published 1690)

Lorenz, K. (1965). *Evolution and modification of behavior.* Chicago: University of Chicago Press.

Mendel, G. (1959). *Verhandlungen naturforchender verein in Brunn, Abhand* [Experiments in plant hybridization]. In J. A. Peters (Ed.), *Classic papers in genetics* (pp. 2–26). Englewood Cliffs, NJ: Prentice-Hall. (Original work published 1865)

Miller, G. A. (1956). The magical number seven, plus or minus two: Some limits on our capacity for processing information. *Psychological Review, 63,* 81–97.

Moore, B. R. (1973). The role of directed Pavlovian reactions in simple instrumental learning in the pigeon. In R. A. Hinde & J. Stevenson-Hinde (Eds.), *Constraints on learning: Limitations and predispositions* (pp. 159–186). New York: Academic Press.

Moore, B. R., & Stuttard, S. (1979). Dr. Guthrie and *Felis domesticus* or tripping over the cat. *Science, 205,* 1031–1033.

Muller, J. (1848). *The physiology of senses, voice, and muscular motion, with the mental faculties* (W. Baly, Trans.). London: Taylor, Walton, & Maberly. (Original work published 1838)

Palmerino, C. C., Rusiniak, K. W., & Garcia, J. (1980). Flavor-illness aversion: The peculiar roles of odor and taste in memory for poison. *Science, 208,* 753–755.

Pavlov, I. (1955). *Lectures on conditioned reflexes* (S. Belsky, Trans.). Moscow: Foreign Languages Publishing House. (Original work published 1903)

Pedersen, P. E., Williams, C. L., & Blass, E. M. (1982). Activation and odor conditioning of suckling behavior in 3-day-old albino rats. *Journal of Experimental Psychology, 8*(4), 329–341.

Poulton, E. B. (1887). The experimental proof of the protective value of color and marking in insects in reference to their vertebrate enemies. *Proceedings of the Zoological Society of London* (pp. 191–274).

Premack, D. (1965). Reinforcement theory. In D. Levine (Ed.), *Nebraska symposium on motivation* (pp. 123–180). Lincoln, NE: University of Nebraska Press.

Richter, C. P. (1942–1943). Total self-regulatory functions in animals and human beings. *Harvey Lecture Series, 38,* 63–101.

Rusiniak, K. W., Garcia, J., Palmerino, C. C., & Cabral, R. (1983). Developmental flavor experience affects utilization of odor, not taste in toxiphobic conditioning. *Behavioral and Neural Biology, 39,* 160–180.

Rusiniak, K. W., Palmerino, C. C., Rice, A. G., Forthman, D. L., & Garcia, J. (1982). Flavor-illness aversions: Potentiation of odor by taste with toxin but not shock in rats. *Journal of Comparative and Physiological Psychology, 96,* 527–539.

Sahakian, W. S. (Ed.). (1968). *History of psychology.* Itasca, IL: F. E. Peacock.

Sahley, C. L., Rudy, J. W., & Gelperin, A. (1984). Associative learning in a mollusk: A comparative analysis. In D. L. Alkon & J. Farley (Eds.), *Primary neural substrates of learning and behavioral change* (pp. 243–258). New York: Cambridge University Press.

Shepher, J. (1983). *Incest: A biosocial view.* New York: Academic Press.

Skinner, B. F. (1938). *Behavior of organisms: An experimental analysis.* New York: Appleton-Century-Crofts.

Skinner, B. F. (1959). A case history in scientific method. In S. Koch (Ed.), *Psychology—A study of a science* (pp. 359–379). New York: McGraw-Hill.

Skinner, B. F. (1966). The phylogeny and ontogeny of behavior. *Science, 153,* 1205–1213.

Smotherman, W. P. (1982). Odor aversion learning by the rat fetus. *Physiology and Behavior, 29,* 769–771.

Spence, K. W. (1947). The role of secondary reinforcement in delayed reward learning. *Psychological Review, 54,* 1–8.

Staddon, J. E. R., & Simmelhag, V. L. (1971). The "superstition" experiment. *Psychological Review, 78,* 3–43.

Stickrod, G., Kimble, D. P., & Smotherman, W. P. (1982). In utero taste/odor aversion conditioning in the rat. *Physiology and Behavior, 28,* 5–7.

Thorndike, E. L. (1911). *Animal intelligence.* New York: Macmillan.

Tinbergen, N. (1974). Ethology and stress disease. *Science, 185,* 20–27.

Twain, M. (1893). *Pudd'nhead Wilson.* New York: Harper.

von Frisch, K. (1967). *The dance language and orientation of bees.* Cambridge, MA: Harvard University Press.

Watson, F. (1915). The father of modern psychology. *The Psychological Review, 12*(5), 333–353.

Watson, F. (1922). *Luis Vives: El gran Valenciano.* Oxford, England: Oxford University Press.

Watson, J. B. (1925). *Behaviourism.* New York: Norton.

Williams, D. R., & Williams, H. (1969). Auto-maintenance in the pigeon: Sustained pecking despite contingent non-reinforcement. *Journal of the Experimental Analysis of Behavior, 12,* 511–520.

Wiltschko, W., & Wiltschko, R. (1972). Magnetic compass of European robins. *Science, 176,* 62–69.

Zilborg, G. (1941). *A history of medical psychology.* New York: Norton.